REVIEW of PERSONALITY and SOCIAL PSYCHOLOGY:3

REVIEW OF
PERSONALITY AND SOCIAL PSYCHOLOGY

REVIEW
of
PERSONALITY
and
SOCIAL
PSYCHOLOGY

3

Edited by
LADD WHEELER

*Published in cooperation with the SOCIETY FOR PERSONALITY AND
SOCIAL PSYCHOLOGY (Division 8, American Psychological Association)*

SAGE PUBLICATIONS
Beverly Hills / London / New Delhi

For information address:

SAGE Publications, Inc.
275 South Beverly Drive
Beverly Hills, California 90212

SAGE Publications India Pvt. Ltd.
C-236 Defence Colony
New Delhi 110 024, India

SAGE Publications Ltd
28 Banner Street
London EC1Y 8QE, England

Printed in the United States of America

International Standard Book Number 0-8039-1854-2 (hardcover)
0-8039-1855-0 (softcover)

International Standard Series Number 0270-1987

FIRST PRINTING

CONTENTS

REVIEW of PERSONALITY and SOCIAL PSYCHOLOGY:3

Editor's Introduction

I had been following the work of Mihaly Csikszentmihalyi for several years, without being able to pronounce his name, before meeting him the summer of 1981 at Nags Head Conference Center. The result of that meeting is his article on optimal experience, a concept so rich in implications for the development and maintenance of self, and for society, that I won't attempt to summarize it. You should enjoy it without finding it pleasurable, a statement you will understand only if you read the article.

Phillip Shaver and Mary Klinnert are concerned with the development of a theory of emotion within an evolutionary and developmental framework. Schachter's work on affiliation, they argue, can best be explained by the subjects' need for a confident appraisal of the situation rather than a need for self-evaluation. His work on emotion shows largely that artificially induced physiological arousal can augment emotional behavior and that emotions may be dampened by preventing subjects from establishing the normal connections between their feelings and the situation at hand. An adequate theory of emotions must apply in its fundamentals to all higher primates and to preverbal children as well as to human adults.

Jim Blascovich and Edward Katkin are also concerned with physiological arousal because of its importance in many psychological theories. They report large individual differences in the ability to detect autonomic responses. Without taking these individual differences into account through correlations or through training, it is difficult to determine the actual importance of arousal. Moreover, scientists should not postulate arousal that is in principle unverifiable.

Few people have difficulty in detecting those autonomic responses associated with social anxiety, defined by Mark Leary as anxiety resulting from the prospect or presence of interpersonal evaluation in real or imagined social settings. Leary takes a self-presentational approach in reviewing the literature on audience anxiety, shyness, stage fright, dating anxiety, and embarrassment. I was thoroughly convinced by his approach.

Anyone who teaches social psychology knows that students have trouble with the preeminence of exchange theory; they argue that we aren't always just exchanging goods or services with other people. Judson Mills and Margaret Clark have come to the rescue of us all with their distinction between exchange and communal relationships. They note a number of differences between these two types.

In a methodological contribution, Saul Kassin discusses the use of animated films in studying causal attributions, such a technique allowing us to use different kinds of subjects—children, cross-cultural, and clinical. I find this a nice contrast to much of the attribution research in which extremely complicated verbal descriptions are given.

Jerry Suls and Glen Sanders present a developmental analysis of self-evaluation through social comparison in which they suggest that it isn't until about the age of nine that children begin to compare with others who are similar on related attributes. From six to eight, social comparison is indiscriminant, and from 4-5 comparison is temporal with the self rather than social.

There are strong and consistent individual differences in the width of cognitive categories people use, and Thomas Pettigrew reviews more than 20 years of research in this area. Social comparison is one of the areas in which category width should be important, with broad categorizers calling a wider range of others "similar" than do narrow categorizers.

William McKinley Runyan attempts to answer the charges of the critics of psychobiography, discussing problems of inadequate evidence, postdictive reconstructions, reductionism, the effect of childhood experience on adult behavior, and trans-historical and cross-cultural generality of psychological theory. His treatment is balanced and fair.

In the final article, Harry Reis presents the prospects and problems of the use of structural equations in personality and social psychology. What most of us have a vague knowledge of as "path analysis" is now usually referred to as "structural modeling." Reis de-mystifies it for us, showing how it is just an extension of statistics most of us know and love. It is nice to be told in a way I can understand what these techniques can and can't do.

In addition to the Associate Editors and members of the Editorial Board, I thank the following people for their reviews: James William Anderson, Faye Crosby, David Kenny, Christina Maslach, Vincent Nowlis, James Pennebaker, Roland Radloff, and Dolf Zillman.

—Ladd Wheeler
Rochester, New York

1

Toward a Psychology of Optimal Experience

MIHALY CSIKSZENTMIHALYI

Mihaly Csikszentmihalyi, a professor in the Department of Behavioral Sciences and Chairman of the Committee on Human Development at the University of Chicago, is currently completing a study of the daily life of teenagers, and is conducting a 20-year follow-up of a sample of 200 artists. His previous books include *Beyond Boredom and Anxiety* (1975), *The Creative Vision* (1976, with J. W. Getzels), and *The Meaning of Things* (1981, with E. Rochberg-Halton).

It is useful to remember occasionally that life unfolds as a chain of subjective experiences. Whatever else life might be, the only evidence we have of it, the only direct data to which we have access, is the succession of events in consciousness. The quality of these experiences determines whether and to what extent life was worth living.

Optimal experience is the "bottom line" of existence. It is the subjective reality that justifies the actions and events of any life history. Without it there would be little purpose in living, and the whole elaborate structure of personality and culture would reveal itself as nothing but an empty shell.

During the past several decades, psychology has neglected experience for the sake of behavior. In so doing it has followed the widespread folk belief about the primacy of action over experience: What people do is more important than how they feel. This assumption is based on the unwarranted merger of two perspectives. For an individual looking out at other persons, it is generally true that behavior takes precedence over inner states. I am less interested in knowing how others will feel than in what they will do. The ability to predict the behavior of others is more useful than the ability to predict their inner states. But this is true only because *other people's behavior has a direct impact on my experience.* In other words, what we need to know about others is their actions, but what counts about ourselves is our feelings. We are all behaviorists when facing outwards, but turn phenomenologists as soon as we reflect.

Not only do other people's actions determine our own inner states more directly than their inner states do, but the former are also more accessible. Strictly speaking, we can never know what another person feels, whereas we do know what he or she does. Thus behavior is a more reliable measure of other people's states than are their reported experiences. But the reverse is true when each person reflects on his or her inner state: Subjective feelings are a more reliable measure of what condition the organism is in than any observable behavior could be.

Despite the importance of what passes in consciousness, psychology has by and large shied away from confronting it. Most psychological research in this century has focused on the periphery of lived experience: on behavior, attitudes, choices; on cognitive processes and performance viewed from an outside, abstract perspective; on relationships between intrapersonal and external events. In studying these epiphenomena it hardly ever asks, how do these feelings relate to the *psyche,* that is, to subjective reality?

The justification usually advanced to explain this state of affairs is that science must deal with objective, tangible, verifiable data, and therefore if psychology is to be scientific it, too, must concentrate on the objective dimensions of human beings. But emphasis on objective qualities in science is only appropriate when dealing with *objects.* It is misplaced when subjectivity is the paramount feature of the object investigated. The chemist need not worry about how the molecule experiences its existence and interprets it to itself. The so-called hard sciences can afford to be parochially anthropocentric, since they are ultimately handmaidens of human purpose. They are expected to fit the world into cognitive categories that make it possible for us to manipulate it.

But psychology is left with the unwieldly task of being objective about subjectivity. Behaviorism manages to evade this task, because by adopting a natural science stance it transforms the experiencing subject into an object of experience and thus fails to come to grips with what is specifically interesting, and essential, about human beings. Psychologists, to the extent that they have adopted the methods of the older sciences, have generally relaxed in the comfortable assumption that they, too, are being scientific. Science, after all, is nothing but method; mastering the latter guarantees that sooner or later one will reach knowledge and understanding. This view, however, is based on a simplification. A method is a means, the adequacy of which cannot be evaluated except with reference to an outcome, or goal.

If the most important aspect of human life is the quality of experience, then the goal of psychology as a science must dictate methods appropriate to the description and understanding of subjective experience.

LIMITING CONDITIONS ON THE INTEGRITY OF EXPERIENCE

Subjective experience exists in consciousness. It consists of thoughts, feelings, sensations—in short, information that effects a discriminable change in awareness. When I think "this is wonderful music" or "this is a boring meeting," consciousness relates information about external events to its own states and attributes positive or negative valences to the relationship. Focusing attention on the interplay of data in consciousness is what we call experience.

It is generally assumed that experiencing presents no problem, that as long as one is alive and awake, one cannot help "experiencing." But this is not true. Relating information from outside sources to states of consciousness must be an ordered process, and therefore it requires inputs of energy. One source of energy is the calories necessary to keep consciousness operating at a physiological level. Important as this input is in the overall economy of the organism, its significance is trivial from the purely psychological viewpoint.

The more relevant source of energy that keeps consciousness in an ordered state is information. Consciousness becomes disorganized when the input of information is either too complex or too simple. This can be due to either external causes—the environment contains too many or too few stimuli—or to malfunctions of attentional processes that allow excessive or inadequate information to reach consciousness (Csikszentmihalyi, 1978; Hamilton, 1981).

External causes of disruption have been researched rather extensively. Studies of stimulus deprivation, for instance, suggest that without inputs of information from outside, consciousness becomes chaotic (Geiwitz, 1966; Zubek, 1969; Hamburg, Pribram, & Stunkard, 1970; Zuckerman, 1964, 1979). Its content—images, feelings, thoughts—become unpredictable and uncontrollable. Consciousness is not ordered "naturally"; it cannot maintain its order from within itself. To keep functioning in a predictable way, it requires inputs of ordered information. For it is not necessary that stimuli merely be available; they must also be compatible with the parameters of expectation established by genes and learning. If the stimuli are too numerous, or contradictory, or unassimilable, experience will be disrupted.

Internal causes that disrupt the ability to process experience are equally well-known, although their existence is usually not related to a theory of experience. Autism, for instance, appears to involve excessively rigid barriers against incoming information. Several other pathologies, like schizophrenia, are characterized by the opposite syndrome: stimulus over-inclusion. Psychiatry is beginning to recognize and label an increasing number of psychic dysfunctions as "attentional disorders" (Harrow, Tucker, Hanover, & Shield, 1972; Harrow, Grinker, Holzman, & Kayton, 1977; Wynne, Cromwell, & Matthysse, 1976; Brumback & Weinberg, 1977).

Thus optimal experience could be defined in formal terms, rather than in terms of content. First, it must be an ordered state of consciousness. As we have just seen, order depends on certain characteristics of the information flow. When information is too little or too much, when it is random or incongruous, consciousness fails to operate. Attention becomes unpredictable and it cannot be used to process experience.

Within the broad range of ordered experience, *optimal* experience may be further defined in terms of two dimensions: what there is to do and what one is capable of doing. Part of the information that gets processed in consciousness consists in an evaluation of the opportunities for action present in a given situation. At the same time, we also tend to be aware of what our abilities are in terms of these opportunities. It is convenient to call the first one of these two parameters of perception "challenges" and the second "skills." Optimal experiences are reported when the ratio of

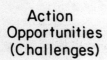

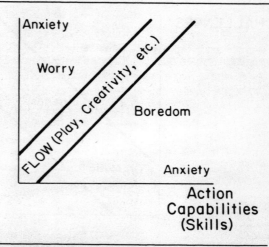

Figure 1: Model of the flow state. When action opportunities are perceived by the
actor to overwhelm his capabilities, the resulting stress is experienced as
anxiety. When the ratio of capabilities is higher, the experience is worry.
The state of flow is felt when opportunities for action are in balance with
the actor's skills. The experience is then autotelic. When skills are greater
than opportunities for using them, the state of boredom results, which
again fades into anxiety when the ratio becomes too large. (Adapted from
Csikszentmihalyi, 1975)

the two parameters approximates unity; that is, when challenges and skills
are equal (see Figure 1).

When artists, athletes, or creative professionals describe the best times
experienced in their favorite activities, they all mention this dynamic
balance between opportunity and ability as crucial. Thus optimal experience—or *flow,* as we came to call it using some of the respondents' own
terminology—is differentiated from states of boredom, in which there is
less to do than what one is capable of, and from anxiety, which occurs
when things to do are more than one can cope with (Csikszentmihalyi,
1975, 1979, 1981a, 1982).

The relationship between the optimal flow experience, boredom, and
anxiety seems to hold not only in peak experiences, but to be diffused
through everyday life. In a study of high school students, Mayers asked
teenagers to rate their favorite activities as well as the high school classes

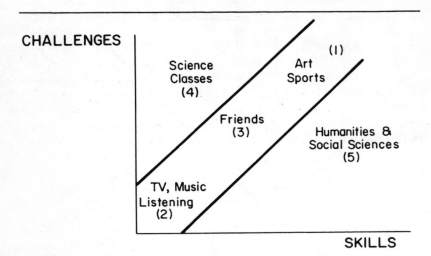

CHALLENGES

Science
Classes
(4)

(1)
Art
Sports

Friends
(3)

Humanities &
Social Sciences
(5)

TV, Music
Listening
(2)

SKILLS

Figure 2: How high school students rate their favorite activities (Nos. 1, 2, 3) and
school classes (Nos. 4 & 5) in terms of challenges and skills. (Adapted from
Mayers, 1978)

they were taking in terms of the challenges and skills present in each. The
ratings he obtained are summarized in Figure 2. The great majority of the
favorite activities were placed in the diagonal "flow channel." Arts (drama,
ballet, playing music) and sports were rated the most complex, in that
they were seen to use many skills in dealing with high challenges. TV
watching and music listening were rated as equally enjoyable, although
lower in complexity because they required the use of few skills to meet
negligible challenges. Friends, on the other hand, were listed all along the
flow diagonal, because interaction with them is flexible: It can be either
very relaxing or quite demanding. In contrast to these favorite activities,
school classes tended to be placed consistently off the diagonal; "hard"
subjects like math and sciences typically in the region of anxiety, while
humanities and social science classes often fell in the area of boredom
(Mayers, 1978).

A more exhaustive study of the relationship between the ratio of
challenges and skills on the one hand and optimal experience on the other
is one in which a sample of 107 adult workers participated (Csikszent-

mihalyi & Graef, 1980; Csikszentmihalyi & Kubey, 1981). In this study respondents carried an electronic pager (or "beeper") on their persons for a week. At random times within two-hour blocks between 8 a.m. and 10 p.m. a transmitter sent a signal which caused the pagers to "beep." At the signal, respondents were to fill out a standard rating sheet bound in a booklet they also carried. Each sheet contained questions about the respondent's location, activity, thoughts, and semantic differential-type scales for rating internal states such as "happy-sad" and "active-passive." In addition, respondents were asked to rate each situation in which they were paged in terms of the challenges present, and in terms of the skills available, on two 10-point scales. A total of 4791 responses were collected from the 107 adults.

The question was, do people who tend to perceive challenges and skills as balanced report higher levels of optimal experience? Optimal experience was operationalized in terms of individual mean scores, aggregated over a week of self-reports, on two dependent variables: Affect (sum of items "happy," "cheerful," and "sociable") and Activation (sum of items "active," "alert," and "strong"). We used 27 predictor variables, including demographic and personality data. The theoretically relevant predictors were four variables consisting of the percentage of time each person reported being in Flow (Challenge = Skills > 0), in a state of Boredom (Challenge < Skills), in Anxiety (Challenge > Skills), and in a fourth state that might be best called Stagnation, where both challenges present and skills available were rated "0."

Table 1 shows what happens when the average level of affect reported is regressed against the 27 predictors. Thirty-one percent of the variance in how happy, cheerful, and sociable people feel is explained in terms of seven predictors. The single best predictor of overall affect is the "alienation from self" subscore on a shortened version of Maddi's Alienation Scale (Maddi, Kobasa, & Hoover, 1979). The second is the amount of flow-like experiences reported. The third—with a negative sign—is the amount of stagnation experienced. And after level of education (negative) and amount of time spent in public places, the sixth predictor is the proportion of time a person is bored (negative). The best predictor of a person's level of Activation—of how active, alert, and strong he or she feels over the week—is the frequency with which flow is reported. The flow variable is the first to enter the regression and accounts for 8% of the variance in activation. Another 11 predictors explain only 21% more of

TABLE 1
Stepwise Multiple Regression of Mean
Self-Reported *AFFECT* (Happy, Cheerful, Sociable)

Variable	Multiple Correlation (R)	Cumulative Explained Variance (R²)	R^2 Change	Beta
Alienation from self	.36	.13	.13	.37
Challenges = Skills (FLOW)	.44	.20	.07	.23
Challenges–Skills = 0 (STAGNATION)	.47	.23	.03	−.18
Education	.51	.26	.03	−.19
Time spent in public	.53	.28	.02	.19
Challenges < Skills (BOREDOM)	.54	.30	.01	−.11
Age	.56	.31	.01	.11

Note: The regression was computed on the 107 individual mean scores based on 4791 repeated measures.

the variance; fifth among these is stagnation, again with a negative sign (Gianinno, Graef, & Csikszentmihalyi, 1979).

The Experience Sampling Method, which this and similar studies have used, makes subjective states accessible to systematic investigation. Specifically, the study referred to above showed that the level of perceived challenges and skills can be measured in ongoing everyday activities, and that the ratio between these two is an important component of the quality of life. Moreover, the pattern of results in Table 1 hints at a relationship between the self, the ability to be in flow, and the quality of experience, which is a topic that will be developed in more detail later.

THE SUBJECTIVE EXPERIENCE OF FLOW

The fact that a certain ratio of information input, or a balance between challenges and skills, is involved in optimal experience seems quite clear. But this relationship does not say anything about what the experience is like from the inside, so to speak; about how it feels subjectively. To answer that question, we relied on extensive interviews with people who were likely to report optimal experiences (Csikszentmihalyi, 1975, 1979, 1981a).

At first sight, it might seem that severe methodological problems must be involved in identifying optimal experience. The task is, however, not that difficult. It is safe to assume that quality of experience is positively related to the probability of it being sought out regardless of external contingencies. In other words, a positive experience is its own reward; one keeps attending to it even if nothing else happens as a result.

Needless to say, most people's experience is not optimal, most of the time, by this definition. For instance, average workers said that they wanted to do whatever they were doing on the job only 17% of the time their experiences were sampled (Csikszentmihalyi & Graef, 1980; Rubinstein, Csikszentmihalyi, & Graef, 1980). Presumably the remaining 83% of the time at work they attended to experience not because it was rewarding in itself but because extrinsic rewards like money or social pressures justified an experience that in and of itself was not worth having.

Nevertheless, there are situations in which people keep attending to information for intrinsic reasons. One plays, for instance, generally because the experience is enjoyable. There might be a variety of ulterior, extrinsic reasons motivating the activity, but even when these are absent people keep playing for the sheer fun of it. Art, creative work of any kind, sports, and religious practices also often provide this kind of self-justifying, optimal experience. Thus in our early studies we interviewed people involved in such activities to see if some common features were present despite the often glaring differences between activities like playing chess and playing basketball, composing music or climbing rocks.

The interviews confirmed the expectation that intrinsically rewarding experience is distinguished by common parameters regardless of the nature of the activity. Later investigations have found that these parameters apply to optimal experiences outside of leisure contexts; that they are present in those relatively rare instances when work is enjoyable, or when the classroom becomes engrossing (Csikszentmihalyi, 1975, 1981a; Mayers, 1978).

At the most abstract level, an optimal subjective state is experienced when conscious processes proceed in an ordered way, without inner conflict or interruptions. In other words, optimal experience is simply experience that flows according to its own requirements. It seems that when experience is ordered, it is self-contained or autotelic.

Most of the time inner states fall far short of this criterion. Everyday life constantly presents stimuli that need to be attended to, whether we like it or not. Order in consciousness is threatened by conflicting goals, unclear expectations, ambiguous desires. Most people most of the time feel constrained to alienate their experience—that is, settle for an inner state that is far from optimal, either just to survive or in the hope of more rewarding experiences in the future. Thus we tolerate the boredom of school, of work, of family life, in the expectation that sometime before we die we shall be rewarded with a blissful state of enjoyment.

Optimal experience stands out against this background of humdrum everyday life by excluding the noise that interferes with it in normal existence. Thus the first characteristic mentioned by people who describe how they feel at the height of enjoyment is a *merging of action and awareness*; a concentration that temporarily excludes irrelevant thoughts, feelings from consciousness. This means that stimuli outside the activity at hand have no access to consciousness; past and future cease to exist subjectively. This continuous focus on the present produces a *distortion of time* perspective. Minutes seem to stretch for hours, or hours elapse in minutes: Clock time is replaced by experiential sequences structured according to the demands of the activity.

Deep concentration on the ongoing present is possible only because *the goals of the activity are clear.* Ambiguity and conflict, so typical of everyday life, are replaced by undivided intentionality. Not only are goals sharply defined, but *the means to reach them are also clear:* The rules of the game leave no doubt about what can or cannot be done. Finally, pursuit of the goal is helped by *clear feedback* which helps the actor adjust his or her behavior as the interaction proceeds.

Immersion in the activity produces as one of its consequences *a loss of self-consciousness.* There is neither need nor opportunity to reflect on oneself—the self as an object of awareness recedes while the focus of attention is taken up by the demands of the activity and by the responses given to them.

Although one often gets involved in activities that produce optimal experiences either accidentally or for extrinsic reasons, once a person has had a taste of the exhilaration produced by the ordered interaction, he or she will continue the involvement for intrinsic reasons. Thus optimal experience is *autotelic,* or intrinsically rewarding. With time it might become addictive. In any case, it is experienced as something one chooses to do freely and for its own sake.

These are the conditions that define a *flow experience,* as we came to call the well-ordered, fully functioning dynamic state of consciousness. They are generally found in most cases where a person describes his or her experience as optimal or intrinsically rewarding. We might call activities that tend to produce such experiences *flow activities.* It does not matter what the activity is. It could be a race for the runner, chess for the chess master, dance for the dancer; in each case the complexities and contradictions of the world are filtered out until only a limited set of well-ordered goals and means are left in awareness.

In everyday life, flow experiences occur in a great variety of contexts. To get a better sense of what these are, we interviewed 82 adult workers. Each person was read three quotations describing flow experiences, originally collected from a rock climber, a composer of music, and a dancer. After reading each statement, the respondent was asked whether he or she ever felt an experience similar to the one described in the quote. If the answer was yes, they were asked what they were doing when the experience occurred, and to estimate how often they had such an experience in the activity.

The three quotations were the following:

(1) "My mind isn't wandering, I am not thinking of something else; I am totally involved in what I am doing. My body feels good . . . I don't seem to hear anything, the world seems to be cut off from me . . . I am less aware of myself and my problems."

(2) "My concentration is like breathing. . . . I never think of it. I am really quite oblivious to my surroundings after I really get going. I think that the phone could ring, and the doorbell could ring, or the house burn down or something like that. . . . When I start, I really do shut out the whole world. Once I stop I can let it back in again."

(3) "I am so involved in what I am doing . . . I don't see myself as separate from what I am doing."

As it turned out, 87% of the respondents said they knew the feelings described in the above statements. Thirty percent reported that they experienced something like it less often than once a week; 40% that they

TABLE 2
Frequency of Activities Mentioned as Having
Produced Flow Experiences (N = 71 adults)

	Percent of Ss mentioning
1. Social Activities (Vacationing with family; being with children, wife, or lover; parties; traveling)	16
2. Passive Attending Activities (Watching TV, going to the theatre, listening to music, reading)	13
3. Work Activities (Working, electrical work, challenging problems at work)	31
4. Hobbies and Home Activities (Cooking, sewing, photography, singing, etc.)	22
5. Sports and Outdoor Activities (Bowling, golf, dancing, swimming, etc.)	18
	100

Note: For each S, the one activity mentioned most often in response to the three quotes was selected.

felt something like it every week, and 30% reported that they experienced it daily. Only 11 respondents, or 13% of the sample, could not identify with the experiences at all. Those who identified with one statement tended also to respond to the other two; the average correlation between the reported frequency of the three experiences was .58.

Contrary to expectations, the activity most often associated with flow experiences was work (see Table 2). One-third of the respondents said that the intense concentration, involvement, and loss of self-consciousness occurred most frequently when they were working. Next came more predictable hobbies like cooking or carpentry; then sports and outdoor recreations. Each of these was mentioned most often by about one-fifth of the respondents. Interpersonal relations were prime occasions of flow for 16% of the sample, and 13% singled out passive leisure-type activities as conduits for the flow experience. The variety of activities, ranging from solitary to gregarious, from physical to cognitive, from obligatory to voluntary, each of which is capable of producing the intense involvement of the flow experience, is the most impressive message of Table 2.

How frequently people reported experiencing flow was related to several aspects of their lives. If one looks, for instance, at the data obtained from the pager-induced self-reports of the Experience Sampling Method, one finds that those adults who claimed to have more frequent flow experiences also spent more time on the job actually working (r. = .38, p < .001), and less time "goofing off" (r. = -.26, p < .01). Of the total 1274 responses filled out while on the job, the 71 workers were actually working only in 828 instances, or 64% of the time. The rest was spent daydreaming, chatting, or talking to co-workers about personal matters. But respondents who were above average on the reported frequency of flow spent about 25 minutes more each day actually working than the respondents who experienced flow infrequently. Assuming that time spent working results in increased productivity, and extrapolating this finding to the entire working force, one might conclude that the flow experience contributes tens of billions of dollars to the Gross National Product each year. To compensate for greater involvement in work, those who report more frequent flow spend significantly less time idling and socializing outside of work as well. What is perhaps more important, flow frequency has a significant inverse relationship to "wishing to be doing something else" in ten out of eleven main life activities (Csikszentmihalyi & Graef, 1979). Thus subjective as well as objective involvement with one's actions is related to the ability to experience flow.

These results are somewhat counterintuitive, in that they suggest that hard work and involvement with life are related to a kind of experience that is typical of playful, intrinsically motivated activities. Apparently concentrated engagement is a trait that cuts across the work/leisure distinction. The capacity to experience flow seems to be an extremely important personal skill. At the same time, it is also clear that the way society structures action opportunities will affect the ease with which people may find optimal experiences in their daily lives.

SOCIAL STRUCTURE AND FLOW

The attraction of art, religion, sport, and science—of all the intrinsically rewarding action-systems developed by culture—is that they allow this intense concentration to occur by providing a self-contained world with clear limits. Within those limits consciousness can run loose without being challenged or interrupted by information with which it cannot cope.

Life is generally too unwieldy to make optimal experience possible. Thus historically a great deal of ingenuity has gone into making it more manageable by shaping it into self-contained systems of action and information. It is questionable, for instance, that science has improved the quality of life in any absolute sense, or whether it even has the slightest potential of doing so. But as a self-contained symbol system science is an excellent activity for providing optimal experiences to those who accept its rules and lose their consciousness in pursuing its byways. Science is good for the scientist, like religion for the mystic or art for the artist, because it provides a world in which to act with total concentration and thus experience order in consciousness.

A central task of any human community is to make flow experience available to its members within productive, prosocial activities. In many ways, hunting and gathering societies seem to have been more effective than later cultures at making work and maintenance activities enjoyable (Firth, 1929; Sahlins, 1972). With the invention of farming, and even more during the past two hundred years since the Industrial Revolution restructured everyday survival tasks, people have had to work more while enjoying it less (Thompson, 1963; Wallace, 1978). Organized leisure has evolved to compensate for the dreariness of productive life. Whereas in past cultures art, music, dance, play, and religion were intertwined with serious work and could not be separated out of the matrix of everyday experience, now these activities have become trivialized therapeutic adjuncts to a "real" life which in its stark meaninglessness cannot justify itself any longer.

Confronted with barren work and empty leisure, many people turn to "cheap thrills" in their search for optimal experiences. The Balinese fascination with cockfighting, the Hiberian awe of the bullfight, our willingness to pay for spectacles of destruction in the boxing ring or the demolition derby are some instances of how instant immersion in a compelling activity can be accomplished. The "Russian roulette" theme in

The Deerhunter is an excellent symbol of what might happen when a culture disintegrates: The only activity left that attracts people's attention long enough to forget the chaos of life and experience a semblance of order is the sight of a person methodically blowing his brains out.

For many teenagers, juvenile delinquency is the only activity that provides enjoyment. Compared to the dullness of school and home life, the attractions of burning down a school or stealing a car are often irresistible (Csikszentmihalyi & Larson, 1978). To get a teenager to grow up, he or she must believe that becoming an adult is a worthwhile goal. If confusion and boredom are all one can look forward to, why bother? The 300% increase in adolescent suicide rates over the past three decades suggests that more and more young people find the prospect of growing up less than persuasive. Others turn to drugs or "cheap thrills" in an effort to recapture optimal experience as they shuffle reluctantly into adulthood (Csikszentmihalyi, 1981b).

Of course, such failures to provide optimal experience as part of the warp and woof of daily life is not unique to our time and place. Rome had to resort to the circus to spark up the graying lives of her citizens, and Byzantium made chariot-racing into a great popular placebo. Alienation from subjective experience is not a consequence of capitalistic social relations, as leftist theoreticians would like us to believe. It is not an exclusive malady of ruling castes and cultures, nor is it unique to contemporary technological conditions. It seems to happen every time the way of life of a group of people is disrupted, either by outside forces or by internal processes of development, to the extent that flow becomes more and more difficult to experience within the routines of everyday life.

It does not follow, however, that optimal experiences are more readily available in societies where life is comfortable, affluent, or pleasurable. Conceptually as well as empirically, pleasure and enjoyment are likely to be inversely related (Csikszentmihalyi, 1982). Pleasure is a homeostatic experience following on the satisfaction of physiological needs. Enjoyment occurs typically as a result of activity that involves the use of skills in response to increasingly complex challenges, and thus satisfied emergent needs. The function of pleasure is contentment, whereas enjoyment leads to change and growth.

Of course, homeostatic experiences are as necessary as, and certainly more eagerly sought after than, enjoyment. For instance, food, probably the earliest source of pleasure and reward, is still responsible for the best subjective times in the daily cycle of experiences. Of the dozen or so major activity categories, "eating" is associated with the highest scores of self-reported happiness, cheerfulness, and satisfaction. Of the twelve most frequent types of thought people think about in an average week, thoughts about food are associated with the most positive self-reports (Graef, Gianinno, Csikszentmihalyi, & Rich, 1978; Csikszentmihaly & Figurski, in press). During an average day, moods peak around mealtimes, resulting in a daily curve that looks somewhat like the Golden Gate bridge in profile.

Similarly, processes that produce homeostasis in consciousness by directly manipulating information seem to be more attractive than enjoyable experiences. Television is the major purveyor of pleasurable information in our culture. When watching TV people rate their subjective states more "relaxed" than at any other time of the day. They are also quite happy, cheerful, and satisfied. They say that they chose the activity freely. At the same time, they rate their level of cognitive and conative involvement lower than in any other activity. Self-reported concentration, control, alertness, strength, and activation are abysmal (Csikszentmihalyi & Kubey, 1981). Adolescents describe their experiences in active leisure—for example, when playing sports or games—as very significantly more enjoyable than watching television. Yet they spend two and a half as many hours a week in front of the TV set as they do in active leisure (Csikszentmihalyi, Larson, & Prescott, 1977). Apparently the low level, predictable, undemanding information provided by television results in a soothing experience which for most people takes precedence over the more involving experiences produced by flow activities.

The contrast between comfortable pleasure on the one hand and often strenuous enjoyment on the other can best be seen in historical perspective. The early culture of the Puritans, renowned for shunning pleasure and levity, was in fact very effective in providing a lifestyle full of flow experiences for those who abided by its rules. Puritan culture created one inclusive goal to give order to all of life (i.e., salvation); it specified clear rules to obtain that goal (i.e., self-discipline); and it defined worldly success as the feedback by which progress toward the goal could be measured (Weber, 1958). In other words, Calvin and his successors were able to reduce all of life to a do-able, internally consistent game. Those who followed its rules could process experience as ordered information and therefore were able to enjoy life even though they found no pleasure in it.

But the game the early Puritans invented and played by choice soon turned into a burdensome necessity. As Weber wrote in the gloomily prophetic ending of his analysis of the Protestant ethic, what had been a freely chosen set of goals and rules became an "iron cage" constraining those who were born into it. "The Puritan wanted to work in a calling; we are forced to do so" (Weber, 1958, p. 181). This petrification of flow activities appears to be a historical constant. Patterns of action are first institutionalized by free choice because they provide optimal experiences; successive generations find those patterns already established and are bored by them (Berger & Luckmann, 1967). The dialectic between freedom and necessity was described by Hegel as the alternation between what he called the "world as history" and the "world as nature." The founding fathers wrote the Constitution and designed the American political system as a spontaneous, creative act. They were making history. We face the Constitution and the government as external givens; almost as natural forces like the weather or like the force of gravity. Activities that were enjoyable to those who first created its rules may be tiresome to those who feel obliged to follow them.

Even though this is not why he said it, Jefferson was right in claiming that each generation must make its own revolution. Mao Tse Tung arrived at the same conclusion about the need for a permanent revolution. Politically their ideas are probably unworkable, but they point at a vital psychological need: namely, the necessity to restructure life activity to make optimal experiences possible.

FLOW AND THE SELF

The relationship between optimal experiences and the self is fraught with apparent paradox. On the one hand, the self is hidden during a flow experience; it cannot be found in consciousness. On the other hand, the self appears to thrive and grow as a result of such experiences. This anomaly suggests that further exploration of the relationship might prove theoretically fruitful.

Experimental social psychology has amply documented the fact that objective self-awareness is an aversive experience. This has been explained in terms of self-awareness inevitably involving self-evaluation and a failure to live up to expected standards (Duval & Wicklund, 1972; Wicklund, 1975). In an earlier volume in this series, it was pointed out that self-awareness produces negative affect only when the discrepancy between the actual and the ideal states is unlikely to be reduced (Carver & Scheier 1981). In other words, the problem with focusing attention on the self is that it reveals depressing inadequacies.

A recent study using the Experience Sampling Method replicated outside the laboratory this negative association between self-awareness and affect, but found it contingent on whether the person was involved in a voluntary or obligatory activity. Self-awareness was associated with a negative experience only when the person felt he or she had freely chosen to do an activity. When doing something that had to be done, focusing attention on the self made no difference in the moods reported (Csikszent-mihalyi & Figurski, in press). These findings suggest an alternative explanation for why being aware of the self is not a positive experience: because self-awareness interrupts involvement in an enjoyable activity. To explore this issue further, it might be helpful to develop a model of the self that will account for the findings.

The self shows itself as a pattern of information in consciousness; more specifically, it is information that stands for, or represents, the information-processing organism itself. It is composed of past experiences strung together by acts of intentionality and shaped by feedback (Csikszent-mihalyi & Rochberg-Halton, 1981).

Being a pattern, the self requires inputs of energy to keep its order intact. Like consciousness itself, of which it is is one of the contents, the self does not keep its shape unless appropriate information is constantly provided to perpetuate its existence. To put it in the simplest possible terms, the self survives by assimilating feedback to intentions.

Whenever a desire arises in consciousness and the self identifies with it, turning it into an intention, the stage is set for potential self-building feedback. If the intention is accomplished, the information will be incorporated into the self, which will appear to be that much stronger the next time it shows up in consciousness. Of course, if the intention fails, the feedback will usually result in a weakening of the self.

This constant interchange, which takes place below the threshold of awareness, results in the gradual modification of the self as the feedback to intentions moves from a positive to negative balance, or vice versa. Without intentions or without feedback, the self would cease to exist as an ordered pattern of information. This is the reason why religions that try to abolish the self prescribe giving up desires and purposeful actions.

Renouncing worldly attachments is the central method used to destructure the self in Zen, Sufi, Yoga, Judeo-Christian, and several other spiritual traditions (Ornstein, 1977, p. 135).

Most people in most cultures, however, learn to develop their selves rather than aiming to dismantle them. In fact, once a self system is established in consciousness, it will try to maintain itself and increase its power. It can do so by directing the energies of the organism to produce feedback congruent with its intentions.

If this is true, then attention turned inwards on the self tends not to be productive. Self-consciousness does not accomplish anything—it does not produce feedback. (There are some quite important exceptions to this statement, but they can be saved for a later treatment. The statement seems to be true most of the time, and for people who are not trained to use reflection in a systematic and constructive way. The exceptions would include philosophers, both natural and professional; artists; mystics, and psychoanalysts.) Paradoxically, when we focus attention on the self, by so doing we deprive it of the sustenance it needs.

By contrast, concentration on an activity produces feedback which nurtures the self. This is especially true if the activity is freely chosen, if it presents opportunities for complex interactions and allows the formulation of increasingly unpredictable intentions. As a result of such an activity—and assuming it was moderately successful—the self emerges strengthened from the evidence of its accomplishments. So the self gets lost when we search for it, and reveals itself when we forget it. Presumably this is the pattern hinted at by the first two rows of Table 1, where we see that a nonalienated self and the ability to find flow are the best predictors of happiness. Another way to view this pattern is within Mead's conceptual framework. Attending to the self reveals the "me," or the self as object. Strictly speaking, the "I" can never be found in consciousness. We can only sense it in action, so to speak; we know of it through its works. At best the "I" appears as a flicker at the periphery of vision as we pursue some difficult or improbable task. For only then is the "I," or the active, self-determining agency of the self, revealed.

In routine, determined, predictable activities there is no necessity to postulate the "I"; a "me" will do very well. In other words, as long as actions can be explained by outside forces or by probabilistic statements that apply to all men, or to all Americans living now, or to members of my profession, a freely acting self is an unnecessary assumption. By Ockham's law, it becomes superfluous and we need not consider it. Only when actions depart from expectations, when unlikely intentions are fulfilled, does an "I" become justified as an explanatory construct. In subjective experience at least, the free self becomes a reality when action bears witness to its existence.

After successfully coping with unlikely challenges, the "I" might reappear in consciousness as the "me." But it is a different "me" from what it had been before; it is now stronger and more competent (Smith, 1968, 1978; White, 1959).

In terms of this model, it might be easier to explain the hide-and-seek of the self in flow experiences. Intense involvement in a complex activity provides the most concentrated feedback for the nourishment of the self. The higher the challenges of the activity, the more unlikely it is that one can meet them, and therefore the greater the experience of order that follows upon success. Enjoyment builds the self. But the self destroys enjoyment; that is, when we reflect on the self, the interaction is interrupted, concentration collapses, and the feedback stops. Thus in the long run self-awareness is inimical to the self, because it interferes with the flow of information that is necessary to maintain it.

TEMPORARY CONCLUSIONS

In the hundred years since the first men assembled at Leipzig to study psychology systematically, much was learned about human behavior, the workings of the nervous system, and the symptomatology of mental disorders. But we still have very little solid knowledge about the dynamics of conscious experience, the *psyche* itself. Only in the past few years has the study of consciousness received a certain academic respectability (Ornstein, 1977; Pope & Singer, 1978).

Yet as I have tried to argue, the information unfolding therein constitutes our life and should therefore be at least of passing interest to students of humankind. Of all the information contained in consciousness, perhaps the most intriguing is the self, or the bundle of signs that represents the experiencer in experience.

The study of flow suggests that consciousness and the self are fragile structures of order that need constant inputs of information energy to expand or even to keep their form intact. The kind of information which can do this has certain common properties: it can be assimilated with neither too little nor too much difficulty; it presents opportunities for interaction with clear goals, rules and feedback; it allows concentration without distraction or ambiguity.

Involved in such an ordered interaction system, consciousness flows without hindrance, bringing into play the "I," the active dimension of the self. Optimal experience is simply this freeing the organism to experience its own freedom. In retrospect, as we look back on our life, these are the experiences that make living worthwhile.

One common misunderstanding about this theory (in the original meaning of the word, as a viewpoint, or encompassing sight, rather than in the contemporary meaning of a logical network of universal statements) is that by emphasizing the quality of experience it encourages a hedonistic, even decadent attitude. After all, as every thinker from Plato to Freud agreed, civilization is built on the harnessing of pleasure, on the postponement of gratification.

But the evidence suggests that this particular Gordian knot need not baffle us further: The old dichotomy was a false one. We might have to forfeit a certain amount of pleasure to accomplish complex tasks, but we need not forego enjoyment. And enjoyment rather than pleasure makes life rewarding. The pessimistic conclusions of former psychologies follow from the failure to distinguish between pleasure and enjoyment—the first homeostatic, conservative, and genetically limited; the second open, growth-producing, and evolutionary. It bears repeating that according to this perspective the hard-working dour Puritans must have enjoyed their lives much more than the playboys who spend their days between Cortina and Cozumel.

What would it take to develop this theory of enjoyment from being just a point of view into a useful scientific tool? First, the relationships described in this chapter should be stated in more formal ways. For instance: "The strength of the self will be directly proportional to the amount of enjoyment experienced." Or "The strength of the self will be inversely proportional to the amount of self-consciousness experienced." When an adequate number of such statements are generated, they must be related to each other and to statements derived from other psychological theories. It is essential, for instance, that the relationships predicated by this theory be reconciled with the regularities uncovered by even widely divergent explanatory systems such as behaviorism or psychoanalytic psychology. Finally, the conditions that set thresholds and limits to the theoretical relationships will have to be discovered and codified. It is clear, for example, that there are striking individual differences in the ability to derive enjoyment from information. Are these due to temperamental differences or to prior experience? Can they all be accounted for in terms of how the self is organized?

This kind of systematic appraisal of consciousness has not been started. Yet there is no scientific theory without a logical network of empirically validated statements. Will one be built in this field? It will if enough people have fun trying to build it.

REFERENCES

Berger, P. L., & Luckmann, T. *The social construction of reality*. Garden City, NY: Doubleday, 1967.

Brumback, R. A., & Weinberg, W. A. Relationship of hyperactivity and depression in children. *Perceptual and Motor Skills*, 1977, *45*, 247-251.

Carver, C., & Scheier, M. F. A control-systems approach to behavioral self-regulation. In L. Wheeler (Ed.), *Review of personality and social psychology* (Vol. 1), Beverly Hills, CA: Sage, 1981.

Csikszentmihalyi, M. *Beyond boredom and anxiety*. San Francisco: Jossey-Bass, 1975.

Csikszentmihalyi, M. Attention and the wholistic approach to behavior. In K. S. Pope & J. L. Singer (Eds.), *The stream of consciousness*. New York: Plenum, 1978.

Csikszentmihalyi, M. The concept of flow. In B. Sutton-Smith (Ed.), *Play and learning*. New York: Gardner, 1979.

Csikszentmihalyi, M. Intrinsic motivation and effective teaching. In J. Bess (Ed.), *The Motivation to Teach*. San Francisco: Jossey-Bass, 1981. (a)

Csikszentmihalyi, M. Leisure and socialization. *Social Forces*, 1981, *60*, 332-340. (b)

Csikszentmihalyi, M. Education and life-long learning. In R. Gross (Ed.), *Invitation to life-long learning*. New York: Follett, 1982.

Csikszentmihalyi, M., & Figurski, T. The experience of self-awareness in daily life. *Journal of Personality*, in press.

Csikszentmihalyi, M., & Graef, R. Flow and the quality of experience in everyday life. Unpublished manuscript, University of Chicago, 1979.

Csikszentmihalyi, M., & Graef, R. The experience of freedom in daily life. *American Journal of Community Psychology*, 1980, *8*, 401-414.

Csikszentmihalyi, M., & Kubey, R. Television and the rest of life. *Public Opinion Quarterly*, 1981, *45*, 317-328.

Csikszentmihalyi, M., & Larson, R. Intrinsic rewards in school crime. *Crime and Delinquency,* 1978, *24,* 322-335.

Csikszentmihalyi, M., Larson, R., & Prescott, S. The ecology of adolescent activity and experience. *Journal of Youth and Adolescence,* 1977, 6 181-294.

Csikszentmihalyi, M., & Rochberg-Halton, E. *The meaning of things: Domestic symbols and the self.* New York: Cambridge University Press, 1981.

Duval, S., & Wicklund, R. A. *A theory of objective self-awareness.* New York: Academic Press, 1972.

Firth, R. *Primitive economics of the New Zealand Maori.* New York: Dutton, 1929.

Geiwitz, P. J. Structure of boredom. *Journal of Personality and Social Psychology,* 1966, *3,* 592-600.

Gianinno, S., Graef, R., & Csikszentmihalyi, M. Well-being and the perceived balance between opportunities and capabilities. Paper presented at the 87th American Psychology Association Convention, New York, 1979.

Graef, R., Gianinno, S., Csikszentmihalyi, M., & Rich, E. Instrumental thoughts and daydreams in everyday life. Paper presented at the 86th American Psychology Association Convention, Toreonto, 1978.

Hamburg, D., Pribram, K. H., & Stunkard, L. (Eds.). *Perception and its disorders.* Baltimore: Williams & Wilkins, 1970.

Hamilton, J. A. Attention, personality, and the self-regulation of mood: Absorbing interest and boredom. In B. A. Maher (Ed.), *Progress in experimental personality research* (Vol. 10). New York: Academic Press, 1981.

Harrow, M., Tucker, G. J., Hanover, N. H., & Shield, P. Stimulus overinclusion in schizophrenic disorders. *Archives of General Psychiatry,* 1972, *27,* 40-45.

Harrow, M., Grinker, R. R., Holzman, P. S., & Kayton, L. Anhedonia and schizophrenia. *American Journal of Psychiatry,* 1977, *134,* 794-797.

Maddi, S. R., Kobasa, S. C., & Hoover, M. An alienation test. *Journal of Humanistic Psychology,* 1979, *19,* 73-76.

Mayers, P. L. Flow in adolescence and its relation to school experience. Unpublished Ph.D. dissertation, University of Chicago, 1978.

Ornstein, R. E. *The psychology of consciousness.* New York: Harcourt Brace Jovanovich, 1977.

Pope, K. S., & Singer, J. L. *The stream of consciousness.* New York: Plenum, 1978.

Rubinstein, B., Csikszentmihalyi, M., & Graef, R. Attention and alienation in daily experience. Paper presented at the 88th American Psychology Association Convention, Montreal, 1980.

Sahlins, M. *Stone age economics.* Chicago: Aldine, 1972.

Smith, M. B. Competence and socialization. In J. Clausen (Ed.), *Socialization and society.* Boston: Little, Brown, 1968.

Smith, M. B. Perspectives on selfhood. *American Psychologist,* 1978, December, 1053-1063.

Thompson, E. P. *The making of the English working class.* New York: Vintage, 1963.

Wallace, A.F.C. *Rockdale.* New York: Knopf, 1978.

Weber, M. *The Protestant ethic and the spirit of capitalism.* New York: Scribner, 1958.

White, R. W. Motivation reconsidered: The concept of competence. *Psychological Review*, 1959, *66*, 297-333.

Wicklund, R. A. Objective self-awareness. In L. Berkowitz (Ed.), *Advances in experimental social psychology* (Vol. 8). New York: Academic Press, 1975.

Wynne, L. C., Cromwell, R. L., & Matthysse, S. (Eds.). *The nature of schizophrenia*. New York: John Wiley, 1976.

Zubek, J. P. (Ed.). *Sensory deprivation: Fifteen years of research*. New York: Appleton, 1969.

Zuckerman, M. Perceptual isolation as a stress situation: A review. *Archives of General Psychology*, 1964, *11*, 225-276.

Zuckerman, M. *Sensation seeking: Beyond the optimal level of arousal*. Hillsdale, NJ: Lawrence Erlbaum, 1979.

Schachter's Theories of Affiliation and Emotion:

IMPLICATIONS OF DEVELOPMENTAL RESEARCH

PHILLIP SHAVER

MARY KLINNERT

Phillip Shaver, Associate Professor and head of graduate studies in personality and social psychology at the University of Denver, is co-author of *Measures of Social Psychological Attitudes* (Michigan) and of the recently published *In Search of Intimacy* (Delacorte). His research interests include relationship formation and dissolution, loneliness, emotion, social motivation, self-awareness, and sex-role orientation.

Mary Klinnert, a recent graduate of the University of Denver, is a child clinical psychologist at National Jewish Hospital and Asthma Research Center in Denver, and an instructor at the University of Colorado Health Sciences Center. Her research has focused on emotional communication between parents and infants—specifically on infants' search for and use of emotional signals from their mothers' faces.

Research on affiliation, social comparison, and emotion—and on the relationships between them—has proceeded apace during the past 20 years, spurred in part by Schachter's early contributions (1959; Schachter &

AUTHORS' NOTE: We are grateful to Albert Bandura, Donna Bradshaw, Joseph Campos, Robert Emde, Harry Reis, and Lawrence Wrightsman for helpful comments on earlier drafts of this chapter.

Singer, 1962). Unfortunately, most of the existing research has been based exclusively on college student subjects. Until recently, little attention was paid to social comparison of emotions in early childhood or to the developmental course of the processes identified by Schachter: affiliation under stressful conditions and social comparison of emotional states. Nor has much effort been directed toward the integration of Schachterian research with studies of the social and emotional behavior of nonhuman primates, even though, at least since the publication of Darwin's (1872) *Expression of Emotions in Man and Animals,* it has been evident that humans and animals share basic emotions and basic patterns of emotional expression. As Plutchik (1980) noted recently,

> The beginnings of a new integration are slowly becoming evident, one that is relevant not only to the behavior of college students but also to the behavior of infants, children, adults, . . . higher primates, and lower animals. . . . The basic idea . . . is that emotions must be conceptualized within an evolutionary framework.

Questions have already been raised about the place, if it has one, of Schachter's work in this emerging "psychoevolutionary synthesis." Plutchik's (1980) verdict, for example, was quite damning: "The Schachter-Singer theory is not about naturally occurring emotions." Combined with recent methodological critiques and reported failures to replicate Schachter and Singer's (1962) results (Maslach, 1979; Marshall & Zimbardo, 1979), conclusions like Plutchik's suggest that emotion theorists are about to set Schachter's work aside. Though we, too, intend to criticize some of his conclusions, we believe it is a mistake to neglect certain features of his work, especially the origins of his emotion theory in research on affiliation and social comparison. Since the current trend in emotion research is to emphasize the social context of emotion and emotional expression, and to speculate about the role of social processes in the evolutionary history of emotion (e.g., Campos & Stenberg, 1981; Ekman, 1972; Izard, 1977; Klinnert, Campos, Sorce, Emde, & Svejda, 1982; Sroufe, Waters, & Matas, 1974), it seems likely that Schachter's ideas, having been "social" from the start, will be relevant. It is ironic that Schachter's ideas emerged from a social psychological context and then over time became less and less social, finally culminating in a theory about physiological arousal and cognitive labeling (Schachter, 1971), while emotion theorists who at first neglected social processes now express great interest in them. The result is a little like the proverbial ships passing in the night.

This chapter grew out of a comparison of the results of Schachter's studies and the results of recent research and theory concerning the emotional and social behavior of human and other primate infants. The comparison illuminates certain basic features of emotion and calls into question some widely accepted implications of Schachter's experiments. Unlike Maslach, Marshall, and Zimbardo, we do not question the validity or replicability of Schachter's results; in fact, we find them to be in line with recent developmental studies and quite plausible in their own right. Our claim will be that the data were misleadingly interpreted in terms of Festinger's (1954) social comparison theory while other more plausible interpretations were neglected. To make this case, we will (1) review evidence from recent studies of infants and primates which shed light on the relationship between social processes and emotion; (2) examine carefully the now relatively neglected development of Schachter's thinking about affiliation, social comparison, and emotion, giving special attention to his 1959 book, *The Psychology of Affiliation* (which was not cited by Maslach, Marshall and Zimbardo, or Plutchik); (3) reconsider two goals of affiliation—anxiety reduction and cognitive clarity—which Schachter mentioned but neglected in favor of a third possible goal, "self evaluation"— the conceptual precursor of the cognitive labeling component of his two-factor theory of emotion; and (4) outline certain features which a general or integrative theory of emotion must eventually include. Our larger aim is to contribute to a theory of emotion which fits within an evolutionary and developmental framework. Although Schachter made few explicit efforts in this direction, much of his work is compatible with it.

ATTACHMENT AND SOCIAL REFERENCING

Schachter (1959) considered four reasons for affiliation under stressful conditions: direct anxiety reduction (due simply to the presence of others), indirect anxiety reduction (due to distraction), increased cognitive clarity (due to information provided by others), and self-evaluation (based on comparisons with others). He clearly favored the latter alternative. In thinking about recent research involving nonhuman primates and human infants, we have had reason to question Schachter's preference. There is now overwhelming evidence (to be reviewed below) for the calming effects of social contact on distressed infants (and adults as well), and for the idea that infants, at least, consult others in order to gain information about the environment. In contrast, self-labeling of emotional states is presumably not a goal, or even a possibility, for nonverbal primates and preverbal, cognitively immature human infants. Since there are clear emotional similarities between nonhuman and human primates, and between human infants and adults, it seems sensible to look first for commonalities before inventing an "adults only" theory of emotion. (This is not to say there are no special features of adult emotionality, due for example to cognitive development, increased self-awareness, or extensive enculturation.)

Our tack will be, first, to review primate and infant research in order to identify certain basic features of emotionality and emotional communication, and then to reevaluate Schachter's work with these findings in mind. At the end we will talk briefly about adult complexities which need to be considered when constructing a more complete theory of human emotion.

Attachment

Ten years after the publication of Schachter's affiliation book, Bowlby (1969) issued the first volume of his well-known series on attachment and loss, which marked a change in the way many behavioral scientists thought about social relationships.[1] Combining ideas and evidence from ethology and psychoanalysis, Bowlby argued that the first social bond in a person's life, the attachment between mother and infant, is based on inherited mechanisms designed by evolution to assure the infant's survival. Infants come equipped to capture their mother in a web of attachment; they cry, respond dramatically to rocking, feeding, and cuddling, and within the first few months of life make eye contact and smile—responses which win the attention and affection of most parents. The infant develops a special relationship with its main caretaker; only mother (or a regular mother substitute) can easily calm the infant when it is distressed. The infant becomes upset when separated from mother (the "attachment object," in Bowlby's terminology) and typically expresses joy and initiates physical contact upon reunion (Ainsworth, Blehar, Waters, & Wall, 1978). Mother's presence facilitates the infants' exploration of the environment, an effect which appears to be mediated by a feeling of security (Sroufe & Waters, 1977). Attached infants maintain a certain average distance from mother, balancing the desire for security against the attraction of exploring the surrounding environment. The "set goal" for proximity (a term borrowed by Bowlby from cybernetic control theory) is automatically adjusted downward when the infant is tired, frightened, or in pain; under these conditions he or she seeks closer contact with mother. Bowlby cited studies of rhesus monkeys, baboons, chimpanzees, and gorillas to show that attachment behavior is probably universal among primates, serving, among other purposes, the goal of protection of nearly helpless infants from predators.

In his second volume, Bowlby (1973) expanded his ideas concerning the "attachment system" and its relation to the "fear system." He pointed out that while the two systems differ (e.g., the fear system involves avoidance of some object or situation), both involve seeking the presence of conspecifics and touching or clutching them. Bowlby listed a number of "natural clues to danger," including strangeness or novelty, sudden changes in stimulation, height, and simply being alone, which (in the natural environment) are often associated with predators and other threats to life. Evolution has rewarded animals for sticking together and for seeking each other out when danger is imminent.

Many of the central tenets of attachment theory have now been extensively tested in the laboratory and in naturalistic observations of humans and other animals. The idea that infants and young children remain close to mother has received considerable support (summarized by Maccoby, 1980). When in a familiar environment, with no threats or unexpected disruptions, older infants and toddlers freely wander away from mother (older children daring to go further, as Rheingold & Eckerman, 1970, have shown). Especially where the environment is novel, however, young children repeatedly "check back" with mother visually, vocally, or through locomotion (Mahler, Pine, & Bergman, 1975), resulting in closer average proximity to mother in strange as compared with familiar settings (e.g., Castell, 1972).

Bowlby's (1969) claim that proximity-seeking increases under threatening or frightening conditions has also received ample support. In a "strange situation" paradigm designed expressly for the purpose of assessing infant attachment behavior, Ainsworth, Bell, and Stayton (1971; see also Ainsworth et al., 1978) placed 12-month-old infants and their mothers in a room which, following a few minutes for acclimation, was unexpectedly entered by a stranger. When this happened, many infants quickly moved closer to mother, some clinging to her or hiding safely behind her.

This retreat to mother is exaggerated when the stimulus is frightening as well as novel. Maccoby and Jacklin (1973) reported that 13- to 14-month-olds who played happily with toys at a considerable distance from mother when in an emotionally neutral baseline condition retreated quickly to her side when an angry male stranger's voice was projected into the laboratory. The infant's beeline to mother was even faster when the voice was made more intense. Once in contact with mother, infants in these threat conditions clung to her tenaciously.

This behavior is remarkably similar to what has been observed in nonhuman primates. Mason and his associates (summarized in Mason, 1967) conducted a series of experiments in which chimpanzees were exposed to a variety of stressful conditions, including unfamiliar surroundings, separation from cagemates, intense noise, and—interestingly, in light of Schachter and Singer's (1962) study—ingesting amphetamine. In every case, the young chimps clung to their mothers or to a familiar companion and drastically reduced the time they spent playing. Similar behavior had previously been reported by Harlow (1961), who studied rhesus monkeys' attachment to surrogate mothers. When a novel and threatening stimulus was introduced into their cages, the monkeys ran to their cloth "mothers" and clutched and clung. Since the artificial mothers had never protected the infants from danger, and in fact had done no more than passively provide what Harlow called "contact comfort," it seems likely that proximity-seeking and clinging in response to frightening or novel events is largely innate.

Research has shown that contact with mother dramatically reduces infant anxieties. In studying reactions to strangers, several investigators have found that human infants exhibit less distress when approached by a stranger if they are seated in their mothers' laps than if they are seated several feet away from her (Bronson, 1972; Morgan & Ricciuti, 1969). However, the baby does not have to be touching mother for her to have a comforting effect. Campos, Emde, Gaensbauer, and Henderson (1975) subjected 9-month-old infants to a stranger-approach situation, either with mother present (four feet away) or with her out of the room. The infants' heart rate was continuously monitored. Accelerations were found to be significantly more frequent and more extreme in the infant-alone condition.

Again, results from animal research parallel the results from studies of human infants. Mason and Berkson (1962) administered electric shock to infant chimpanzees both while they were alone and while they were securely held by a familiar experimenter. As shock level increased, the solitary monkeys' distress cries increased proportionately, while the same monkeys when held remained relatively calm and quiet. At the highest shock levels, solitary monkeys' distress level was more than eight times as high as the level when they were held. The calming effect of contact with a caretaker following a period of separation has also been measured physiologically. Mendoza, Coe, Smotherman, and Levine (1979) reported a rise in the stress-related hormone cortisol in both mother and infant rhesus monkeys when they were separated, followed by a sharp drop back to normal levels when the two were reunited.

Social Referencing

While proximity-seeking and clinging are prototypical signs of attachment, Bowlby (1969, 1973) and others (e.g., Ainsworth, 1974; Sroufe & Waters, 1977) have emphasized that attachment behaviors are diverse and to some extent interchangeable. For example, when faced with strangers, infants do not always move physically closer to mother. Instead, they often look alternately at mother and at the environmental event. Such looking behavior has been noted in the "strange situation" (Bretherton & Ainsworth, 1974) and in other stranger-approach studies (Emde, Gaensbauer, & Harmon, 1976; Schaffer, 1966). Looks to mother also occur in relation to environmental events that do not involve strangers. Anderson (1972) observed infants aged 15 to 30 months as they left and returned to their caretakers in a park. When the infants moved away from their mothers they looked back frequently. "The best way to identify a mother-infant pair is to see whom a child looks at when he is astonished or startled by external events like a noise in the distance or a passing animal; only the mother's attention is sought in such circumstances."

For a long while it was thought that the purpose of this looking behavior was solely to confirm that mother was present. Presumably, an infant who had become emotionally attached to its mother would be calmed by knowing that she was available should she be needed. While mother's presence does, by itself, have a calming effect, recent studies have revealed another important function of looking behavior.

In a 1975 study, Carr, Dabbs, and Carr placed two-year-olds in a laboratory room which contained some attractive toys attached to a corner opposite to where mother was seated. In one condition she was in view and facing the infant; in another, she was in view but not facing the infant. When mother's face was visible in this novel situation, infants played happily at a distance from her. When she was visible but facing away, however, they tended to forego the toys and move to places in the room where they could see her face.

Going a step further, Sorce and Emde (1981) showed that sight of mother's face alone is not satisfying if she pays no attention to the infant. They compared the proximity of infants to mother when she either paid attention to them (without talking) or intently read a magazine. In the latter condition, the 15-month-olds stayed closer to mother, especially when a mechanical robot toy entered the room. In contrast, when mothers continued to attend to their infants, the infants approached and explored the robot more, as if they felt relatively safe as long as mother was watching and indicated no danger.

This suggests another interpretation of infants' desire to be close to mother and look toward her in novel or potentially threatening situations. They may be looking to her for *information about the environment* as well as for comfort. Since young infants cannot communicate verbally, information must be provided nonverbally—for example, by mother's facial expressions.

In fact, two recent studies indicate that infants of 12 months and beyond not only reliably look to mother when presented with novel stimuli, but also use information from her facial expression to decide how to react. Klinnert (1981) created a situation in which three uncertainty-arousing stimuli (a remote-controlled dinosaur, a large remote-controlled spider, and a life-size model of the Incredible Hulk's head) appeared while a 12- or 18-month-old infant played in a corner. The room was arranged so that the infant was at some distance from mother and had to turn to see her after noticing one of the experimental stimuli. Most of the infants looked questioningly at their mother on all three trials. Mothers (who had previously received careful instructions) posed one of three facial expressions—approval (smile), fear, or neutral—when a particular stimulus appeared and her child turned to consult her. The infant's first move after observing mother's face was toward her if she showed a fearful face and toward the stimulus if she seemed pleased.

Sorce, Emde, Campos, and Klinnert (1981) created an uncertain situation for 12-month-old infants by modifying a "visual cliff"—an apparatus designed originally to study infants' and animals' perception of heights.

The "cliff" is like a table top, half of which is a solid checkerboard; the other half is a thick plexiglas sheet through which can be seen a checkerboard some distance below. In the Sorce et al. study, the apparent vertical drop-off was altered until a distance was found which caused indecisiveness in infants when they reached the "edge." An infant's mother stood at the far end of the apparatus alongside an attractive toy; she had been instructed to show either fear or a smile when the infant stopped at the "edge" and consulted her face. Of the 17 infants who received the fear signal, *none* of them crossed the plexiglas surface. Of the 19 who received a smile, 14 crossed to the end where mother was standing.

This pattern of behavior—looking to mother and then using information provided by her facial expressions of emotion—has been termed *social referencing* by Campos and Stenberg (1981). Infants, when they "reference," appear to be requesting information about an environmental event and adjusting their behavior accordingly. Campos and Stenberg suggest that social referencing occurs when an infant is faced with an event which exceeds his or her own intrinsic appraisal capacities. (The term "appraisal," when used in connection with emotion, is borrowed from Arnold, 1960.) The infant's lack of understanding seems to create a feeling of uncertainty and apprehensiveness which can be relieved or resolved by seeking the opinion of a trusted "expert" (in this case, mother).

In the Klinnert and Sorce et al. studies it was necessary to do considerable pilot testing before hitting upon stimulus conditions that created optimal ambivalence between the tendency to approach an interesting or attractive object and the tendency to avoid danger. If the Hulk head was made more realistic by attaching a shirt to it, for example, infants tended to become distressed and scrambled for mother without stopping to consider her expression. Similarly, if the visual cliff was too deep, infants looked down and backed up, regardless of mother's beaming face. If the cliff was too shallow, on the other hand, infants seemed to view it as a familiar-sized step and turned around to scoot "down" it without the benefit of mother's nonverbal advice. In other words, infants sometimes appraised the situation confidently on their own, and in such cases were not much affected by mothers' emotional signals.

Affiliation Beyond Infancy

So far we have reviewed evidence that both primate and human infants seek contact with others in times of uncertainty and distress. This early form of affiliation serves two distinct but related functions: direct anxiety (or fear) reduction and reduced uncertainty (increased cognitive clarity). There is obviously a long developmental path between infancy and adulthood, but for both human and nonhuman primates the relationship between distress and affiliation is evident all through life.

Rowell and Hinde (1963) exposed 17 rhesus monkeys, most of them adults, to an unfamiliar, threatening person draped in a sheet and wearing a mask; each monkey underwent this stress both alone and in a familiar group. When alone, the behavior of the monkeys, both adults and children, indicated more distress than when they encountered the costumed human together. When alone, their hair stood on end more, they made more threat noises, and more often looked through a window to view companions from whom they were temporarily estranged. The stressor was not merely isolation (as shown in a baseline condition) but being alone under stress. For adults as well as infants, "isolation is best regarded not merely as an additional stress-producing factor acting equally under all circumstances, but rather as one which while producing relatively little effect on undisturbed animals can strongly accentuate the effect of other stress-producing agents."

Observers of primates in the wild have noted similar phenomena. Eibl-Eibesfeldt (1970) reported that "even high-ranking [adult] animals, when frightened, will clasp a lower-ranking animal for reassurance. . . . Bodily contact has a calming effect." Lawick-Goodall (1968) noticed that both adult and infant chimpanzees reach to touch each other when frightened. Kummer (1967) made similar observations of baboons; when under stress, both adults and infants cling to their companions.

There is also a growing literature on the stress-moderating effect of social support in adult humans. Bowlby (1973) reviewed evidence showing that humans, especially friends and members of the same family, seek each other out when natural disasters strike. Henderson (1977) says: "Subjects commonly report that the presence of others, particularly immediate kin, lessens the anxiety and distress occasioned by the situation and promotes purposeful behavior." Cobb (1976), in an extensive review of the medical consequences of stressful life events, concluded that

> social support can protect people in crisis from a wide variety of pathological states: from low birth weight to death, from arthritis through tuberculosis to depression, alcoholism, and the social breakdown syndrome. Furthermore, social support may reduce the

amount of medication required, accelerate recovery, and facilitate compliance with prescribed medical regimens.

Researchers have yet to agree on a precise definition of "social support," but the various working definitions are fairly similar. Cobb (1976) tentatively defined it in terms of "information" leading to certain beliefs—that one is cared for and loved, esteemed and valued, and integrally involved in a network of communication and mutual obligations. In an influential paper entitled "The Provisions of Social Relationships," Weiss (1974) listed, among other provisions, intimacy, shared concerns, nurturance, reassurance of worth, a feeling of "reliable alliance," and guidance (i.e., information and advice).

There is less direct research evidence for "social referencing" beyond infancy because the concept is new, but we might view observational learning in childhood (Bandura & Walters, 1963), conformity and nonverbal social influence in adults (Asch, 1956, Milgram, Bickman, & Berkowitz, 1969), and social comparison of opinions and abilities (Cottrell & Epley, 1977; Festinger, 1954) as examples of this phenomenon. The literature on "reference groups" (e.g., Hyman, 1968; Merton & Kitt, 1950) is also relevant, of course. Studies of children's modeling of other people's behavior (reviewed by Bandura, 1971) clearly indicate that children pay most attention to *well-liked* and *competent* models. Similarly, a host of social influence experiments have shown that adults are most influenced by well-liked and knowledgeable or prestigious communicators (reviewed by Freedman, Sears, & Carlsmith, 1981). It seems safe to conclude, then, that humans of all ages "reference" others whom they expect to be friendly (or sympathetic) and knowledgeable.

The same tendencies are evident in nonhuman primates. Observational learning is well-documented in studies of both child and adult chimpanzees and rhesus monkeys. When these primates witness an event that causes pain to a member of their group, they learn to avoid that event themselves, and when a clever group member discovers a new and useful trick, his or her companions are likely to adopt it (see the review by Hinde, 1974). When faced with a novel or threatening event, lower status primates tend to look to more dominant members of their group for an "authoritative" reaction (Lawick-Goodall, 1972).

To summarize, when infant or adult primates, including humans, are fearful or apprehensive, they tend to seek comfort from others. Early in life, these "others" tend to be primary caretakers, but with development, the circle of reliable others expands. There is considerable evidence that the presence of sympathetic, comforting others in a fearful situation is anxiety-reducing. Beyond comforting, however, conspecifics provide information about the degree of threat inherent in particular situations and model appropriate behavioral responses. Even infants seek information from others when their own appraisals are uncertain. Finally, we have noted that social referencing can occur nonverbally; in fact, for human infants and nonhuman primates it cannot occur in any other way.

RETRACING SCHACHTER'S STEPS

We are now ready to examine Schachter's research in light of recent work on attachment, anxiety reduction, and social referencing. In order to show why we believe that a reinterpretation of some of Schachter's key results is warranted, we will provide a step-by-step exegesis of the 1959 affiliation book and the 1962 emotion paper. A close reading reveals where certain mistaken emphases in the emotion theory originated.

Affiliation

The Psychology of Affiliation begins very generally: "Despite the importance of the study of the affiliative needs, almost nothing is known of the variables and conditions affecting these needs. We have no precise idea of the circumstances that drive men either to seek one another out or to crave privacy, and we have only the vaguest and most obvious sort of suggestions concerning the kinds of satisfaction that men seek in company." Early in the book Schachter drew an a priori distinction between two general classes of reasons for affiliation, (1) mediation of personal goals (e.g., getting help to lift a log off the pathway, "a peculiarly asocial sort of affiliation") and (2) fulfilling "needs which can be satisfied *only* in interpersonal relations," such as needs for approval, support, friendship, and prestige. Schachter intended to focus only on the latter class, the truly social needs.

In discussing these needs at greater length, he focused on social comparison processes, quoting Festinger (1954):

To the extent that self evaluation can only be accomplished by means of comparison with other persons, the drive for self evaluation is a force acting on persons to belong to groups, to associate with others. And the subjective feelings of correctness in one's opinions and the subjective evaluation of adequacy of one's performance on important abilities are some of the satisfactions that persons attain in the course of these associations with other people.

While reviewing evidence which supported Festinger's theory, Schachter said: "If one broadens this 'drive for evaluation of opinions and abilities' into a more general 'drive for cognitive clarity,' one does find additional evidence for the proposition that evaluative or cognitive needs are an important source of affiliative behavior." This additional evidence included, prominently, a 1955 study by Schachter and Burdick in which a bizarre experimentally staged event in a girls' school led students to gossip and speculate wildly about possible causes. Notice that "cognitive clarity" referred primarily to cognitions about the environment, not to self-evaluation.

From the start, then, Schachter's work on affiliation—and hence on emotion, since his emotion theory grew out of the affiliation studies—took shape within a theoretical context which included social comparison processes, needs for cognitive clarity, and reactions to novel and inexplicable events. This angle of approach seems to have greatly influenced his interpretation of data and his choice of what to study further.

Toward the end of the first chapter, Schachter (1959) summarized the available literature on social isolation—for the most part anecdotal reports from prisoners and religious hermits. Common to many reports, he noticed, was an initial stage of fear bordering on panic.

[T]he reported 'pain' of the isolation experience seems typically to bear a nonmonotonic relationship to time—increasing to a maximum and then, in many cases, decreasing sharply. This decrease in pain is frequently marked by onset of a state of apathy sometimes so severe as to resemble a schizophrenic-like state of withdrawal and detachment.

(It's interesting to note that a similar sequence—agitated, anxious protest followed by quiet despair and, eventually, by emotional detachment— occurs in human infants separated from their mothers [Bowlby, 1973] and in human adults following the death of a loved one [Bowlby, 1980].) Schachter summarized the anecdotal reports and his own pilot studies of social isolation by saying, "[I]t is evident that anxiety, in some degree, is a fairly common concomitant of isolation." He then speculatively reversed this relationship and launched the series of experiments which would lead, in time, to his theory of emotion: "For a variety of frankly intuitive reasons, it seemed reasonable to expect that if conditions of isolation produce anxiety, conditions of anxiety would lead to the increase of affiliative tendencies."

To arouse anxiety in college student females, Schachter threatened them with painful electric shock. He found, as most readers already know, that greater anxiety, or fear, was associated with a greater desire to affiliate with other girls who were participating in the study.

To test whether the need for affiliation was "directional" (i.e., partial to certain kinds of companions), Schachter next conducted an experiment in which females who were threatened with painful shock could affiliate either with fellow subjects or, in another condition, with female students who were not part of the experiment. Subjects clearly preferred the company of other subjects. In our opinion, Schachter drew an incorrect conclusion from this result: "Whatever the needs aroused by the manipulation of anxiety, it would seem that their satisfaction demands the presence of others in a similar situation. . . . Misery doesn't love just any kind of company, it loves only miserable company."

If we think about possible parallels between the behavior of Schachter's subjects and the behavior of infants in, say, Ainsworth's "strange situation," it is obvious that "miserable" (frightened) infants do not seek "miserable company." They seek someone who, past experience indicates, is likely to be both *sympathetic* and *knowledgeable* in times of uncertainty or distress. College students might very well do the same, if given the opportunity. A fellow subject in Schachter's experiment was likely to be more sympathetic than an outsider, we would guess, and possibly more knowledgeable about the threatening situation at hand. Besides being familiar with the experiment itself, some fellow subjects might have had relevant information to share concerning the likely effects of electric shock. One of Schachter's internal analyses revealed, in fact, that subjects who had had less experience with electricity were more likely to seek affiliation with other subjects. Schachter failed to consider "nonmiserable" people who might have been viewed as desirable companions for his frightened subjects—people known to be sympathetic (for example, friends or family members), or people with special knowledge about electricity.

Following the directionality experiment, one plausible explanation for affiliation under conditions of anxiety—namely, that anxious subjects wished to distract themselves by conversing with other people about virtually anything—was eliminated. The remaining explanations included (1) that subjects wanted to hatch a rebellion against the experimenter, (2) that they wanted to gain cognitive clarity with respect to a novel and unexpected situation, (3) that they hoped the presence of others would directly reduce their anxiety, and (4) that they wanted to evaluate and understand their own feelings through social comparison. Schachter acknowledged the similarity between cognitive clarity and self-evaluation, which earlier he had placed in a single conceptual category, but he now decided to separate them theoretically: "For the moment, . . . we would prefer to keep these two categories distinct, with cognitive clarity referring strictly to information gathering of the order of gossip or newspaper reading and self evaluation referring to the attempt via social comparison processes to place and evaluate one's own opinions and feelings."

Schachter reasoned—incorrectly, we believe—that adding a no-talk condition to his experiment would rule out the cognitive clarity hypothesis. (It would also, and did, rule out the rebellion hypothesis, but that is of less concern here.)

> Either to escape from the situation or to satisfy one's curiosity and achieve some degree of cognitive clarity requires the opportunity to talk to one's fellow subjects. On the other hand, verbal communication, though certainly helpful, is probably not indispensable for either self evaluation or anxiety reduction. An exchange of sympathetic glances or a friendly pat on the back may indeed be anxiety reducing. Similarly, no great perspicacity is required to surmise, just by looking, the reactions of people to anxiety-provoking situations, and a glance may tell a good deal about how other members of an experimental group are reacting as compared with oneself.

Schachter ignored the possibility that the reason for wanting to know other people's reactions might be not to scrutinize and label oneself, but to assess the objective danger of the external threat.

Recall for a moment the recent studies of social referencing in infancy. Infants look to mother when they are uncertain about the malignity or benignity of a novel or puzzling object or situation. They seek nonverbal cues concerning whether they should be frightened or bold. But they are not, we assume, attempting to self-label an emotional state; they are simply trying to appraise a potential threat in the environment. Nothing in Schachter's No Talk experiment rules out the possibility that his young adult subjects were doing the same thing. (This is important because Schachter's ideas about emotion stem from a self-labeling interpretation of the affiliation studies.)

In the No Talk study, Schachter for the first time asked subjects, at the end of the experiment, why they had chosen to wait together or alone. The following is one of the few answers quoted: "I wanted to wait with other people to see how they would react while waiting for the experiment. By seeing that they weren't worried then I wouldn't be." Says Schachter: "Certainly self-evaluative and possibly anxiety-reducing motives are evident in such a statement." We would say, in contrast, that the desire to reduce anxiety is certainly evident and that the need for cognitive clarity concerning the danger inherent in the situation is as likely an explanation as is the need for self-evaluation. This is one of several places where Schachter's desire to apply social comparison theory to the self-labeling of emotions seems to have run ahead of his actual results.

In order to see whether the relationship between anxiety and affiliation would hold for another "drive" state, Schachter repeated the basic experiment, this time manipulating hunger instead of fear. As it turned out, intense hunger, like intense fear or anxiety, increased the tendency to affiliate. In earlier experiments, firstborn subjects had proven to be more affiliative than laterborns, but in the hunger experiment no such relationship was discovered. Schachter thought this might be because firstborns, during infancy, receive more attention from their parents, especially when they are frightened or injured. In contrast, firstborns and laterborns are probably equally likely to be fed. Schachter reviewed available evidence, further corroborated since then (e.g., Nisbett, 1968), that firstborns have lower pain thresholds than laterborns, more easily become anxious, and even with anxiety held constant are more prone to affiliation.

In all of Schachter's experiments, subjects merely indicated a desire to wait alone or together. The study ended once this preference was expressed. While the 1959 monograph was being written, however, Wrightsman (1959, 1960) conducted a dissertation experiment, under Schachter's sponsorship, in which subjects in an anxiety-provoking situation actually waited either alone, together with no talking allowed, or together with talking allowed. The reasoning behind this study was as follows:

> If the presumed anxiety-reducing property of group membership is a potent determinant of the choice of 'Together,' it should be anticipated that being with others will actually reduce anxiety. If evaluative needs are major determinants of the relationship between anxiety and affiliation, it should be anticipated that being with others will lead to homogeneity of emotional intensity among the group members and to relative stability of emotions.

Wrightsman's experiment (which, incidentally, was the first to include both male and female subjects) supported *both* hypotheses. Especially for firstborn subjects, anxiety reduction occurred in the "together" conditions, whether or not talking was allowed. Over and above this effect, both firstborn and laterborn subjects showed "homogenization" of anxiety levels—that is, increased emotional similarity to other group members—as a result of waiting together. This homogenization was not due solely to the general downward trend of anxiety levels; and, interestingly, it occurred whether or not talking was allowed. (There were no sex differences.)

Schachter emphasized that "there were no externally imposed pressures to uniformity. There was no group goal, no reward for conformity, and no penalty for nonconformity. The subjects . . . made their judgments of their own emotional state in complete privacy. In short, there is every indication that the conformity . . . is a manifestation of a genuine individual need for appraisal of a state of emotion or feeling." Apparently he had convinced himself by this point that the conformity was due to a *self-evaluative* process, rather than to an *appraisal of the environment* influenced by social referencing.

While accepting the experimental results, we remain unconvinced of the self-evaluation hypothesis. Nothing in Schachter's book indicates that self-evaluation rather than anxiety reduction and "cognitive clarity"—or, as we prefer to say, anxiety reduction and confident appraisal of the situation—was the goal of affiliating with others in his and Wrightsman's studies. Thus, the three major plausible causes of affiliation with which Schachter began his explorations—anxiety reduction, cognitive clarity, and self-evaluation—are still viable, and of them, the one he chose to emphasize seems least convincing.

That subjects who were more familiar with electricity were less eager to affiliate when threatened with electric shock, and that (as the hunger experiment showed) experienced lunch-skippers were less eager than other fasting subjects to affiliate when hungry, need not imply, as Schachter thought, that inexperienced subjects wanted to evaluate their own feelings. It is just as reasonable to guess that they wanted more information about a threat to their well-being—painful electric shock in one case, prolonged food deprivation in the other.

Nevertheless, the idea that people might not always be able to label their feelings correctly appealed to Schachter and seemed to fit with available summaries of research on the physiology of emotion. Woodworth and Schlosberg (1954) said:

> Psychologists and physiologists have made extensive investigations of many physiological functions in the hope that they would find some patterning to correspond to the common-sense distinctions among the various emotional states. . . . [W]e may as well warn the reader now that he will discover very little evidence for differentiation among emotions when he looks inside the skin.

Even earlier, Woodworth had decided: "The several emotions are distinguished, in practice, by stating the external situation in which each occurs and the type of overt response demanded. Any particular emotion is the stirred-up state appropriate to a certain situation and overt response" (Woodworth & Marquis, 1948). Schachter asked: "[J]ust how does the emoter 'decide' which is the appropriate state? Exactly what does determine whether a person will label his feelings as anger, vexation, impatience, or fury?" This question set the stage for the famous Schachter and Singer (1962) experiment and the two-factor theory of emotion.[2]

Before turning to that experiment, it might be worthwhile to mention just how limited in application Schachter originally considered his budding theory to be.

> [T]he immediate situation as interpreted by past experience furnishes the framework within which one understands and labels his own feelings. [T]he emotions precipitated by many situations are *completely clear-cut*. But what of *disturbing situations which are more ambiguous and unfamiliar*?" [emphasis added].

Consider, as a prime example, the situation facing a subject in one of our anxiety-affiliation experiments. Partly out of interest, partly to get extra class credit, a student volunteers to take part in a psychological experiment. She comes at her appointed hour to find herself surrounded by electrical apparatus, facing a doctor who rather ominously tells her that she will be shocked—an unexpected and unfamiliar situation. Without any doubt the subject is disturbed and uneasy. But what precisely *does* she or, perhaps, *should* she feel? . . . In the case of an emotion, when the precipitating situation is ambiguous or uninterpretable in terms of past experience, . . . pressures arise to establish a social reality.

In the beginning, then, Schachter was talking about *special cases*—cases in which a person's own enviromentally directed appraisal processes fail to produce an unambiguous emotional reaction. Unfortunately, these special cases quickly became the paradigm for *all* emotional experiences.

The Schachter-Singer Experiment

Because Schachter had begun to think about social influences on the labeling of an already partly existing emotional state, he and Singer (1962) designed an experiment in which arousal of a subject's sympathetic nervous system by adrenalin occurred *independently* of the subject's situation-based cognitive appraisal. They did this even though they explicitly acknowledged that in most emotion-inducing situations, "the two factors [cognition and arousal] are completely interrelated. Imagine a man walking alone down a dark alley, a figure with a gun suddenly appears. The perception-cognition 'figure with a gun' in some fashion initiates a state of physiological arousal." In this example, clearly, cognitive appraisal *precedes* and somehow *causes* the arousal state.

In planning their experiment—which, as most readers know, involved injecting subjects with adrenalin and placing them in the presence of a giddy or angry "stooge"—Schachter and Singer realized that the situationally induced cognition had to come *before* the artificially augmented arousal state: "It was, of course, imperative that the sequence with the stooge begin before the subject felt his first symptoms, for otherwise the subject would be virtually forced to interpret his feelings in terms of events preceding the stooge's entrance." This crucial feature of the experiment was reemphasized in Schachter and Singer's (1979) rebuttal to Maslach (1979) and Marshall and Zimbardo (1979).

Yet Schachter and Singer (1962) also referred to "a state of arousal for which the individual has no immediate explanation," as if the arousal state existed in suspended animation while the subject searched for an explanation of it. They also revealed a tendency to view the arousal state as coming *before* the situational appraisal, saying, for example, that the "cognition exerts a steering function" (as if the vehicle, arousal, already existed to be driven) and that "precisely *the same state of physiological arousal* could be labeled 'joy' or 'fury' or 'jealousy' or any of a great diversity of emotional labels" [italics added]. If appraisal comes first, however, it is a mistake to talk about "the *same* state of physiological arousal." The arousal state, like the "same" notes in different melodies, is part of an emotional Gestalt. It doesn't 'wait' for a post hoc label and in fact doesn't even exist as a separate subjective entity to be labeled. Nor was it appropriate for Schachter and Singer to place at the center of their theory "a person in a state of physiological arousal for which no immediately explanatory or appropriate cognitions are available," a person with "evaluative needs" (i.e., with "pressures to understand and label his bodily feelings"). Subjects in the Schachter-Singer experiment did have, by design, a plausible context in which to feel happy or angry.

What, then, do the results of the experiment mean? Most of the data simply show that when a person is happy or angry, adding to his or her natural level of adrenalin will *amplify* his or her feelings and intensify behavior related to those feelings. This is also an adequate interpretation of the other studies cited by Schachter and Singer in support of their theory. For example, Schachter and Wheeler (1962) showed that adrenalin injections caused subjects to laugh especially hard at an already funny slapstick movie, while chlorpromazine, a sympatholytic agent, caused them to laugh less hard than usual. In explaining such effects there is no need to call upon "evaluative needs" or arousal states which require labeling or interpretation. An emotional person tends to act emotionally; if artificially aroused, he or she may act more emotional than usual; if artificially tranquilized, less emotional than usual. These findings are not surprising and do not require all the baggage of Schachter and Singer's theory.

One result does seem to support their line of reasoning, however, and it is the one that has inspired many subsequent "misattribution" studies: Subjects who were told honestly that the adrenalin injection would have "side effects" ("your hands will start to shake, your heart will start to pound, and your face may get warm and flushed") did not become as emotional as other subjects. Why? In our view, these appropriately informed subjects had been given an *additional correct appraisal of the situation*—one which short-circuited or blocked the simpler and more natural pathway from situational appraisal to emotion and emotional behavior. In effect the experimenter said: If you begin to feel anything like intense emotion don't get carried away; the cause is this injection, not something in the environment." What the Schachter-Singer experiment demonstrates, then, is that information given to subjects can affect their situational appraisals and decrease their emotional responsiveness to the environment. The same kind of effect has been demonstrated subsequently, under a very different theoretical banner (but using the same term we have used, "short-circuiting"), by Lazarus and his co-workers (Lazarus & Alfert, 1964; Lazarus & Opton, 1966).[3]

How powerful are such cognitive blocks on feelings? In a well-known study by Nisbett and Schachter (1966), subjects were given a series of electric shocks which progressively increased in intensity. For each subject the series continued until a shock level was reached which the subject declared to be the maximum tolerable. All subjects were first given a placebo pill, half being told that it would produce arousal side effects (tremor, palpitations, etc.), half that it would have side effects unrelated to arousal. Half of each of these groups was led to believe that the shocks would be very painful (the High Fear condition), half that they would be quite mild (the Low Fear condition). To bolster the fear manipulation, high fear subjects were given a sample shock that was twice as strong as the sample given to the low fear subjects. Results indicated that, within the Low Fear condition, subjects who attributed some of their feelings to the pill rather than to the threat and pain of the shock reported less pain and tolerated higher shock levels. Within the High Fear condition, however, the attribution manipulation had absolutely no effect. The truly fearful subjects could not be convinced that their feelings were due to a pill.

This reminds us of the infant social-referencing studies described earlier. Infants can be induced to look at mother for clues regarding the appropriate emotional reaction *if they are uncertain or ambivalent about their own appraisal.* When a stimulus really frightens them, however, they are not affected by mother's experimentally manipulated smiling face. This may be one reason why Maslach's (1979) and Marshall and Zimbardo's (1979) attempts to replicate the Schachter-Singer experiment failed. They

gave more ominous instructions than Schachter and Singer did, implied
that the arousal experience would be unpleasant and perhaps dangerous,
and held their studies in more medically and scientifically imposing environments—all factors which might suggest to subjects that a negative
situational appraisal was warranted. No mild attributional hocus-pocus
could overcome this initial appraisal.[4]

To summarize, the design of the Schachter-Singer experiment did not
fit their labeling-of-unexplained-arousal theory very well, since it provided
subjects with a situational appraisal *before* their arousal level was artificially augmented. There was no reason for subjects to experience "evaluative needs" or to "label" their arousal state after the fact. Their arousal
occurred within an emotion-inducing context, as indicated by the fact that
placebo subjects became almost as aroused as the subjects who had been
injected with adrenalin. The study *does* show that the normal causal
sequence—from appraisal to arousal and emotional behavior—can be
augmented by artificially induced physiological arousal and short-circuited
by telling subjects not to establish the normal connection between their
feelings and the situation at hand. Such short-circuiting of the normal
appraisal process is probably limited; if a situation is truly funny or
frightening or anger-provoking, subjects will become truly emotional
despite an experimenter's attributional instructions. In this sense, Marshall
and Zimbardo were right when they paraphrased the TV commercial:
"It's not easy to fool Mother Nature."

ISSUES FOR A THEORY OF EMOTION

In this section we indicate briefly some of the implications of our
approach for a general, integrative theory of emotion. Most of our points
are similar to ones made previously by other emotion theorists, but they
look somewhat different in the context of the present argument.

The Nonverbal Nature of Primary Appraisal

Throughout, we have used the term "appraisal" to refer to the *initial*
phase of an emotional reaction, the rapid, intuitive evaluation of a situation or object as beneficial or harmful to the self. The term was first used
in this way by Arnold (1960) and later was adopted by Bowlby (1969),
Lazarus (1968), and others. Arnold (1960) distinguished between two
kinds of appraisal—primary and secondary. Primary appraisal, to which we

have been applying the general term appraisal, is an immediate, probably unconscious, and not necessarily verbal process which results in emotional experiences and expressions. This is evidently the process Zajonc (1980) was referring to in his recent article, subtitled "Preferences Need No Inferences," in which he criticized overly elaborate cognitive models of emotion. Secondary appraisal was Arnold's term for the processes that augment or reduce the intensity of an emotion caused initially by a primary appraisal.

Since human infants and nonhuman primates clearly react emotionally to a variety of events and express their emotions in ways that adults reliably recognize (Emde, Kligman, Reich, & Wade, 1978; Hiatt, Campos, & Emde, 1979; Izard, Huebner, Risser, McGinnes, & Dougherty, 1980; Stenberg, Campos, & Emde, in press), we are certain that basic emotional processes do not require labels or higher-order cognitive interpretations of the kind Schachter and Singer (1962) thought necessary. Moreover, since social referencing, a secondary appraisal process, also occurs in infancy, we can be sure that at least some forms of secondary appraisal are preverbal. (We call social referencing a secondary appraisal process because infants in the referencing studies clearly have an initial reaction—wonder, wariness, or pleasant surprise—which must depend on an initial appraisal of some kind, but they often alter this reaction in light of mother's facial expression.)

This does not mean, however, that human adults have no special secondary appraisal abilities. Adults certainly are much more capable than infants of self-monitoring and self-regulation, and adults undoubtedly make more complex inferences about situations and recognize subtle nuances in their own experiences. But a general theory of emotion should begin by explaining what nonhuman primates, human infants, and human adults have in common (Plutchik, 1980), and only then tackle the question of how the basic processes get elaborated or altered as a human being develops. Schachter's question—essentially, "How do adults label their emotions?"—should not be at the center of a general theory of emotional processes. Monkeys and human infants do not label their emotions (verbally at least), but this does not prevent them from expressing feelings and behaving emotionally.

When Schachter first began thinking and writing about emotion, he probably did not mean "labeling" in a verbal or higher cognitive sense; otherwise, he would not have freely mixed animal and human evidence in his 1962 paper with Singer. At times, Schachter and Singer sound as if by "cognition" they mean what we are calling primary appraisal—the kind of appraisal any higher mammal could make. At other times, however, the cognitive component of their theory is called a "label" and seems to be a result of complex self-observations and inferences, hence quite secondary and unique to older humans. Most subsequent work (Bem, 1972; Kleinke, 1978) has followed this second lead, focusing on self-observation rather than on primary appraisal of the environment.

Schachter's theory never has fit well with the idea that there are basic emotions or fundamental emotional expressions. If emotions are merely arousal-plus-a-label, the number of labels would seem to be arbitrary and potentially limitless. Why, then, do anger, fear, joy, sadness, surprise, and a few other basic emotions stand out in studies of nonhuman primates and human infants? Why are the basic emotions (Ekman, Friesen, & Ellsworth, 1972; Izard, 1977; Plutchik, 1980) associated with genetically "hard-wired" expressions which infants (even blind ones; see Eibl-Eibesfeldt, 1970) express early in life and also react to appropriately when their mothers display them? Why do infant monkeys that have been reared in isolation during their first few months of life respond appropriately to slides of monkey threat expressions (Kenney, Mason, & Hill, 1979; Sackett, 1966)? Why do two of the major negative emotions, fear and anger, come attached to two such different behavioral reactions as flight and attack? Although many details remain to be worked out, one conclusion seems evident already: The general causal pathway from stimulus to primary appraisal and on to emotional reactions and expressions is innate for certain stimuli and certain reactions and expressions. These innate emotional "packages" obviously have something to do with harm avoidance, self-protection, and social communication. No theory of emotion that neglects these facts can possibly be on the right track.

The Role of Higher Cognitive Processes

Higher cognitive processes—elaborate anticipation, inference, self-monitoring and self-regulation—obviously influence adult emotional experience and behavior. As Lazarus and Opton (1966) have shown, an interpretation of an event given *before* the event occurs can augment or reduce one's emotional reaction to it. (We believe this is what happened in some of the conditions in Schachter and Singer's experiment, as explained earlier.) Reinterpreting an emotion-inducing event can also dampen or completely dispel an initial emotional reaction. As soon as one's interpretation changes, emotional experience and behavior change as well. This is the gist of many important attribution experiments inspired by Schachter's work (Bem, 1972; Shaver, 1975).

Emotional intensity can also be influenced by self-attention. Scheier (1976) found that mirror-induced self-awareness intensified the angry behavior of already angered subjects (see also Scheier & Carver, 1977). On the other hand, self-awareness, if it interferes with primary appraisal of an event in the environment, can block the normal emotional reaction to that event (Carver & Scheier, 1981; Thompson & Collins, 1980; Vallacher, 1978). Finally, self-awareness can invoke secondary appraisal processes. One of us has noticed that if he laughs aloud while solitarily reading a comic novel, he becomes self-conscious and immediately stops laughing. (The other, less self-conscious author laughs aloud and experiences no such diminution in response.) If attention shifts from the environment (a funny passage in a book) to oneself, and one has learned to disapprove of the behavior in progress, the circuit from environment to emotion is broken. One's appraisal of oneself replaces the previous appraisal of the environment, and the emotion changes accordingly.

Presumably, such complex processes are less common, perhaps absent entirely, in human infants and nonhuman primates. Just how emotional self-regulation develops systematically in humans between infancy and adulthood remains to be discovered (Harter, in press).

Arousal and Amplification

Schachter and Wheeler (1962) demonstrated that emotional behavior ("belly-laughing") becomes more intense when subjects are injected with adrenalin and less intense when they are injected with chlorpromazine. Similar effects have been obtained in social facilitation experiments, where arousal was manipulated socially rather than through chemical injections (e.g., Cottrell, 1972; Zajonc & Sales, 1966). The amplification of behavior due to arousal has also been noted in other species (Hull, 1943; Mason, 1967; Zajonc, 1966). Thus, a general theory of emotion must contain an arousal construct even though at present it is not clear that *high* arousal is either necessary or sufficient as a cause of emotional experience (Harris & Katkin, 1975; Plutchik, 1980). Increased arousal intensifies emotional behavior but seems not to be essential for emotional experience.

The biggest mystery at present, and a prime topic for research and theory, is how primary appraisal processes lead to a particular emotional experience, an associated pattern of behavior (or behavioral tendencies), and a degree of arousal appropriate to the situation—for example, a feeling of surprise, a surprised expression, and the arousal level necessary to attend carefully to an unexpected stimulus; or a mixture of fear and anger, a behavioral response compatible with one or the other, and the arousal level necessary to attack forcefully or run full-speed away. Solution of this mystery must logically precede a complete answer to the question that interested Schachter: What determines how a person will label his or her emotional state? If we knew how appraisal triggered a particular experience-expression-action package, the answer to Schachter's question might be that the label usually follows fairly automatically from knowledge of the situation's meaning—that is, from the appraisal—and, to a lesser extent perhaps, from observation of one's own reactions.

When Might Schachter's Ideas Apply?

Undoubtedly there *are* times when we don't know for sure what we are or should be feeling. In such cases, we may look to other people (as babies in social referencing studies do) for "expert appraisals," or we may infer an explanation of our feelings from situational and personal clues. In other words, while in our opinion Schachter misinterpreted some of his affiliation data and offered an inadequate general explanation of emotion, he certainly pointed to some interesting and practically important special cases. In such cases, people probably do experience "evaluative needs."

Infants in the social referencing experiments needed further information about a novel object or event, and they looked to their mother's facial expressions for this information. They are typical of humans at any age who, feeling uncertain of the harmfulness of a novel stimulus or situation, defer to others who have relevant knowledge. Schachter emphasized the role of uncertainty in his 1959 affiliation experiments but was not clear about the distinction between environment and viscera as the focus of uncertainty. Subjects had, we think, a need for what Schachter called cognitive clarity, not a need to evaluate their internal processes. Still, their uncertainty (lack of clarity) caused them to "reference" others.

Higher animals react to novel stimuli with increased arousal and behavioral signs of wariness (Bronson, 1968), and seem to trade wariness for acceptance, or even liking, after several unharmful exposures to once-novel stimuli (Bischof, 1975; Zajonc, 1968, 1980). It is worth noting that Zajonc's (1980) claim that "preferences need no inferences"—that is, that primary appraisal requires almost no intervening cognition—was based largely on research into the attitudinal effects of repeated exposures to novel stimuli. The perceptual judgment that a stimulus is unfamiliar, hence possibly dangerous, or familiar and acceptable is probably one of the most primitive of our appraisal processes. When a situation is appraised as novel, animals seem prone to seek further information about it (at first from a safe distance). One prominent source of information is the emotional reactions of conspecifics.

A different form of evaluative need is evoked by situations that are complex enough to elicit a number of contradictory or incompatible appraisals. In the face of contradiction, the "emoter" needs further information, or some way of selecting among stimulus attributes, before he or she can experience a clear emotion and act decisively. When we witness a person slipping on ice and falling, for example, we may experience both enjoyment because of the person's humorously sudden loss of dignity and pity because the person might be hurt or embarrassed. Under such circumstances it is common to see adults "socially reference" one another to determine the appropriate reaction. If everyone else is grave, the referencer's chuckle will quickly be suppressed. A similar process of referencing is evident in studies of bystander intervention (or nonintervention) in emergencies (Latané & Darley, 1970; Latané & Nida, 1981).

The arousal of evaluative needs by complex situations can also be seen in cases where a person comes away from an important event, say a job interview, with a vague feeling of uneasiness. It may be difficult to identify the precise *cause* of the feeling, perhaps because many unconscious appraisals contributed to it. Notice, however, that the problem in this case is not *labeling* the feeling—the job candidate knows roughly what it is (certainly that it is distressful, not pleasant). The problem is being unable to identify the environmental cause. Misattribution researchers often seem to confuse these two very different forms of uncertainty. Schachter made it sound as if we don't know *what* we are feeling, when instead the problem is often that we don't know for sure *why* we are experiencing a particular feeling.

Psychoanalytic theory and clinical observations inspired by it reveal another class of instances in which a person might "experience" a particular emotion but not consciously label it correctly. Suppose a young woman has a history of being punished by her father whenever she displays anger. Her angry feelings are gradually forced underground, and rarely surface in the presence of men. When faced with a difficult male supervisor, the young woman's primary appraisal processes trigger anger, including the associated muscle tension and physiological arousal. She feels vaguely "upset" or "out of sorts"—may even scream at neighbors or kick her dog—but still does not interpret the causes of her feelings and behavior appropriately. In general, people who repress their feelings (or are insensitive to them) would seem to be good candidates for attribution manipulations, since they are in a sense looking for false explanations of their own behavior. (Notice that the psychoanalytic formulation assumes that there are real emotions which can be quite different from an emoter's conscious labels—an impossibility according to Schachter and Singer's theory.)

Finally, in line with Schachter's ideas, a person could, under unusual circumstances, misunderstand the causes of his or her own feelings for physical rather than psychodynamic reasons. Some people become mildly depressed if they go without food for several hours, but are unaware of the connection between low blood sugar and emotion. They concoct reasons for their sadness—guessing, for example, that it is because their work isn't going well—even though the imagined environmental causes are unrelated to their feelings. Similar effects can be caused by physiological malfunctions, illnesses, unexpected prescription drug side effects, drinking too much coffee, and so on. In such cases, a person has no environmental appraisal at first but invents one in response to bodily feelings; or his or her internal "environment" becomes the focus of the emotional appraisals (Am I getting the flu? Am I having a heart attack?). These cases, while important when they occur, are misleading if taken as the prototype for all emotional experiences.

In fact, all of the examples given of situations in which Schachter's ideas might apply comprise, we would guess, a minority of emotional experiences. They are therefore not a solid basis for a general theory of emotion.

CONCLUDING COMMENTS

When Schachter began his studies of affiliation, he correctly noted that "almost nothing [was] known . . . of the circumstances that drive men to seek one another out." Today the body of available research findings is much greater than it was then, and the entire intellectual context of questions concerning affiliative behavior has changed. We are much more aware than we were 20 years ago of the desirability of considering the evolutionary significance of the behaviors we study.

As Henderson (1977) remarked,

It is commonplace in science that phenomena of fundamental significance may escape recognition through being submerged in familiarity. [W]ithin the social fabric of day-to-day life the phenomenon of social bonding has not been recognized for what it is, a process of fundamental importance to both the social sciences and to psychiatry, and a behavior essential for the maintenance of health. It is revealed in the phylogenetic origins and present structure of the social network, in the maintenance of affectional bonds within the individual's primary group and in the derivation from this group of . . . 'support.'

We would add that it is also revealed in phenomena as diverse as the human infant's desire to be near its mother, especially when danger or novelty threatens, and the college student's wish to wait with peers when under the threat of painful shock or prolonged fasting. Schachter deserves credit for rescuing the latter cases of affiliation from submersion in familiarity, just as Harlow and Bowlby warrant recognition for calling attention to the amazing process of mother-infant attachment.

When affiliation is viewed within a suitably broad framework, Schachter's experimental findings fit very well, but some of his interpretations and emphases need to be reconsidered. Affiliation in times of stress, regardless of the subject's age, seems to serve mainly needs for anxiety reduction and cognitive clarity, and only secondarily a need for self-evaluation through social comparison. Since Schachter's emotion theory developed out of a very selective, albeit highly provocative, reading of his affiliation studies, it is not surprising that his emotion theory focuses on special cases, skirting the central mystery of emotion: How do brief, intuitive, largely unconscious appraisal processes determine appropriate feelings, expressions, and action sequences? This problem still needs research attention, even though it has been around at least since William James's day.

If the problem is ever solved, the answer will undoubtedly apply, at least in its fundamentals, to all higher primates and to preverbal children as well as to human adults. Of course, this does not mean that the uniquely human phenomenon of labeling emotions verbally is unimportant or undeserving of research attention. Answering what we regard as the central cross-species questions about emotion would still leave unanswered many interesting questions about verbal labeling and about misattribution of feelings to incorrect causes. In fact, the conceptual problems surrounding self-consciousness of emotion are so difficult that they will probably keep us busy for many decades.

Regardless of scientific discoveries, people will probably always marvel at the complexity, subtlety, and variety—indeed, the ultimate indescribability—of human emotional experience. It is, for good evolutionary reasons, truly beyond words.

NOTES

1. It is not fair to give Bowlby all the credit. Before his book was published, ideas about attachment had been circulating for some time (see, for example, Arsenian, 1943, and Harlow & Zimmerman, 1959), but Bowlby's integration of existing literature from several disciplines and his theoretical innovations brought attachment to the attention of a much wider audience of social scientists. For our purposes it will be sufficient to refer to Bowlby's volumes.

2. The first question might be mistaken for one that we believe is crucial: How does perception of a situation lead to a particular emotional reaction? But Schachter's second question indicates that he was thinking instead about how a person *verbally labels* an emotion after it has already begun to occur. Confusion between these two issues is also evident in the Schachter-Singer paper.

3. Lazarus and Alfert (1964) used the term "short-circuiting" to refer to the decrease in stress reaction which occurred when subjects were given a benign interpretation of a shocking film *before* the film was shown. Lazarus and Opton (1966) referred to this procedure as "prior prophylactic indoctrination." Many of the Lazarus group's studies have shown that reaction to a stressful event is strongly affected by subjects' cognitive appraisals, and that these appraisals can be manipulated more effectively before rather than during the stressful event.

4. We agree with Maslach and with Marshall and Zimbardo when they argue that *unexplained* arousal is likely to be inherently unpleasant or anxiety-producing. (As mentioned earlier, Mason and his co-workers have found that amphetamine causes infant monkeys to cling anxiously to their mothers in the same way that externally manipulated threats do.) This is all the more reason why an experimental setting must be both very convincingly positive and arranged so that environmentally

oriented emotional appraisals begin *before* the arousal symptoms appear. As we have attempted to show, arousal in the Schachter-Singer experiment was not really "unexplained," coming as it did after appraisal was under way. Subjects had to be saying to themselves (consciously or unconsciously), "This guy's a riot" or (in the anger condition) "He's right, we deserve to be mad at the experimenter"; otherwise, the arousal manipulation would not have had the intended effect. As Schachter and Singer (1979) noted, timing was absolutely critical in their study.

REFERENCES

Ainsworth, M. Infant-mother development and social attachment: Socialization as a product of reciprocal responsiveness to signals. In M. Richards (Ed.), *The integration of the child into the social world.* Cambridge: Cambridge University Press, 1974.

Ainsworth, M., Bell, S., & Stayton, D. Individual differences in strange situation behavior of one-year-olds. In H. Schaffer (Ed.), *The origins of human social relations.* London: Academic Press, 1971.

Ainsworth, M. D., Blehar, M. C., Waters, E., & Wall, S. *Patterns of attachment: Assessed in the strange situation and at home.* Hillsdale, NJ: Lawrence Erlbaum, 1978.

Anderson, J. W. Attachment behavior out of doors. In N. Blurton Jones (Ed.), *Ethological studies of child behavior.* Cambridge: Cambridge University Press, 1972.

Arnold, M. B. *Emotion and personality: Volume I. Psychological Aspects.* New York: Columbia University Press, 1960.

Arsenian, J. M. Young children in an insecure situation. *Journal of Abnormal and Social Psychology,* 1943, *38,* 225-249.

Asch, S. E. Studies of independence and conformity: A minority of one against a unanimous majority. *Psychological Monographs,* 1956, *70* (9, Whole No. 416).

Bandura, A. *Social learning theory.* Morristown, NJ: General Learning Press, 1971.

Bandura, A., & Walters, R. H. *Social learning and personality development.* New York: Holt, Rinehart & Winston, 1963.

Bem, D. J. Self-perception theory. In L. Berkowitz (Ed.), *Advances in experimental social psychology* (Vol. 6). New York: Academic Press, 1972.

Bishof, N. A systems approach toward the functional connections of fear and attachment. *Child Development,* 1975, *46,* 801-817.

Bowlby, J. *Attachment and loss: Vol. I, Attachment.* New York: Basic Books, 1969.

Bowlby, J. *Attachment and loss: Vol. II, Separation: Anxiety and anger.* New York: Basic Books, 1973.

Bowlby, J. *Attachment and loss: Vol. III, Loss: Sadness and depression.* New York: Basic Books, 1980.

Bretherton, I., & Ainsworth, M.D.S. Responses of one-year-olds to a stranger in a strange situation. In M. Lewis & L. A. Rosenblum (Eds.), *The origins of fear*. New York: John Wiley, 1974.

Bronson, G. W. The fear of novelty. *Psychological Bulletin*, 1968, *69*, 350-358.

Bronson, G. W. Infants' reactions to unfamiliar persons and novel objects. *Monographs of the Society for Research in Child Development*, 1972, *37* (3, Serial No. 148).

Campos, J. J., Emde, R., Gaensbauer, T., & Henderson, C. Cardiac behavioral interrelations in the reactions of infants to strangers. *Developmental Psychology*, 1975, *11*, 589-601.

Campos, J. J., & Stenberg, C. Perception, appraisal, and emotion: The onset of social referencing. In M. E. Lamb & L. R. Sherrod (Eds.), *Infant social cognition: Empirical and theoretical considerations*. Hillsdale, NJ: Lawrence Erlbaum, 1981.

Carr, S., Dabbs, J., & Carr, T. Mother-infant attachment: The importance of the mother's visual field. *Child Development*, 1975, *46*, 331-338.

Carver, C. S., & Scheier, M. F. *Attention and self-regulation: A control-theory approach to human behavior*. New York: Springer-Verlag, 1981.

Castell, W. Effect of familiar and unfamiliar environments on proximity behavior of young children. *Journal of Experimental Child Psychology*, 1972, *9*, 342-347.

Cobb, S. Social support as a moderator of life stress. *Psychosomatic Medicine*, 1976, *38*, 300-314.

Cottrell, N. B. Social facilitation. In C. B. McClintock (Ed.), *Experimental social psychology*. New York: Holt, Rinehart & Winston, 1972.

Cottrell, N. B., & Epley, S. W. Affiliation, social comparison, and socially mediated stress reduction. In J. M. Suls & R. L. Miller (Eds.), *Social comparison processes: Theoretical and empirical perspectives*. Washington, DC: Hemisphere, 1977.

Darwin, C. *The expression of the emotions in man and the animals*. London: John Murray, 1872.

Eibl-Eibesfeldt, I. E. *Ethology: The biology of behavior*. New York: Holt, Rinehart & Winston, 1970.

Ekman, P. (Ed.). *Darwin and facial expression: A century of research in review*. New York: Academic Press, 1972.

Ekman, P., Friesen, W., & Ellsworth, P. *Emotion in the human face: Guidelines for research and an integration of findings*. New York: Pergamon, 1972.

Eibl-Eibesfeldt, I. E. *Ethology: The biology of behavior*. New York: Holt, Rinehart & Winston, 1970.

Emde, R. N., Gaensbauer, T. J., & Harmon, R. J. Emotional expression in infancy: A biobehavioral study. *Psychological Issues* (Vol. 10, No. 37). New York: International Universities Press, Inc., 1976.

Emde, R. N., Kligman, D. H., Reich, J. H., & Wade, T. D. Emotional expression in infancy: I. Initial studies of social signaling and an emergent model. In M. Lewis & L. A. Rosenblum (Eds.), *The development of affect*. New York: Plenum, 1978.

Festinger, L. A theory of social comparison processes. *Human Relations*, 1954, *7*, 117-140.

Freedman, J. L., Sears, D. O., Carlsmith, J. M. *Social psychology* (4th ed.). Englewood Cliffs, NJ: Prentice-Hall, 1981.

Harlow, H. F. The development of affectional patterns in infant monkeys. In B. M. Foss (Ed.), *Determinants of infant behavior* (Vol. 1). New York: John Wiley, 1961.

Harlow, H. F., & Zimmermann, R. R. Affectional responses in the infant monkey. *Science*, 1959, *130*, 421.

Harris, V. A., & Katkin, E. S. Primary and secondary emotional behavior: An analysis of the role of autonomic feedback on affect, arousal, and attribution. *Psychological Bulletin*, 1975, *82*, 904-916.

Harter, S. Developmental perspectives on the self system. In P. Mussen (Ed.), *Carmichael's manual of child psychology*. New York: John Wiley, in press.

Henderson, S. The social network, support and neurosis. *British Journal of Psychiatry*, 1977, *131*, 185-191.

Hiatt, S., Campos, J. J., & Emde, R. N. Facial patterning and infant emotional expression: Happiness, surprise, and fear. *Child Development*, 1979, *50*, 1020-1035.

Hinde, R. A. *Biological bases of human social behavior*. New York: McGraw-Hill, 1974.

Hull, C. L. *Principles of behavior*. New York: Appleton-Century-Crofts, 1943.

Hyman, H. H. The psychology of status. In H. H. Hyman & E. Singer (Eds.), *Readings in reference group theory and research*. New York: Free Press, 1968.

Izard, C. E. *Human emotions*. New York: Plenum, 1977.

Izard, C. E., Huebner, R., Risser, D., McGinnes, G., Dougherty, L. The young infant's ability to produce discrete emotion expressions. *Developmental Psychology*, 1980, *16*, 132-140.

Kenney, M., Mason, W., & Hill, S. Effects of age, objects, and visual experience on affective responses of rhesus monkeys to strangers. *Developmental Psychology*, 1979, *15*, 176-184.

Kleinke, C. L. *Self-perception: The psychology of personal awareness*. San Francisco: W. H. Freeman, 1978.

Klinnert, M. D. Infants' use of mothers' facial expressions for regulating their own behavior. Paper presented at the meeting of Society for Research in Child Development, Boston, April, 1981.

Klinnert, M. D., Campos, J. J., Sorce, J. F., Emde, R. N., & Svejda, M. J. Emotions as behavior regulators: Social referencing in infancy. In R. Plutchik & H. Kellerman (Eds.), *Emotions in early development: Vol. II. The emotions*. New York: Academic Press, 1982.

Kummer, H. Tripartite relations in hamadryas baboons. In S. A. Altman (Ed.), *Social communication among primates*. Chicago: University of Chicago Press, 1967.

Latané, B., & Darley, J. M. *The unresponsive bystander: Why doesn't he help?* New York: Appleton-Century-Crofts, 1970.

Latané, B., & Nida, S. Ten years of research on group size and helping. *Psychological Bulletin*, 1981, *89*, 308-324.

Lawick-Goodall, J. van. The behavior of free-living chimpanzees in the Gombe Stream Reserve. *Animal Behavior Monographs*, 1968, *1*, 161-311.

Lawick-Goodall, J. van. A preliminary report on expressive movements and communication in the Gombe Stream chimpanzees. In P. Dothinow (Ed.), *Primate patterns*. New York: Holt, Rinehart and Winston, 1972.

Lazarus, R. S. Emotions and adaptation: Conceptual and empirical relations. In M. Arnold (Ed.), *Nebraska symposium on motivation*. Lincoln: University of Nebraska Press, 1968.

Lazarus, R. S., & Alfert, E. The short-circuiting of threat by experimentally altering cognitive appraisal. *Journal of Abnormal and Social Psychology*, 1964, *69*, 195-205.

Lazarus, R. S., & Opton, E. M., Jr. The study of psychological stress: A summary of theoretical formulations and experimental findings. In C. D. Spielberger (Ed.), *Anxiety and behavior*. New York: Academic Press, 1966.

Maccoby, E. E. *Social development: Psychological growth and the parent-child relationship*. New York: Harcourt Brace Jovanovich, 1980.

Maccoby, E. E., & Jacklin, C. N. Stress, activity, and proximity seeking: Sex differences in the year-old child. *Child Development*, 1973, *44*, 34-42.

Mahler, M. S., Pine, F., & Bergman, A. *The psychological birth of the human infant: Symbiosis and individuation*. New York: Basic Books, 1975.

Marshall, G. D., & Zimbardo, P. G. Affective consequences of inadequately explained physiological arousal. *Journal of Personality and Social Psychology*, 1979, *37*, 970-988.

Maslach, C. Negative emotional biasing of unexplained arousal. *Journal of Personality and Social Psychology*, 1979, *37*, 953-969.

Mason, W. A. Motivational aspects of social responsiveness in young chimpanzees. In H. W. Stephenson, E. H. Hess, & H. L. Rheingold (Eds.), *Early behavior: Comparative and developmental approaches*. New York: John Wiley, 1967.

Mason, W. A. Regulatory functions of arousal in primate psychosocial development. In C. R. Carpenter (Ed.), *Behavioral regulators of behavior in primates*. Lewisburg, PA: Bucknell University Press, 1973.

Mason, W. A., & Berkson, G. Conditions affecting vocal responsiveness of infant chimpanzees. *Science*, 1962, *137*, 127-128.

Mendoza, S. P., Coe, C. L., Smotherman, W. P., & Levine, S. Functional consequences of attachment: A comparison of two species. In W. P. Smotherman & R. W. Bell (Eds.), *Maternal influences and early behavior*. New York: Spectrum Press, 1979.

Merton, R. K. & Kitt, A. S. Contributions to the theory of reference group behavior. In R. K. Merton & P. F. Lazarsfeld (Eds.), *Continuities in social research: Studies in the scope and method of "The American soldier."* New York: Free Press, 1950.

Milgram, S., Bickman, L., & Berkowitz, L. Note on the drawing power of crowds of different sizes. *Journal of Personality and Social Psychology*, 1969, *13*, 79-82.

Morgan, G. A., & Ricciuti, H. N. Infants' response to strangers during the first year. In B. M. Foss (Ed.), *Determinants of infant behaviour* (Vol. 4). New York: Barnes & Noble, 1969.

Nisbett, R. E. Birth order and participation in dangerous sports. *Journal of Personality and Social Psychology*, 1968, *8*, 351-353.

Nisbett, R. E., & Schachter, S. Cognitive manipulation of pain. *Journal of Experimental Social Psychology*, 1966, *2*, 227-236.

Plutchik, R. *Emotion: A psychoevolutionary synthesis*. New York: Harper & Row, 1980.

Rheingold, H. L., & Eckerman, C. O. The infant separates himself from his mother. *Science*, 1970, *168*, 78-83.

Rowell, T. E., & Hinde, R. A. Responses of rhesus monkeys to mildly stressful situations. *Animal Behavior*, 1963, *11*, 235-243.

Sackett, G. P. Monkeys reared in visual isolation with pictures as visual input: Evidence for an innate releasing mechanism. *Science*, 1966, *154*, 1468-1472.

Schachter, S. *The psychology of affiliation*. Stanford: Stanford University Press, 1959.

Schachter, S. *Emotion, obesity, and crime*. New York: Academic Press, 1971.

Schachter, S., & Burdick, H. A field experiment on rumor transmission and distortion. *Journal of Abnormal and Social Psychology*, 1955, *50*, 363-371.

Schachter, S., & Singer, J. E. Cognitive, social, and physiological determinants of emotional state. *Psychological Review*, 1962, *69*, 379-399.

Schachter, S., & Singer, J. E. Comments on the Maslach and Marshall-Zimbardo experiments. *Journal of Personality and Social Psychology*, 1979, *37*, 989-995.

Schachter, S., & Wheeler, L. Epinephrine, chlorpromazine, and amusement. *Journal of Abnormal and Social Psychology*, 1962, *65*, 121-128.

Schaffer, H. R. The onset of fear of strangers and the incongruity hypothesis. *Journal of Child Psychology and Psychiatry*, 1966, *7*, 95-106.

Scheier, M. F. Self-awareness, self-consciousness, and angry aggression. *Journal of Personality*, 1976, *44*, 627-644.

Scheier, M. F., & Carver, C. S. Self-focused attention and the experience of emotion: Attraction, repulsion, elation, and depression. *Journal of Personality and Social Psychology*, 1977, *35*, 625-636.

Shaver, K. G. *An introduction to attribution processes*. Cambridge, MA: Winthrop, 1975.

Sorce, J. F., & Emde, R. N. Mother's presence is not enough: The effect of emotional availability on infant exploration. *Developmental Psychology*, in press.

Sorce, J. F., Emde, R. N., & Klinnert, M. D. Maternal emotional signaling: Its effect on the visual cliff behavior of one-year-olds. Paper presented at the meeting of the Society for Research in Child Development, Boston, April, 1981.

Sroufe, L. A., & Waters, E. Attachment as an organizational construct. *Child Development*, 1977, *48*, 1184-1199.

Sroufe, L. A., Waters, E., & Matas, L. Contextual determinants of infant affective response. In M. Lewis & L. A. Rosenblum (Eds.), *The origins of fear*. New York: John Wiley, 1974.

Stenberg, C., Campos, J., & Emde, R. N. The facial expression of anger in seven month olds. *Child Development*, in press.

Thompson, S. C., & Collins, B. E. The effects of self-awareness on the social detection process. Paper presented at the annual meeting of the American Psychological Association, Montreal, 1980.

Vallacher, R. R. Objective self-awareness and the perception of others. *Personality and Social Psychology Bulletin*, 1978, *4*, 63-67.

Weiss, R. S. The provisions of social relationships. In Z. Rubin (Ed.), *Doing unto others*. Englewood Cliffs, NJ: Prentice-Hall, 1974.

Woodworth, R. S., & Marquis, D. G. *Psychology*. New York: Holt, 1948.

Woodworth, R. S., & Schlosberg, H. *Experimental psychology.* New York: Holt, 1954.

Wrightsman, L. S. The effects of small-group membership on level of concern. Unpublished doctoral dissertation, University of Minnesota, 1959.

Wrightsman, L. S. Effects of waiting with others on changes in level of felt anxiety. *Journal of Abnormal and Social Psychology,* 1960, *61,* 216-222.

Zajonc, R. B. Social facilitation. *Science,* 1966, *149,* 269-274.

Zajonc, R. B. Attitudinal effects of mere exposure. *Journal of Personality and Social Psychology,* 1968, *9* (Monograph Supplement), 1-29.

Zajonc, R. B. Feeling and thinking: Preferences need no inferences. *American Psychologist,* 1980, *35,* 151-175.

Zajonc, R. B., & Sales, S. M. Social facilitation of dominant and subordinate responses. *Journal of Experimental Social Psychology,* 1966, *2,* 160-168.

Arousal-Based Social Behaviors:

DO THEY REFLECT DIFFERENCES IN VISCERAL PERCEPTION?

JIM BLASCOVICH

EDWARD S. KATKIN

Jim Blascovich is Research Associate Professor of Family Medicine and Adjunct Associate Professor of Psychology at the State University of New York at Buffalo. He is Director of Research and Evaluation for the Department of Family Medicine. His research interests include social psychology, behavioral medicine, and self-esteem.

Edward S. Katkin is Professor and Chairman of the Department of Psychology at the State University of New York at Buffalo. His research interests focus on autonomic responses and behavioral medicine.

In order to explain social behaviors, social psychologists often rely on concepts, mechanisms, processes, and theories that have evolved primarily from other psychological subdisciplines. Thus, principles of cognition, development, personality, and psychophysiology are embedded in many important social psychological theories. This is not to suggest that social psychology is devoid of its own theoretical contributions, nor do we imply that basing explanations of certain social behaviors on principles discovered outside of social psychology is less than desirable. It does suggest, however, that multiple psychological processes are intrinsic to social behavior.

In the decade or so since Shapiro and Crider's (1969) review of psychophysiological approaches in social psychology, social psychologists have become increasingly interested in examining bodily or psychophysiological processes in order to explain many social behaviors (see Cacioppo & Petty, in press; Waid, in press). Indeed, the "body" seems to be in vogue in social psychology. What will come of this increased interest in psychophysiology by social psychologists is an open question. If Shapiro and Crider's hope that "fruitful explorations of previously untouched areas may result" (1969, p. 2) is to be realized, then social psychologists will have to become more concerned with testing the validity of the psychophysiological constructs that are incorporated into their explanations of social behavior.

This chapter proposes an integration of recent work in psychophysiology and social psychology. Specifically, we present a model of the self-perception of autonomic responses (i.e., visceral perception) associated with arousal. Based on this model, the impact of individual differences in such perception for a wide variety of social behaviors for which theorists have suggested arousal as a primary component will be discussed.

The goals or objectives of this chapter are the following: (1) to clarify what is meant by arousal-based social behaviors; (2) to consider theories of arousal-based social behavior as a class of theories covering a wide variety of behaviors; (3) to present a model of the self-perception of arousal (i.e., visceral responses); (4) to present and review methods of assessing and training the self-perception of visceral responses (i.e., visceral perception); and (5) to argue that individual differences in visceral perception have important implications for arousal-based social behaviors and suggest empirical tests of this argument. To the extent that this chapter accomplishes these goals, we believe it will contribute to a worthwhile theoretical integration of social psychological and psychophysiological processes—that is, one that can be empirically tested.

AROUSAL-BASED SOCIAL BEHAVIORS

What are "arousal-based social behaviors"? There are no simple criteria. Although there are probably several decision rules that could be defended on an a priori basis according to one's definition of the concept of "arousal," there are many instances of social psychological theories in which the arousal aspects of social behaviors are left vague, ambiguous, or even completely unspecified. Hence, relying on any single set of definitional criteria for what is meant by arousal-based social behaviors is arbitrary.

Instead, we suggest a different strategy. We propose classifying arousal-based social behaviors as a function of the type or degree of specificity concerning "arousal" in the theoretical explanation of the behavior. In developing this classification scheme, we have relied on three principles elucidated by Harré (1972):

1. Some theoretical terms can be used to make reference to hypothetical entities.
2. Some hypothetical entities are candidates for existence (i.e., some could be the real things, qualities, and processes in the world).
3. Some candidates for existence, for reality, are demonstrable, i.e., can be indicated by some sort of gesture of pointing in the appropriate directions [p. 91].

Following from these principles, the theoretical arousal basis of a social behavior may be *purely hypothetical, potentially demonstrable,* or *demonstrable.*

The arousal basis of a social behavior is limited to a *purely hypothetical* sense if the nature of the arousal is *unspecifiable* in concrete terms. "Arousal" of this type cannot be measured or assessed. The use of arousal as part of a theoretical explanation of a social behavior in a purely hypothetical sense is often subtle, as in the case of "psychic" or "general arousal" which "may or may not have measurable somatic or psychological substrates." In Averill's (1974) terminology, arousal used in this sense is an "extrinsic symbol."

The arousal basis of a social behavior is *potentially demonstrable* if the nature of the arousal is potentially specifiable in concrete terms. "Arousal" used in this sense is based on speculative or abstract reasoning. Although concrete specifications or criteria for measuring or assessing arousal used are not actually made, *it is assumed that such specifications can or will be made at some future time.* The use of arousal in this sense is very common in social psychological theories. Specification of criteria for measuring arousal in these theories may be lacking for a variety of reasons; for example, the theoretical explanation may be in a relatively

simple stage of development; the theoretician may not have the necessary
expertise; or the theoretician may assume that an adequate measurement
methodology does not yet exist even if the criteria for arousal were
specified.

A social behavior is theoretically arousal-based in a *demonstrable* sense
if the nature of the arousal is specified in concrete terms. That is, the
decision to accept arousal as an explanation or part of an explanation of a
social behavior is based on empirical test. Although there are certainly
fewer explanations of social behavior which are arousal based in a demonstrable sense than a potentially demonstrable sense, many do exist.

We believe this categorization is valuable because it helps us to separate
demonstrable explanations of arousal-based social behavior from those
that are potentially demonstrable or purely hypothetical. If an explanation
of a social behavior rests on the assumption of a kind of arousal that is
unspecifiable in concrete terms, we cannot evaluate it; that is, choose to
accept or reject it, on an empirical basis. On the other hand, if an
explanation of a social behavior rests on an assumption or an implied
assumption of a kind of arousal that is potentially or actually demonstrable in concrete terms, that explanation is potentially or actually
scientific and is material for further elucidation and investigation.

Before considering actual social psychological theories which postulate
arousal as the basis for social behaviors, a few additional points require
clarification. First, a given behavior may have a number of alternative
antecedents; that is, a *plurality* of causes, only one of which might be
arousal. For example, as Harris and Katkin (1975) have suggested, emotional behaviors in some instances may be primarily arousal based and in
other instances may not. Accepting a social behavior as arousal based, even
on the basis of empirical verification, does not preclude other antecedents
of the particular behavior.

Second, that the nature of the arousal basis of a social behavior may
have been empirically verified does not necessarily establish the validity of
the theoretical explanation of which it is a part. Theories quite different in
other respects may specify the same or similar arousal processes. For
example, although the emotional labeling theories of Marshall and Zimbardo (1979) and Maslach (1979) differ in some critical ways from
Schachter and Singer's theory (1962), all three rest on the same assumption of physiological arousal.

Third, the arousal basis of a particular social behavior may have several
theoretical explanations across which the use of arousal differs in the

senses suggested above (i.e., purely hypothetical, potentially demonstrable, and demonstrable). Regarding the latter two, we believe it is useful to transform potentially demonstrable concepts into demonstrable concepts as appropriate knowledge and methods accumulate. Fazio and Cooper (in press) make this kind of transformation regarding the nature of cognitive dissonance. This permits empirical investigation of the nature of "dissonance" itself, a concept originally introduced in a hypothetical sense.

THEORIES OF AROUSAL-BASED SOCIAL BEHAVIORS

Arousal has been postulated as an intervening variable for many types of social behaviors in numerous social psychological theories. These theories take this general form:

$$\text{ANTECEDENT(S)} \longrightarrow \text{AROUSAL} \longrightarrow \text{BEHAVIOR(S)}$$

The nature of the "arousal" in these theories is often described only in a hypothetical sense. If the nature of arousal is described more explicitly, it is not often a very specific description. Hence, social psychological theories are more likely to specify a type of "drive" or "tension" or "distress" or "general arousal" or perhaps "general physiological arousal" rather than a specific, complex pattern of autonomic or central nervous system responses. Nevertheless, most of these theories do not preclude more specific descriptions, and various investigators have postulated such descriptions in order to investigate empirically the arousal component of the theories (see Fazio & Cooper, in press).

The specific nature of "arousal" has itself been the focus of substantial controversy among psychophysiologists. Although such theorists as Duffy (1962) and Malmo (1959) popularized the general concept of arousal as a facilitator of behavior, the concept fell into some disrepute after Lacey and Lacey's (1958) discovery of "directional fractionation." The Laceys observed that when subjects were engaged in preparation for a reaction time task, their skin conductance would show elevations typical of sympathetic arousal but their heart rate would slow down, as if parasympathetically activated. This observation, they argued, weighs against glib assumptions about a unidimensional concept of arousal and suggests that the construct must be specified more precisely. The current status of the concept of arousal, even among psychophysiologists, is controversial; for these reasons, it is important for social psychologists as well to strive for greater precision in the use of the construct in their theory building.

In this section, we will review briefly a sample of social behaviors for which arousal has been a significant theoretical component although by no means a usually well-defined component. Our intention is to be neither exhaustive nor detailed, but rather to support the argument that theories of arousal-based social behaviors represent a large class of social psychological theories covering a wide range of social behavior. Indeed, a more exhaustive and detailed review of theories of arousal-based social behaviors might lead one quickly to the conclusion that arousal is the sine qua non of social behavior.

Emotional Labeling

Arousal-based theories of emotion are well-known. The arousal basis of emotion can be traced to William James's emphasis (1884) on bodily processes as a determinant of emotional experience. Although the nature of the arousal as specified by James (i.e., discrete patterns of arousal for each pattern of emotional experience) was not empirically verified, the notion of arousal as a mediator of emotional experience was planted firmly.

So-called Neo-Jamesians revived Jamesian theory. Not only did they revise the arousal component of emotion, but they added an essential social psychological component. Schachter and Singer (1962) postulated that individuals experience different emotions not on the basis of a specific type or pattern of physiological arousal, as James postulated, but on the basis of undifferentiated general physiological arousal and the social context in which it occurs.

Some theorists (e.g., Marshall & Zimbardo, 1979; Maslach, 1979) have criticized Schachter and Singer's theory and have suggested that emotional labeling is not as much a function of the immediate social context as Schachter and Singer theorized. Nevertheless, these critics share the assumption of physiological arousal as an essential component of emotional experience. Although others (e.g., Harris & Katkin, 1975; Valins, 1966) have suggested that actual physiological arousal is not always necessary for emotional behavior, these theorists maintain that arousal is a primary component of emotional experience.

Attitudes

Perhaps no concept has received more attention in social psychology than the concept of attitude and the notion of attitude change. Arousal has been regarded implicitly or explicitly as an integral component of attitude and attitude change by many theorists. In fact, tracing the use of the concept of arousal by attitude theorists provides an interesting case history of the transition from a hypothetical concept to a more demonstrable, scientific one.

Consistency theories have been the most frequently and popularly emphasized explanations of attitude and attitude change in social psychology. The causal sequences specified by these theories fit the form illustrated above. The essential and distinguishing feature of consistency theories is a state of "inconsistency" (or "balance" or "incongruity" or "dissonance," etc.). The individual is driven to strengthen or change attitudes in order to reduce or eliminate the inconsistency. Not surprisingly, the nature of most kinds of inconsistency has been explained in terms of arousal. Dissonance theory (Festinger, 1957) provides a good illustration. Festinger originally provided little description of the nature of "dissonance," although he did suggest that it was a kind of "tension." Later, Brehm and Cohen (1962) characterized dissonance as an arousal state. Although a few researchers (e.g., Buck, 1970; Gerard, 1967; Gleason & Katkin, 1979; McMillan & Geiselman 1974) subsequently investigated the physiological arousal properties of the state of dissonance, only recently have the physiological arousal properties of dissonance been theoretically integrated into dissonance theory in a demonstrable and comprehensive way (Fazio & Cooper, in press).

Still further work on the relationship between physiological arousal and attitudes has been provided by Cacioppo and his colleagues (Cacioppo, 1979; Cacioppo & Petty, 1979). Their work focuses on the role of physiological arousal, not in terms of its drive properties, but in terms of its relationship to various cognitive processes such as the role of physiological arousal in resistance to persuasion.

Antisocial and Prosocial Behavior

Aggression. Since the relationship between arousal and aggression is so widely assumed (see Berkowitz, 1969), we will not dwell on a review of theories that postulate arousal as a component of aggressive behavior. Arousal is a critical feature in most theories of aggressive behavior, including both biological and social psychological theories. It is a major link in "frustration leads to aggression" theories. Research has repeatedly demonstrated a relationship between physiological arousal and aggressive behavior. Indeed, research on physiological arousal has demonstrated the powerful effect of arousal on the likelihood of aggressive behavior even when the arousal is created in a nonfrustrating, nonaggression context (e.g., Baron & Bell, 1977; Donnerstein & Barrett, 1978; Mueller & Donnerstein, 1977; Tannenbaum & Zillman, 1975; Zillman, 1971, 1978).

Helping behavior. In addition to an important role in antisocial behaviors such as aggression, arousal has been postulated as a component of prosocial behaviors such as helping behavior. Piliavin, Piliavin, and Rodin's (1975) cost-arousal model of helping behavior is a case in point. According to their model, "observation of an emergency arouses the bystander.... Physiological components may include ... rapid and heavy heart beat, shortness of breath, 'butterflies' in the stomach, and a variety of other reactions associated with startle and shock. ... The bystander will choose the response to an emergency that most rapidly and most completely reduces his arousal, incurring as few net costs ... as possible in the process" (p. 430). To date there have been no direct empirical tests of the physiological arousal component of the cost-arousal model of helping behavior. However, the theory does suggest that helping behavior, at least in emergency situations, is arousal based.

Social justice. Arousal has also been suggested as a component in another category of prosocial behavior—justice-oriented behavior. Proponents of equity theory (e.g., Austin & Walster, 1974; Walster, Berscheild, & Walster, 1976; Walster, Walster & Berscheid, 1978) suggest that the perception of inequity or injustice leads to a kind of arousal or "distress" which the individual is motivated to reduce by restoring "equity," "fairness," or "justice" in the situation. If the individual perceives himself or herself to be underbenefited, the distress or arousal is labeled "anger." If the individual perceives him or herself to be overbenefited, the distress or arousal is labeled "guilt." Presumably these same feelings are aroused when the individual observes others in an inequitable or unjust situation. Austin and Walster (1974) attempted to measure this distress physiologically but concluded that the conditions under which the physiological measurements were made were inappropriate.

Interpersonal Behavior

Social facilitation. Even the first of the social influence processes to be investigated empirically—that is, social facilitation (Triplett, 1897)—is explained theoretically on the basis of drive or arousal. Modern theoretical explanations of social facilitation effects (Zajonc, 1965, 1968; Cottrell, 1968, 1972; Sanders, 1981) take the general form suggested above.

According to Zajonc's "drive" theory of social facilitation, the presence of others leads to increased general arousal or drive, which in turn facilitates "dominant" responses in an individual's behavior. Cottrell (1968, 1972) contended more specifically that increased arousal is elicited by the presence of others to the extent that the performing individual feels evaluation apprehension; that is, that others are judging the performance. Sanders and his colleagues (Baron, Moore, & Sanders, 1978; Sanders, 1981; Sanders & Baron, 1975; Sanders, Baron, & Moore, 1978;) in their "distraction-conflict" theory specify that distractions, such as those caused by the actual presence of others, which conflict with performance of the task at hand produce arousal which often facilitates performance.

While these three explanations differ on the antecedents of arousal which underly social facilitation effects and have created much theoretical debate (see Geen, 1981; Markus, 1981; Sanders, 1981), all three include or imply arousal as a major component. None of the theories, however, specifies the nature of arousal explicity or concretely.

Interpersonal attraction. Arousal-based theories have been proposed to explain various types and aspects of social behavior that can be classified under the general heading of interpersonal attraction, includint affiliation and liking and loving behavior.

Schachter (1959) proposed and demonstrated that fear arousal increases an individual's desire to affiliate with others. Later, Sarnoff and Zimbardo (1961) demonstrated that if the arousal was caused by "anxiety" rather than fear, the desire to affiliate was decreased. Still later, others (see Fish, Karabenick, & Heath, 1978; Teichman, 1973) suggested that "embarrassment" is a better label than "anxiety" for the type of arousal leading to a decrease in affiliation. Thus, arousal has been hypothesized to play an important role in causing an individual either to seek (affiliate) or to avoid (nonaffiliate) the company of others. In a study which examined, in part, physiological reactions to fear and embarrassment and the presence of others, Buck and Parke (1972) demonstrated that the presence of another person has a calming effect physiologically on an individual when his or her arousal is caused by fear rather than embarrassment.

Arousal also plays a role in social psychological explanations of liking and loving. To the extent that emotions and emotional labeling play a role in theoretical explanations of liking and loving, arousal is an important component. Stephan, Berscheid, and Walster (1971), Berscheid and Walster (1974), and Carducci, Cozby, and Ward (1978), for example, have investigated the relationship of arousal, especially sexual arousal, and interpersonal attraction, demonstrating that arousal often forms the basis for attributions or misattributions of attraction.

Social Ecology

The influence of the environment on social behavior, especially the physical presence of others, has often been tied theoretically to the notion of arousal. Perhaps the most general theoretical statement in this regard is that of Mehrabian (1976), who asserted that behavior is a function of arousal, affect, and dominance/submissiveness. According to Mehrabian, the extent to which the physical environment contributes to feelings along these three dimensions of behavior influences behavior.

Others have relied on the concept of arousal in less sweeping ecological theories. For example, Patterson (1976) proposed an arousal model of interpersonal intimacy. According to his model, changes in the immediacy (i.e., "closeness") of the communicative and nonverbal behaviors of an individual toward another will lead to a change in the arousal level of the other person which the other person will label positively or negatively. If the individual labels the arousal positively, the individual will reciprocate the new level of intimacy. If the arousal is labeled negatively, the individual will compensate by reducing the immediacy of other communicative and nonverbal behaviors. The arousal aspect of Patterson's theory has been supported at least partially in terms of physiological measurement in a study by Coutts, Schneider, and Montgomery (1978).

Explanations of reactions to spatial invasions have also relied on arousal (see Evans, 1978; Middlemast, Knowles, & Matter, 1976; Smith & Knowles, 1978). These explanations take the general form suggested above. Invasion of personal space is an antecedent of arousal, which in turn leads to some behavioral reaction. Given the reliance on arousal as an intervening variable in explanations of invasion of personal space, it is not surprising that a number of theoretical explanations of the effects of crowding also rely on arousal (Aiello, DeRisi, Epstein, & Karlin, 1977; Patterson, 1977; Schaeffer & Patterson, 1980; Worchel & Teddlie, 1976).

Implications

We have reviewed broad categories of social behavior for which arousal is an important theoretical component. We could have included many more categories and types of social behavior—for example, evaluation apprehension (Rosenberg, 1965), self-focused attention (Fenigstein & Carver, 1978; Wegner & Guilano, 1980), cooperative and competitive decision making (Blascovich, Nash, & Ginsburg, 1978; Van Egeren, 1979), empathy (Sapolsky & Zillman, 1978), and obesity (Rodin, 1977). The preceding review is selective and limited. In addition, there are many explanations of social behaviors, including the categories we reviewed above, which may not rely at all on even an implicit notion of arousal.

Nevertheless, what is clear is the *arousal is an important construct for many theories covering a wide variety of social behaviors.* What is less clear is the degree to which awareness of perception of such arousal is important. For many, if not most, arousal-based theories of social behavior, some level of awareness or perception of internal or visceral arousal is assumed or at least implied. Many theories are based on an assumption that individuals are accurate perceivers of arousal (e.g., Schachter & Singer 1962; Maslach, 1979; Piliavin et al., 1975). Others have suggested that such an assumption is unjustified (Valins, 1966; Zillman, 1980; Pennebaker, 1981). The critical point is that the perception of arousal and the relationship of the accuracy of such visceral perception are open to empirical test. Furthermore, it is likely that what we learn about the relationship between visceral perceptual accuracy and arousal-based social behaviors will facilitate understanding individual differences in such behaviors.

A MODEL OF THE SELF–PERCEPTION OF VISCERAL RESPONSES

While it is clear that a rather large and diverse body of theoretical literature in social psychology incorporates the notion of arousal, it is equally clear that relatively little attention has been paid empirically to the nature of such arousal. As we have argued above, if we are to examine these arousal-based theories of social behavior in scientific ways, the nature of the arousal must be specified. We suggest as a starting point the assumption that such arousal involves physiological activity in general, including particularly autonomic or visceral activity. For a more thorough justification of this assumption, especially as it relates to arousal-based theories of emotion, we refer the reader to Averill (1974) and Buck (1970).

If autonomic or visceral arousal is an important component of a social behavior, then the issue of the individual's *perception* of that arousal should be addressed. As mentioned above, the accurate perception of arousal is clearly implied in some theoretical explanations (e.g., Schachter & Singer's [1962] notion of "unexplained arousal"), while in others the implication is that accurate perception is unnecessary (Valins, 1966). If both the nature of the autonomic or visceral arousal is specified and the accuracy of visceral perception can be assessed, then the dual issues of visceral arousal and visceral perception can be examined empirically. Experiments that incorporate a manipulation of individual differences in visceral sensitivity as well as a manipulation of arousal can shed some light on whether the assumption of visceral perception is necessary for an arousal-based theoretical explanation of social behavior, whether the assumption of arousal is necessary, or whether both are necessary.

The general notion of visceral perception is quite plausible and easy to grasp. In common terms, we perceive some somatic change; for example, "butterflies" in the stomach, a "pounding" heart, a full bladder, and so on. However, there are variations in our ability, as individuals, to perceive these responses. At times we are more sensitive to our viscera than at other times. In addition, it seems likely that there are differences in our sensitivity to different visceral sensations; for example, some people seem to be more sensitive to cardiovascular changes, others to gastrointestinal activity, some to both, and some to neither. If we are to bring the issue of visceral perception under scientific scrutiny, we must not rely solely on implicit notions of visceral perception. Rather, we must be more explicit. Consequently, Whitehead, Drescher, Heiman, and Blackwell (1977) propose using the signal detection model (Green & Swets, 1966) as a guide to understanding the nature and measurement of visceral perception and its impact on arousal-based social behaviors.

According to the signal detection model:

$$\text{Sensitivity to a Visceral Signal} = f \text{ (discriminability (signal/noise))}$$

$$\text{Signal} = f \text{ (Physiological Response)}$$

The accuracy of the perception of a specific visceral response depends on physiological, cognitive, and environmental factors. Variations in any of those factors can lead to differences in perceptual accuracy both within and between individuals. It is assumed that at very high levels of visceral arousal the signal strength of a visceral response is high and therefore visceral perception should be accurate irrespective of individual differences. At very low levels of arousal the signal strength of the visceral response is low and therefore visceral perception should be inaccurate irrespective of individual differences. However, at "moderate" levels of arousal—the most likely level of arousal underlying various social behaviors—the picture is not quite so clear. Individual differences in the accuracy of perception of a particular visceral response may be maximized. The question of how to define relative levels of arousal (i.e., low, moderate, high) is an important one for which there is no definite answer at the present time. However, Lykken, Rose, Luther, and Maley (1966) have argued that there are empirical ways to quantify a person's arousal level.

The antecedents of the detection of autonomic or visceral signals are intricate. The causes of autonomic arousal are many, varied, and complex. The arousal of a particular response may be a reaction to either or both internal or external stimuli. However, in the case of social behaviors, the arousal-generating stimuli are likely to be external; for example, another person or verbal material, or internal representations (i.e., cognitive) of external stimuli. Sensitivity to autonomic responses is not likely to be completely "hardwired" or innate, but rather learned to some extent. Finally, background ,noise can result both from other biological and cognitive activities within the person and from external environmental events.

Obviously, there is plenty of room within this model for both intra-individual and interindividual differences in perceptual accuracy of any given visceral response. A variety of possible visceral responses may be aroused to varying degrees in any number of combinations; competing biological and environmental stimuli; varying levels of neurological efficiency; and past experience. Thus, the assessment of visceral perceptual accuracy across individuals becomes quite difficult.

Thus, to conduct experiments in which some nonextreme level of arousal is induced and manipulated as an independent variable without considering the ramifications of individual differences in the ability to detect or perceive that arousal is to invite a set of inconclusive results. Hence, it is not surprising that the reliability of Schachter and Singer's (1962) data have been repeatedly questioned (see Maslach, 1979; Marshall & Zimbardo, 1979). Nor is it surprising that the results of experiments which provide false physiological feedback without consideration of individual differences in the perception of actual physiological activity such as Valins's (1966) have been debated (Harris & Katkin, 1975). We suggest that experimental manipulation or statistical control of individual differences in the ability to detect the particular autonomic response or responses under investigation will potentially eliminate a large source of measurement error and consequently make the test of any such hypothesis clearer.

METHODS OF ASSESSING AND TRAINING
VISCERAL PERCEPTION

Although social psychologists have devoted little effort to the topic, visceral perception has been investigated intensively by other scientists, especially psychophysiologists interested primarily in visceral learning (i.e., biofeedback). The assessment and training methods that have evolved can be useful for empirical investigations of arousal-based social behaviors. Visceral perception has been assessed both subjectively and objectively.

Subjective measures. One of the first attempts to measure visceral perception systematically involved subjective report. The Autonomic Rerception Questionnaire (APQ), developed by Mandler, Mandler, and Uviller (1958), is a self-report inventory intended to assess the frequency and intensity of perceptions of autonomic activity. Although APQ scores have been shown to be higher among subjects who show high levels of general arousal (Mandler et al., 1958), the evidence shows no relationship between APQ scores and enhanced visceral perceptual ability (McFarland, 1975; Whitehead et al., 1977).

More recently other subjective, paper-and-pencil instruments have been developed that may be construed to assess visceral perceptual ability. For example, Pennebaker and his colleagues (Pennebaker & Skelton, 1978; Pennebaker, 1981) have examined "symptom reporting." However, they have not been able to determine more than a few weak relationships between symptom reporting measures and actual somatic changes. Others, such as Fenigstein et al. (1975) and Miller, Murphy, and Buss (1981), have developed self-consciousness and bodily awareness scales, respectively. However, no direct relationships to actual somatic activity have as yet been shown.

The failure to find relationships between self-report measures and visceral perception can be explained in many ways. One possibility is the subjectivity of the instruments. Consequently, it is not surprising that some researchers have attempted to develop more objective techniques for assessing visceral perception.

Objective measures. For the most part, investigations of visceral perception have focused on cardiac activity, although other visceral activities such as sweat gland activation (Lacroix & McGowen, 1979) and gastric motility (Whitehead, 1980) also have been investigated. This emphasis on cardiac activity is due to both the importance of the cardiovascular system and the relative ease with which cardiovascular activity can be monitored and measured—perhaps the same reasons cardiac activity has played a central role in studies of arousal-based social behavior (e.g., Maslach, 1979; Marshall and Zimbardo, 1979; Schachter & Singer, 1962; Valins, 1966; Zillman, 1978).

One of the first objective techniques for assessing visceral perception was developed by McFarland (1975), who measured heartbeat perception by instructing subjects to press a button in rhythm with their heartbeats. Detection ability was calculated according to the formula:

$$1 - ((\text{button presses} - \text{heartbeats})/\text{heartbeats})$$

Unfortunately, a high score does not necessarily reflect accurate beat-to-beat perception. More likely, it represents the individual's ability to estimate heart rate over time.

Brener and Jones (1974) set out to develop a measure that would reflect more accurately the perceptual sensitivity of individuals to phasic changes in heartbeat. They developed a discrimination test which assesses the degree to which subjects can discriminate exteroceptive stimuli that are contingent on heartbeats from exteroceptive stimuli that are independent of heartbeats. Briefly, subjects receive either stimuli triggered by their own heartbeats or noncontingent stimuli which are triggered by a pulse generator set to produce a frequency equal to each subject's mean heart rate. Subjects indicate whether they believe the stimuli are contingent or noncontingent. Brener and Jones (1974) used the number of correct detections as an index of cardiac perception. Unfortunately, Brener and Jones's task may be confounded by intentionally or unintentionally created changes in heart rate which would affect the contingent signal but not the noncontingent signal. For example, by moving, or holding his or her breath, a subject could effect a change in cardiac activity, which would in turn change the contingent but not the noncontingent signals. The discrimination thus becomes trivial and does not reflect accurate perception of heartbeats.

Whitehead and his colleagues (1977) developed a discrimination technique in which subjects are required to discriminate between trains of tones which follow after either a 128 msec or 384 msec delay from their heartbeats. Obviously, any intentional or unintentional change in cardiac activity on the part of subjects would affect both sets of tones equally. A subject's ability to make the discrimination depends on his or her ability to perceive heartbeats. Without reference to perceived heartbeats, the trains of tones become indistinguishable. In addition, Whitehead et al. computed a subject's ability to make the discrimination using signal detection analysis methods (McNicol, 1972).

Whitehead and his colleagues discovered that relatively few subjects could make the discrimination. This suggests that either subjects were not very accurate perceivers of their heartbeats or that the discrimination criterion (i.e., the 128 versus 384 msec delay) itself was too difficult. Subsequently, Katkin and his colleagues (Katkin, Blascovich, & Goldband, 1981; Katkin, Morell, Goldband, Bernstein, & Wise, in Press) developed a discrimination task which preserved the important features of the Whitehead task but which presented subjects with an easier discrimination criterion if they were accurate perceivers of the heartbeats.

Briefly, subjects are required to discriminate between trains of tones which are presented at either a fixed or variable interval after their heartbeats. The algorithm used for the variable interval tones is such that the tones vary considerably in the delay from the heart and are easily discriminable from the fixed interval tones if the discriminator is aware of actual heartbeats. However, the fixed and variable trains of tones are indistinguishable from each other if there is no awareness or reference to the heartbeats from which the tones are generated.

Even with the easier discrimination criterion, Katkin and his colleagues demonstrated that only about 15% of their subjects could make the correct discrimination significantly more often than chance. However, by including performance feedback after discrimination trials, they were successful in training male subjects to make the discrimination.

Research. The development and refinement of the heartbeat perception discrimination task by Katkin et al. have included a number of both parametric and paradigmatic studies (reviewed in Katkin, Blascovich, &

Koenigsberg, 1982). Basically, this line of research has demonstrated that, first, the methods developed are sensitive enough to allow objective and quantitative assessment of heartbeat perception. Second, it is clear that relatively few individuals are accurate heartbeat perceivers in an unaroused state without training. Third, these studies indicate that there are substantial individual differences in the ability to learn to discriminate heartbeats. The best predictor of these individual differences in the ability to learn the discrimination is gender, since males learn to discriminate much more readily than females. Fourth, the learned ability to perceive heartbeats is retained for at least a week. Fifth, males and females appear to employ different strategies for perceiving heartbeats. Males are likely to rely on somesthetic cues, while females seem to rely on auditory cues. Sixth, at least for males there is evidence that right hemisphere preference is associated with enhanced heartbeat discrimination.

One major implication of these findings is that visceral perception is indeed a complex phenomenon even when limited to a single autonomic response. Another implication is that much more work needs to be done if we are to understand fully the parameters of visceral perception. For example, the relationship between the perception of one or more specific visceral responses and the perception of general arousal needs to be established empirically. In addition, it seems likely that further paradigmatic research will lead to more refined and perhaps better assessment strategies.

One of the more important parametric questions that needs to be investigated is the relationship between arousal and perception. Although some investigations have found evidence that arousal is related to perceptual accuracy (e.g., Jones & Hollandsworth, 1981; Katkin et al., 1982) the function (e.g., linear, curvilinear, stepwise) of the relationship needs to be more precisely determined. In addition, much work needs to be focused on the relationships among perceptions of various autonomic or visceral responses.

INDIVIDUAL DIFFERENCES IN VISCERAL PERCEPTION AND SOCIAL BEHAVIOR

Despite the fact that the parameters of visceral perception are not now fully understood, and that new assessment and training methods may be developed in the future, we need not wait to apply now what we know about visceral perception and the methods at hand to address the question of the effects of visceral perception on social behaviors. To the extent that various forms of social behavior are dependent on the experience of visceral arousal, visceral perceptual ability is crucial. Therefore, individual differences in the ability to perceive arousal responses should affect the experience and expression of arousal-based social behaviors. Thus, for example, sensitive or accurate perceivers should be more likely to seek labels for unexplained arousal; to experience and reduce dissonance; to be aggressive, helpful, and equitable; to be facilitated by the presence of others; and to react to invasions of personal space. On the other hand, insensitive or inaccurate perceivers should be more likely to be influenced by false physiological feedback; to misattribute arousal; to experience less attitude change; to be less facilitated by the presence of others; and to be more tolerant of invasions of personal space. The general and specific hypotheses implied in the preceding statements can be empirically tested in a variety of ways within traditional empirical paradigms, including both experimental and correlational approaches.

Within an experimental framework, visceral perceptual ability can be manipulated as an independent variable. In order to manipulate visceral perceptual ability, one can train individuals to various criterion levels of visceral perceptual accuracy. With the appropriate procedures, one can easily envision sensitive tests of Schachter and Singer's notion of unexplained arousal, a Valins-like false physiological feedback study, an excitation transfer study, a dissonance study, and so on.

The relationship between visceral perceptual ability and various arousal-based social behaviors can also be examined in a correlational fashion. Using exercise or other arousal-inducing techniques, one could fairly easily determine the accuracy of heartbeat perception at some moderate level of arousal for a cohort of individuals and relate it to other subjective and behavioral measures such as emotional expressiveness, desire to affiliate, body consciousness, symptom reporting, and socially facilitated increments and decrements in performance.

The results of such experimental and correlational studies could be quite important. Specifically, the arousal basis of various explanations of social behaviors could be tested directly, leading to some inference about the validity of each particular theory. Thus, the "black box" role that the perception of visceral arousal has played in social psychology could begin to change. On a more general level, one could begin to assess the relative contribution of this individual difference variable to the variance of social behavior.

REFERENCES

Aiello, J. R., DeRisi, D. T., Epstein, Y.M., & Karlin, R. A. Crowding and the role of interpersonal distance preference. *Sociometry*, 1977, *40*, 271-282.

Austin, W., & Walster, E. Reactions to confirmations and disconfirmations of expectancies of equity and inequity. *Journal of Personality and Social Psychology*, 1974, *30*, 208-216.

Averill, J. R. An analysis of psychophysiological symbolism and its influence on emotions. *Journal for the Theory of Social Behaviour*, 1974, *4*, 147-190.

Baron, R. A., & Bell, P. A. Sexual arousal and aggression by males: Effects of type of erotic stimuli and prior provocation. *Journal of Personality and Social Psychology*, 1977, *35*, 79-87.

Baron, R. S., Moore, D., & Sanders, G. S. Distraction as a source of drive in social facilitation research. *Journal of Personality and Social Psychology*, 1978, *36*, 816-824.

Berkowitz, L. (Ed.). *Roots of aggression: A re-examination of the frustration-aggression hypothesis*. New York: Atherton, 1969.

Berscheid, E., & Walster, E. Physical attractiveness. In L. Berkowitz (Ed.), *Advances in experimental social psychology* (Vo. 7). New York: Academic Press, 1974.

Blascovich, J., Nash, R. F., & Ginsburg, G. P. Heart rate and competitive decision making. *Personality and Social Psychology Bulletin*, 1978, *4*, 115-118.

Brehm, J. W., & Cohen, A. R. *Explorations in cognitive dissonance*. New York: John Wiley, 1962.

Brener, J., & Jones, J. M. Interoceptive discrimination in intact humans: Detection of cardiac activity. *Physiology and Behavior*, 1974, *13*, 763-767.

Buck, R. W., Jr. Relationships between dissonance-reducing behavior and tension measures following aggression. Doctoral dissertation, University of Pittsburgh, 1970.

Buck, R. W., & Parke, R. D. Behavioral and physiological response to the presence of a friendly or neutral person in two types of stressful situations. *Journal of Personality and Social Psychology*, 1972, *24*, 143-153.

Cacioppo, J. T. The effects of exogenous changes in heart rate on the facilitation of thought and resistance to persuasion. *Journal of Personality and Social Psychology*, 1979, *37*, 487-496.

Cacioppo, J. T., & Petty, R. E. Attitudes and cognitive response: An electrophysiological approach. *Journal of Personality and Social Psychology*, 1979, *37*, 2181-2199.

Cacioppo, J. T., & Petty, R. E. (Eds.). *Social psychophysiology*. New York: Guilford Press, in press.

Carducci, B. J., Cozby, P. C., & Ward, C. D. Sexual arousal and interpersonal evalutions. *Journal of Experimental Social Psychology*, 1978, *14*, 499-457.

Cottrell, N. B. Performance in the presence of other human beings: Mere presence, audience and affiliation effects. In E. C. Simmel., R. A. Hoppe, & G. A. Milton (Eds.), *Social facilitation and imitative behavior*. Boston: Allyn & Bacon, 1968.

Cottrell, N. B. Social facilitation. In C. G. McClintock (Ed.), *Experimental social psychology*. New York: Holt, Rinehart & Winston, 1972.

Coutts, L. M., Schneider, F. W., & Montgomery, S. An investigation of the arousal model of interpersonal intimacy. *Journal of Experimental Social Psychology*, 1980, *16*, 545-561.

Donnerstein, E., & Barrett, G. Effects of erotic stimuli on male aggression toward females. *Journal of Personality and Social Psychology*, 1978, *36*, 180-189.

Duffy, E. *Activation and behavior*. New York: John Wiley, 1962.

Evans, G. Human spatial behavior: The arousal model. In A. Baum & Y. Epstein (Eds.), *Human response to crowding*. Hillsdale, NJ: Lawrence Erlbaum, 1978.

Fazio, R. H., & Cooper J. Arousal in the dissonance process. In J. T. Cacioppo & R. E. Petty (Eds.), *Social psychophysiology*. New York: Guilford Press, in press.

Fenigstein, A., & Carver, C. S. Self-focusing effects of hearbeat feedback. *Journal of Personality and Social Psychology*, 1978, *36*, 1241-1250.

Fenigstein, A., Scheier, M., & Buss, A. H. Public and private self-consciousness: Assessment and theory. *Journal of Clinical and Consulting Psychology*, 1975, *43*, 522-527.

Festinger, L. *A theory of cognitive dissonance*. Stanford: Stanford University Press, 1957.

Fish, B., Karabenick, S., & Heath, M. The effects of observation on emotional arousal and affiliation. *Journal of Experimental Social Psychology*, 1978, *14*, 256-265.

Geen, R. G. Evaluation apprehension and social facilitation: A reply to Sanders. *Journal of Experimental Social Psychology*, 1981, *17*, 252-256.

Gerard, H. B. Choice difficulty, dissonance, and the decision sequence. *Journal of Personality*, 1967, *35*, 91-108.

Gleason, J. M., & Katkin, E. S. The effects of cognitive dissonance on heart rate and electrodermal response (abstract). *Psychophysiology*, 1979, *16*.

Green, D. M., & Swets, J. A. *Signal detection theory and psychophysics*. New York: John Wiley, 1966.

Harré, R. *The philosophies of science*. Oxford: Oxford University Press, 1972.

Harris, V. A., & Katkin, E. S. Primary and secondary emotional behavior: An analysis of the role of autonomic feedback on affect, arousal, and attribution. *Psychological Bulletin*, 1975, *82*, 904-916.

James, W. What is an emotion? *Mind*, 1884, *9*, 188-205.

Jones, G. E., & Hollandsworth, J. G. Heart rate discrimination before and after exercise-induced augmented cardiac activity. *Psychophysiology*, 1981, *18*, 252-257.

Katkin, E. S., Blascovich, J., & Goldband, S. Empirical assessment of visceral self-perception: Individual and sex differences in the acquisition of heartbeat discrimination. *Journal of Personality and Social Psychology*, 1981, *40*, 1095-1101.

Katkin, E. S., Blascovich, J., & Koenigsberg, M. R. Autonomic self-perception and emotion. In W. Waid (Ed.), *Sociophysiology*. New York: Springer Verlag, 1982.

Katkin, E. S., Morell, M. A., Goldband, S., Bernstein, G. L., & Wise, J. A. Individual differences in heartbeat discrimination. *Psychophysiology*, in press.

Lacey, J. I., & Lacey, B. C. Verification and extension of the principle of response stereotypy. *American Journal of Psychology*, 1958, *71*, 50-73.

Lacroix, J. M., & McGowen, A. H. The acquisition of autonomic control through biofeedback: The case against an afferent process—and a possible alternative. Paper presented at the annual meeting of the Society for Psychophysiological Research, Cincinnatti, 1979.

Lykken, D. T., Rose, R., Luther, B., & Maley, M. Correcting psychophysiological measures for individual differences in range. *Psychological Bulletin*, 1966, *66*, 481-484.

Malmo, R. B. Activation: A neuropsychological dimension. *Psychological Review*, 1959, *66*, 367-386.

Mandler, G., Mandler, J. M., & Uviller, E. T. Autonomic feedback: The perception of autonomic activity. *Journal of Abnormal and Social Psychology*, 1958, *56*, 367-373.

Markus, H. The drive for integration: Some comments. *Journal of Experimental Social Psychology*, 1981, *17*, 257-261.

Marshall, G. D., & Zimbardo, P. G. Affective consequences of inadequately explained physiological arousal. *Journal of Personality and Social Psychology*, 1979, *37*, 970-988.

Maslach, C. Negative emotional biasing of unexplained arousal. *Journal of Personality & Social Psychology*, 1979, *37*, 953-969.

McFarland, R. A. Heart rate perception and heart rate control. *Psychophysiology*, 1975, *12*, 402-405.

McMillan, D. L., & Geiselman, J. H. Effect of cognitive dissonance on alpha frequency activity: The search for dissonance. *Personality and Social Psychology Bulletin*, 1974, *1*, 150-151.

McNicol, D. *A Primer of Signal Detection Theory*. London: George Allen & Unwin, 1972.

Mehrabian, A. *Public places and private spaces: The psychology of work, play, and living environments*. New York: Basic Books, 1976.

Middlemast, R. D., Knowles, E. S., & Matter, C. F. Personal space invasions in the lavatory: Suggestive evidence for arousal. *Journal of Personality and Social Psychology*, 1976, *33*, 541-546.

Miller, L. C., Murphy, R., & Buss, A. H. Consciousness of body: Private and public. *Journal of Personality and Social Psychology*, 1981, *41*, 397-406.

Mueller, C., & Donnerstein, E. The effects of humor-induced arousal upon aggressive behavior. *Journal of Research in Personality*, 1977, *11*, 73-82.

Patterson, M. L. An arousal model of interpersonal intimacy. *Psychological Review*, 1976, *83*, 235-245.

Patterson, M. L. Interpersonal distance, affect and equilibrium theory. *Journal of Social Psychology*, 1977, *101*, 205-214.

Pennebaker, J. W. Accuracy of symptom perception. In J. E. Singer & A. Baum (Eds.), *Handbook of medical psychology* (Vol. 5). Hillsdale, NJ: Lawrence Erlbaum, 1981.

Pennebaker, J. W., & Skelton, J. A. Psychological parameters of physical symptoms. *Personality and Social Psychology Bulletin,* 1978, *4,* 524-530.

Piliavin, I., Piliavin, J. A., & Rodin, J. Costs, diffusion, and the stigmatized victim. *Journal of Personality and Social Psychology,* 1975, *32,* 429-438.

Rodin, J. Research on eating behavior and obesity: Where does it fit in personality and social psychology? *Personality and Social Psychology Bulletin,* 1977, *3,* 333-355.

Rosenberg, M. When dissonance fails: On eliminating evaluation apprehension from attitude measurement. *Journal of Personality and Social Psychology,* 1965, *1,* 28-42.

Sanders, G. S. Driven by distraction: An integrative review of social facilitation research and theory. *Journal of Experimental Social Psychology,* 1981, *17,* 227-251.

Sanders, G. S., & Baron, R. S. The motivating effects of distraction on task performance. *Journal of Personality and Social Psychology,* 1975, *32,* 956-963.

Sanders, G. S., Baron, R. S., & Moore, D. L. Distraction and social comparison as mediators of social facilitation effects. *Journal of Experimental Social Psychology,* 1978, *14,* 291-303.

Sapolsky, B. S., & Zillman, D. Experience and empathy: Affective reactions to witnessing childbirth. *Journal of Social Psychology,* 1978, *105,* 131-144.

Sarnoff, I. R., & Zimbardo, P. G. Anxiety, fear, and social affiliation. *Journal of Abnormal and Social Psychology,* 1961, *62,* 356-363.

Schacter, S. *Psychology of affection.* Stanford: Stanford University Press, 1959.

Schacter, S. & Singer, J. Cognitive, social and psychological determinants of emotional state. *Psychological Review,* 1962, *69,* 379-399.

Schaeffer, G. H., & Patterson, M. L. Intimacy, arousal, and small group crowding. *Journal of Personality and Social Psychology,* 1980, *38,* 283-290.

Shapiro, D., & Crider, A. Psychophysiological approaches in social psychology. In G. Lindzey & E. Aronson (Eds.), *Handbook of social psychology* (Vol. 3). Reading, MA: Addison-Wesley, 1969.

Smith, R. J., & Knowles, E. S. Attributional consequences of personal space invasions. *Personality and Social Psychology Bulletin,* 1978, *4,* 429-433.

Stephan, W., Berscheid, E., & Walster, E. Sexual arousal and heterosexual perception. *Journal of Personality and Social Psychology,* 1971, *20,* 93-101.

Tannenbaum, P. H., & Zillman, D. Emotional arousal in the facilitation of aggression. In L. Berkowitz (Ed.), *Advances in experimental social psychology* (Vol. 8). New York: Academic Press, 1975.

Teichman, Y. Emotional arousal and affiliation. *Journal of Experimental and Social Psychology,* 1973, *9,* 591-605.

Triplett, N. The dynamogenic factors in pacemaking and competition. *American Journal of Psychology,* 1897, *9,* 507-533.

Valins, S. Cognitive effects of false heart-rate feedback. *Journal of Personality and Social Psychology,* 1966, *4,* 400-408.

Van Egeren, L. Cardiovascular changes during social competition in a mixed-motive game. *Journal of Personality and Social Psychology,* 1979, *37,* 858-864.

Waid, W. (Ed.). *Sociophysiology.* New York: Springer-Verlag, in press.

Walster, E., Berscheid, E., & Walster, G. W. New directions in equity research. In L. Berkowitz (Ed.), *Advances in experimental social psychology* (Vol. 9). New York: Academic Press, 1976.

Walster, E., Walster, G. W., & Berscheid, E. *Equity: Theory and research.* Boston: Allyn & Bacon, 1978.

Wegner, D. M. & Giuliano, T. Arousal-induced attention to self. *Journal of Personality and Social Psychology,* 1980, *38,* 719-726.

Whitehead, W. E. Interoception: Relationship of visceral perception to the voluntary control of visceral responses. *Psychophysiology,* 1980, *17,* 321.

Whitehead, W. E., Drescher, V. M., Heiman, P., & Blackwell, B. Relationship of heart rate control to heartbeat perception. *Biofeedback and Self Regulation,* 1977, *2,* 371-392.

Worchel, S., & Teddlie, C. The experience of crowding: A two-factor theory. *Journal of Personality and Social Psychology,* 1976, *34,* 30-40.

Zajonc, R. Social facilitation. *Science,* 1965, *149,* 269-274.

Zajonc, R. Attitudinal effects of mere exposure. *Journal of Personality and Social Psychology,* 1968, *9,* 1-27.

Zillman, D. The role of excitation transfer in communication-mediated aggressive behavior. *Journal of Experimental Social Psychology,* 1971, *7,* 419-434.

Zillman, D. Attribution and misattribution of excitatory reactions. In J. H. Harvey, W. Ickes, & R. F. Kidd (Eds.), *New directions in attribution research* (Vol. 2). New York: John Wiley, 1971.

Zillman, D. *Hostility and aggression.* Hillsdale, NJ: Lawrence Erlbaum, 1978.

Zillman, D. Paper presented as part of a symposium on social psychophysiology at the annual meeting of the American Psychological Association, Montreal, 1980.

4

Social Anxiety

MARK R. LEARY

Mark R. Leary received his Ph.D. in social psychology from the University of Florida in 1980. He is currently Assistant Professor of Psychology at Denison University, Granville, Ohio. His research interests include social anxiety, self-presentation, and attribution.

Considering that social anxiety is a pervasive psychological phenomenon and that a high proportion of the population reports being troubled by nervousness in interpersonal encounters (e.g., Bruskin, 1973; Bryant & Trower, 1974; Martinson & Zerface, 1970; Zimbardo, 1977), it is surprising that psychologists have devoted relatively little empirical attention to the phenomenon until quite recently. Now, as if to make up for lost time, researchers have generated a considerable quantity of data dealing with the correlates, causes, and consequences of social anxiety, as well as with counseling strategies designed to help people overcome recurring nervousness in social situations. This work has involved the efforts of researchers working within a number of specialties, including social, personality, developmental, and counseling psychology, and speech communication.

AUTHOR'S NOTE: Preparation of this chapter was partially supported by a grant from the Denison University Research Foundation.

As is often the case in research areas that experience a sudden surge of interest and activity, research on the topic of social anxiety has not been accompanied by equally intense efforts to clarify definitional, conceptual, and methodological issues, or to the integration of the growing literature (see, however, Buss, 1980; Cheek & Buss, 1981; Leary & Schlenker, 1981; Zimbardo, 1977, 1981). This chapter will attempt to review and integrate portions of the literature on the topic of social anxiety, while addressing some basic conceptual issues in the area. Central to these issues is the concept of social anxiety itself. Little agreement currently exists regarding how social anxiety should be defined, and problems with existing definitions have created conceptual and methodological quagmires. Thus, I will first examine the construct of social anxiety. After doing so, I will overview and critique the major approaches that have been adopted for understanding social anxiety, along with their supporting literatures. The final section will address the relationship between subjectively experienced social anxiety and common behavioral manifestations of the experience.

WHAT IS SOCIAL ANXIETY?

If one peruses the references at the end of this chapter, one can see that few of them make any mention of "social anxiety" in their titles. Rather, one will see references to constructs such as shyness, stage fright, hetero-social anxiety, social-evaluative anxiety, dating anxiety, speech anxiety, embarrassment, audience anxiety, and communication apprehension. Although these terms are clearly not synonymous, their respective labels obscure the fact that they all refer to a single psychological phenomenon that may be called social anxiety. Unfortunately, this point has seldom been acknowledged by researchers working in their respective areas, resulting in less integration of the literatures on these topics than might otherwise be possible. Part of the problem is that there is no commonly accepted definition of social anxiety that precisely specifies the nature of the experience and that encompasses all of the above terms.

The Concept of Social Anxiety

As I will define it here, social anxiety is anxiety resulting from the prospect or presence of interpersonal evaluation in real or imagined social settings (Schlenker & Leary, 1981). Since this definition is both different from and more explicit than previous ones, a few words should be said about its major features.

First, *anxiety* refers to a cognitive-affective response characterized by physiological arousal (indicative of sympathetic nervous system activation) and apprehension regarding a potentially negative outcome that the individual perceives as impending. Thus, social anxiety is defined here as a *subjective* experience of nervousness and dread. Earlier definitions of social anxiety (and of specific social anxieties, such as shyness or audience anxiety) have included *behavioral* responses as defining characteristics of social anxiety. To cite only two examples, Clark and Arkowitz (1975, p. 211) define social anxiety as "discomfort in social situations, along with a heightened avoidance of social situations," and Buss (1980) defines shyness (which he classifies as one type of social anxiety) as "the relative absence of expected behavior" (p. 184). Nearly every definition that has been proposed for social anxiety or one of its forms includes mention of reticent, hesitant, awkward, or avoidant kinds of behaviors as defining characteristics of social anxiety.

These kinds of definitions create both conceptual and methodological problems. For example, if social anxiety is defined in terms of specific affective *and* behavioral responses, what do we call anxiety precipitated by interpersonal concerns that is *not* accompanied by overt behaviors such as these? Similarly, when attempting to determine the degree to which a particular client or research subject is experiencing social anxiety, should we focus on affect, behavior, or both? Anxiety and behavior are clearly two different, albeit often related, phenomena, and it does not seem judicious to define the former in terms of the latter.

The failure to distinguish between social anxiety and behavior is not only conceptually problematic, it creates difficulties for the measurement of social anxiety. For example, commonly used self-report measures of "dispositional social anxiety" include items that assess *both* affective and behavioral responses (e.g., Fenigstein, Scheier, & Buss, 1975; Paul, 1966; Watson & Friend, 1969). The confounding of the measurement of subjective anxiousness with the degree to which the individual behaves in a reticent, awkward, hesitant, and/or avoidant manner renders these scales inappropriate as pure measures of dispositional social anxiousness. High scorers on these scales tend to be individuals who frequently experience social anxiety *and* engage in behaviors normally considered indicative of it. Highly anxious individuals who participate fully in interpersonal encounters in a poised manner despite their inner distress might not be classified as high in social anxiety, no matter how frequently or intensely they experience anxiety in interpersonal encounters (Leary, in press).[1]

There is, of course, no doubt that episodes of social anxiety are often accompanied by particular patterns of overt behavior. As I will discuss in detail below, when socially anxious, people often speak less, engage in less eye contact with others, appear nervous, withdraw from the encounter, and so on. However, there is not a one-to-one relationship between the subjective experience of social anxiety and these kinds of behavioral reactions, nor is there any reason to expect one (Clevinger, 1959; Farrell, Mariotto, Conger, Curran, & Wallander, 1979; Mulac & Sherman, 1975). On one hand, people are often able to monitor and control overt indices of their anxious state, their poised demeanor concealing a high degree of inner distress (Zimbardo, 1977). On the other hand, behavioral definitions of social anxiety are thwarted by those individuals who have developed characteristically reticent, hesitant, or awkward modes of interacting yet who do *not* typically experience a high degree of anxiety in interpersonal encounters. There is considerable evidence, for example, that although social anxiety and affiliation are negatively related, introversion and low sociability are not always accompanied by social anxiety and vice versa (Cheek & Buss, 1981; Eysenck & Eysenck, 1969; Leary, in press; Pilkonis, 1977a).

In short, the experience of social anxiety can be conceptually and empirically distinguished from specific patterns of behavior that sometimes accompany it. For this reason, the definition proposed above defines social anxiety in terms of subjectively experienced anxiety only. The relationship between this experience and behavioral reactions is then a topic for investigation in its own right. I will return to the relationship between social anxiety and behavior below.

People may become anxious for a wide variety of social and nonsocial reasons. The definition above specifies how social anxiety may be distinguished from other reasons why people become anxious or afraid. Specifically, only *social* anxiety is precipitated by the prospect or presence of *interpersonal evaluation*. During the course of social encounters, people continually form impressions of and implicitly or explicitly evaluate one another. These impressions and accompanying evaluations determine in large part how each interactant responds toward other individuals (Goffman, 1959; Schlenker, 1980; Snyder, Tanke, & Berscheid, 1977). Because their outcomes in life depend heavily on how they are perceived and evaluated by others, most people attempt to control, to a degree, how they are seen by others. Under certain circumstances, which I will discuss below, this concern with interpersonal evaluation is sufficient to cause people to experience social anxiety (Leary & Schlenker, 1981; Zimbardo, 1981).

The centrality of evaluative concern as the defining characteristic of social anxiety is suggested by a wide variety of studies. For example, factor analyses of fear and anxiety inventories have consistently obtained solutions that include factors reflecting socially based anxieties (e.g., Bates, 1971; Braun & Reynold, 1969; Endler, Hunt, & Rosenstein, 1962; Landy & Gaupp, 1971; Lawlis, 1971; Strahan, 1974). The items that typically load on these "social anxiety" factors include situations such as being introduced to new people, giving a speech, being interviewed for a job, going on a date with someone for the first time, being evaluated, being the center of attention, feeling disapproved of, looking foolish, and being watched while working. What these situations appear to have in common is that they all make interpersonal evaluation unusually salient. People involved in such social settings are more cognizant that they are being scrutinized by others and are often more highly motivated to be evaluated positively than in other, more mundane types of encounters.

Also, people who are high in fear of negative evaluation are significantly more likely to experience social anxiety than people who are low in fear of negative evaluation (Leary, 1980; Watson & Friend, 1969). Similarly, people who are more concerned with the kinds of impressions they are making on others experience social anxiety more acutely than those who are less concerned (Leary & Schlenker, 1981; Zimbardo, 1977, 1981). Also, episodes of social anxiety are typically accompanied by self-cognitions regarding how poorly one is being evaluated by others (Glass, Gottman, & Shmurak, 1976; Rehm & Marston, 1968). Much of the social anxiety literature suggests that concerns with others' evaluations seem to be the distinguishing feature of social anxiety.

Although many, if not most, instances of social anxiety occur in the *presence* of others, the mere *prospect* of interpersonal evaluation is often sufficient to make people apprehensive and nervous. For example, public speakers and performers are often more nervous while waiting to go before an audience than they are during their speech or performance itself (Buss, 1980; Jackson & Latané, 1981). Similarly, shy males experience considerable anxiety just from anticipating an upcoming interaction with a female (e.g., Twentyman & McFall, 1975). Similarly, the social settings that elicit anxiety may be either *real or imagined*. People may feel nervous just from imagining what would happen if a particular encounter occurred. Social anxiety always arises due to interpersonal concerns, but other people need not be present in order for a person to feel socially anxious.

To repeat, social anxiety is anxiety arising from the prospect or presence of interpersonal evaluation in real or imagined social settings. When defined in this way, the construct of social anxiety encompasses all of the terms listed above (i.e., audience anxiety, shyness, stage fright, dating anxiety, embarrassment). Thus, these terms refer to what is essentially the same sociopsychological phenomenon, albeit in different kinds of social settings. Some of these terms, such as audience anxiety, speech anxiety, and communication apprehension, are typically used when people experience social anxiety while performing or speaking before others. Other terms—shyness, dating anxiety, heterosocial anxiety—are more applicable when the anxious individual is in a two-way, contingent encounter (usually face-to-face). The term "embarrassment" is reserved for situations in which the person has become anxious because of a specific social predicament that has threatened to result in lowered evaluations and negative sanctions from others. There is nothing wrong with using descriptive terms such as these as long as we remember that they all refer to the same general experience. Any differences that exist in the phenomena referred to are a function of the specific precipitating factors involved and not due to the fact that they are distinct psychological experiences. When this point is kept in mind, it is possible to integrate the findings of a number of research areas that have typically been regarded as distinct.

Dispositional Versus Situational Social Anxiety

While I do not wish to revive the state-trait anxiety issue of a few years ago (Speilberger, 1968), it is necessary to make an explicit distinction between two common usages of the term "social anxiety." On one hand, the term has often been used in the manner we have defined it here—as a *state* of anxiety aroused by certain situational and dispositional factors. In other instances, the term has been used to refer to an individual difference or trait variable—the degree to which an individual tends to experience nervousness in his or her dealings with others. When communicating about social anxiety, it is important that it be made clear to which meaning a particular usage refers. Many writers have done this by using terms such as "dispositional social anxiety," "trait social anxiety," or "social anxiousness" to refer to the frequency and/or intensity with which individuals experience social anxiety (the state) over situations and time. Throughout this chapter, I will use the term "social anxiousness" when a personal characteristic is meant.

THEORETICAL APPROACHES TO SOCIAL ANXIETY

Most research on the topic of social anxiety has stemmed from one of five major theoretical viewpoints. Although space prohibits full discussion of these approaches to social anxiety, I will briefly overview and critique each.

Personality/Individual Difference Approaches

Until the last few years, most research in the area focused on individual difference variables associated with the tendency to experience anxiety in interpersonal encounters (see Crozier, 1979, for a review of many of these studies). Catell (1973), for example, considered shyness to be one aspect of the threctic (H-negative) personality, which is characterized by timidity, restraint, and sensitiveness. He suggested that threctic individuals possess a highly reactive sympathetic nervous system with a low threshold for responsiveness to physical and social threats to the individual. Numerous other factor analyses of personality trait items have obtained "social anxiety" factors, indicating that the degree to which people feel nervous, hesitant, and awkward in social encounters warrants consideration as an important dispositional variable (e.g., Catell, 1965; Comrey, 1965; Comrey & Jamison, 1966; Fenigstein et al., 1975; Layman, 1940).

More recently, a great deal of attention has been devoted to examining cognitive, affective, and behavioral differences among people who differ on trait measures of social anxiousness, such as the Social Avoidance and Distress Scale (Watson & Friend, 1969). For example, people characterized by a tendency to experience anxiety in social encounters have been found to speak and date less frequently (Pilkonis, 1977b; Curran, 1977), have lower self-esteem (Leary, in press; Zimbardo, 1977), make more negative statements about themselves both before and during interactions (Cacioppo et al., 1979; Clark & Arkowitz, 1975; Glass, Merluzzi, Biever, and

Larsen, 1982), have difficulty timing their responses to others appropriately (Fischetti, Curran, & Wessberg, 1977), nod more frequently while listening to others (Pilkonis, 1977b), and are more concerned with how others evaluate them (Leary, 1980; Watson & Friend, 1969). Few attempts have been made to determine precisely how these cognitive and behavioral reactions relate to the subjective experience of social anxiety itself. That is, are these different reactions causes, consequences, or correlates of social anxiety? More will be said about this question below.

The personality-individual difference approach to social anxiety has been a fruitful one. However, by its nature, it deemphasizes situational determinants of social anxiety. Obviously, even those individuals who would not be classified as characteristically socially anxious occasionally experience anxiety in certain social settings.

Classical Conditioning

Several writers, particularly those examining the efficacy of systematic desensitization as a means of reducing problematic social anxiousness, have regarded social anxiety as a classically conditioned emotional response. According to this model, people find certain kinds of social encounters anxiety-arousing because stimuli in those settings have been associated with aversive outcomes in the past. Previously neutral social events have become conditioned stimuli capable of eliciting anxiety. Indeed, many people trace their apprehension about certain kinds of social situations to a specific incident in which they had a highly unpleasant experience (Zimbardo, 1977).

Although research has shown that emotional responses may be classically conditioned (Bandura, 1969; Wolpe, 1973), no studies have specifically attempted to condition *social* anxiety in an individual—for obvious ethical reasons. The strongest evidence in support of a classical conditioning model of social anxiety comes from counseling studies showing that socially based anxieties may be eliminated through treatments based on classical conditioning, such as systematic desensitization (e.g., Bander, Steinke, Allen, & Mosher, 1975; Bandura, 1969; Curran, 1975; Kondas, 1967; Meichenbaum, Gilmore, & Fedoravicius, 1971; Mitchell & Orr, 1974; Paul, 1966). It should be noted, however, that the efficacy of systematic desensitization does not necessarily demonstrate that the individual's anxiousness originally resulted from a classically conditioned association.

The classical conditioning model has some utility for understanding and treating social anxiety. Yet, despite its usefulness, it has been adopted by few personality and social psychologists. Perhaps this is because it does not directly address the kinds of questions about social anxiety likely to be of interest to researchers in these areas.

Skills Deficit Model

Smooth, pleasant, and productive encounters with others require that individuals possess a repertoire of basic social skills. Successful social contacts require people to be able to hold up their end of conversations, provide appropriate cues that facilitate interaction, appear generally poised, interested, and friendly, refrain from interruptive and annoying behaviors, and so on. People who lack these kinds of social abilities are likely to mismanage their interactions with others, occasionally creating awkward, strained, and otherwise aversive encounters. Put another way, social anxiety may sometimes arise as a (somewhat reasonable) reaction to a problematic, aversive situation brought about by one's inability to handle the social demands of a particular encounter (Bellack & Hersen, 1979; Curran, 1977; MacDonald, Lindquist, Kramer, McGrath, & Rhyne, 1975).

There are several reasons why people may fail to execute appropriate social responses. In many cases, people have never had the opportunity to learn and/or practice proper execution of needed skills. Teenagers on a first date might nervously bumble their way through the evening, uncertain of what to say or do, for example. At other times, people may have learned appropriate behaviors but be unable to bring themselves to put them into practice. A person might know *how* to coherently express his or her feelings to others but have difficulty actually doing so when appropriate. Other people may be able to perform appropriate behaviors when needed but execute them improperly. Bellack (1979) observes that individuals may be able to execute an approximation to the proper response but have difficulty with the frequency, duration, intensity, or form of the behavior. An unskilled male might ask a particular female for a date but ask her too often, spend too long making the request, or plead for a date instead of asking casually.

If people with social skill deficits are more likely to create aversive interactions that precipitate anxiety, we would expect to find a negative relationship between social skill and feelings of anxiety. Indeed, numerous studies have shown that observers (e.g., experimenters, confederates, naive subjects) consistently rate socially anxious people as less socially skilled than less anxious individuals (Arkowitz, Lichtenstein, McGovern, & Hines, 1975; Bellack & Hersen, 1979; Curran, 1977; Twentyman & McFall, 1975). Interestingly, most attempts to isolate specific skill deficits among socially anxious subjects have met very limited success. People who differ on measures of social anxiousness have not been found to differ on measures of social skill in any dramatic way (some minor behavioral differences have been found). The failure to identify social deficiencies among the socially anxious only shows that anxious individuals do not all have the same skill problems, not that each individual does not possess some unique deficit.

Fischetti et al. (1977) have suggested that the social problems of highly socially anxious people are not likely to be reflected in the simple frequency measures used in most studies. Rather, social skill deficits are likely to involve problems handling the *contingent, interactive* nature of many social encounters. High and low socially anxious people may differ little in the frequency with which they engage in certain behaviors but differ significantly in the timing or placement of their responses. In support of this hypothesis, their research showed that, while high and low socially anxious men differed little on frequency counts of vocal and gestural responding during an interaction with a female, they differed dramatically in the timing of their responses. Instead of responding at appropriate "choice points" in the woman's conversation as high skill-low anxiety men did, highly anxious males appeared to strew their responses randomly throughout the woman's conversation. Future research on skill deficits might do well to follow Fischetti et al.'s (1977) lead in examining socially anxious people's problems handling the reciprocal, two-way nature of face-to-face encounters.

Much research has demonstrated the efficacy of social skills training for reducing problematic social anxiousness (see Bellack & Hersen, 1979, for reviews). However, it is not clear whether skills training directly reduces anxiety by decreasing the probability that individuals will mismanage their interactions with others, as the skills deficit hypothesis would suggest, or indirectly reduces it by improving people's feelings of confidence in social settings. Related to this question is whether the behavioral differences that have been observed between high and low socially anxious people are best regarded as causes or consequences (or perhaps merely correlates) of subjective social anxiety. The social skills approach would be supported only if it is determined that skill deficits are *antecedents* of social anxiety.

Cognitive Self-Evaluation Model

The self-evaluation model argues that social skill deficits are neither necessary nor sufficient causes of social anxiety. Many people who are judged by others to be quite socially adept experience considerable anxiety in their interpersonal dealings. Conversely, we all know individuals who are consensually regarded as bumbling, boring, abrasive, and generally unskilled but who are relatively anxiety-free. The self-evaluation approach posits that people experience social anxiety, not because they lack important social skills per se, but because they *believe* they are socially inadequate. As Clark and Arkowitz (1975, p. 212) note, "the behaviors of the socially anxious individuals may be reasonably adequate by external standards but evaluated as inadequate by the socially anxious individual." Negative evaluation of one's own ability to deal effectively with others in certain situations produces expectations of unfavorable social outcomes that precipitate anxiety (Clark & Arkowitz, 1975; Meichenbaum et al., 1971; Rehm & Marston, 1968).

There is considerable research support for this hypothesis. For example, compared to people low in social anxiousness, highly socially anxious individuals tend to underestimate their level of social skill, generate more negative self-statements both before and during social interaction, expect to perform poorly and be evaluated more negatively, and chastise themselves more for not behaving more adroitly (Cacioppo, Glass, & Merluzzi, 1979; Clark & Arkowitz, 1975; Efran & Korn, 1969; Glasgow & Arkowitz, 1975; Glass et al., 1982; Smith & Sarason, 1975; Watson & Friend, 1969). In addition, there is a moderate correlation between self-esteem and social anxiety (r's range around -.50; Leary, in press; Zimbardo, 1977). Also, counseling approaches designed to help socially anxious clients modify their negative self-evaluations are quite effective at reducing the frequency and intensity of episodes of social anxiety (e.g., Fremouw & Zitter, 1978; Glass et al., 1976; Kanter & Goldfried, 1979; Malkiewich & Merluzzi, 1980; Rehm & Marston, 1968). It is interesting that socially anxious individuals' negative self-evaluations are limited to socially relevant attributes. They do not rate themselves lower than nonanxious individuals on athletic, intellectual, or artistic dimensions (Efran & Korn, 1969).

If the self-evaluation analysis has a weakness, it is that it does not specify the conditions under which negative self-evaluation does and does not result in social anxiety. Most people recognize that they are deficient in certain social and nonsocial respects, yet they go about their daily lives with only minimal social anxiety. On the other hand, people may feel socially anxious even when they evaluate themselves and their social performance highly. Why? The answer seems to involve the distinction between *self*-evaluation and how one thinks *others* are evaluating one (i.e., self-appraisals versus reflected appraisals). Although these types of evaluations often covary, the critical factor in social anxiety may be a concern with others' evaluations, rather than self-evaluation per se.

Self-Presentation Approach

To remedy weaknesses of earlier approaches, Leary and Schlenker (1981; Leary, 1980; Schlenker & Leary, in press) proposed a social psychological theory that focuses on the interpersonal origins of social anxiety. According to the self-presentation model, social anxiety results from the joint effect of two sets of factors. People are posited to become socially anxious when they (a) are motivated to make particular impressions on others but (b) doubt they will be successful in doing so, thereby creating expectations of less-than-satisfactory reactions from the others.

As discussed above, the impressions an individual projects of him or herself to others greatly affects how he or she is evaluated and treated by others (Goffman, 1959). The projections of self-images that others deem appropriate and desirable tend to result in rewarding social and material outcomes for the individual, whereas self-presentations that are regarded negatively by others are likely to result in unfavorable reactions. As a result, people are often highly motivated to convey particular impressions of themselves to others in the encounter (Goffman, 1959; Jones & Wortman, 1973; Schlenker, 1980). Since the personal consequences of failing to project desired self-presentations are often negative, people who are motivated to make particular impressions become apprehensive—socially anxious—at the prospect of failing to do so.

According to this model, specific antecedents of social anxiety include those situational and dispositional factors that either heighten people's motivation to convey particular impressions of themselves or lead people to doubt that they will be successful at doing so. An examination of the common antecedents of social anxiety supports this proposition (see Leary & Schlenker, in press; Zimbardo, 1977). For example, social anxiety is more frequently experienced when dealing with critical, expert, and evaluative others, in initial encounters with specific individuals, and by people who are high in public self-consciousness, need for approval, and fear of negative evaluation. All of these factors would be expected to increase people's motivation to make particular impressions on others.

Other variables associated with social anxiety appear to affect the second factor in the model by lowering people's confidence in their ability to make the impressions that will result in the reactions they desire: encounters with strangers and novel situations (since they create doubts about how one should behave), scrutinizing audiences, low self-esteem, perceived social skill deficits, previous social failures, and so on. Any factor that leads people to expect to receive less-than-satisfactory evaluative reactions from others is hypothesized to trigger social anxiety, given that the individual is motivated to convey certain self-presentations in order to be evaluated in a personally rewarding manner. If the individual is either not concerned with how he or she is being perceived and evaluated by others or believes he or she is being evaluated as desired, social anxiety should not occur.

This approach seems to have three advantages over the models already discussed. First, it subsumes the personality, classical conditioning, skills deficit, and self-evaluation approaches. The critical factors in these other approaches may be conceptualized as affecting one of the two necessary and sufficient factors that are hypothesized to cause social anxiety. Second, it explicitly acknowledges the interaction of situational and dispositional variables in producing social anxiety. Third, it clearly hypothesizes the necessary and sufficient conditions for all instances of social anxiety.

BEHAVIORAL CONCOMITANTS OF SOCIAL ANXIETY

We have already discussed the necessity for conceptually and methodologically distinguishing between the subjective experience of social anxiety and behaviors that often accompany this state. Social anxiety and specific patterns of behavior are not perfectly correlated, although there are relationships between them. In this section, I will more closely examine the links between social anxiety and interpersonal behavior.

The behaviors that tend to accompany episodes of social anxiety are quite diverse. When socially anxious, people stammer and figit, reduce their verbal output, nod their heads more frequently, reduce their eye contact with others, and attempt to withdraw from the problematic encounter. It seems unlikely that such different types of behavioral reactions all stem from the same factors or are functionally equivalent. In fact, there seem to be at least three relatively distinct classes of overt behavioral responses that occur in situations that precipitate social anxiety.

Arousal-Mediated Responses

First, subjective social anxiety is typically accompanied by what I will call arousal-mediated responses. These are reactions that directly result from the individual's aroused state (see Borkovec, Stone, O'Brien, & Kaloupek, 1974). When anxious, people squirm in their seats, figit, play with their hair, clothes, or other manipulable objects, stutter and stammer as they talk, and generally appear jittery and nervous (e.g., Cheek & Buss, 1981; Paul, 1966; Pilkonis, 1977b; Zimbardo, 1977). The frequency of these kinds of responses varies directly with the intensity of their anxiety in that encounter. Arousal-mediated responses are merely side effects of the activation of the sympathetic nervous system that accompanies all aroused states, but they serve no useful social function for the individual.

One of the more troublesome consequences of anxious arousal is its effect on speech. People who feel anxious often stutter, stammer, vacilate on words, have a quivering voice, use a greater number of pauses in their speech, and generally communicate less effectively (Borkovec at al., 1974; Kasl & Mahl, 1965; Mahl, 1956; Murray, 1971; Pilkonis, 1977b; Porter, 1939; Swartz, 1976; Van Riper, 1939). The precise mechanism by which anxiety interferes with speech is not fully understood. Perhaps the preoccupation that accompanies social anxiety makes it difficult for the speaker to concentrate on what he or she is saying. If parallels may be drawn between social and test anxiety, it has been shown that self-deprecating thoughts detract from the test taker's ability to devote full attention to the task at hand, thus debilitating performance (Mandler & Watson, 1966; Wine, 1971). Alternatively, the debilitating effect of anxiety may result from paying *too much* attention to what one is saying. When evaluation is a salient concern, people may monitor their speech more carefully than usual. Conscious attention to typically "mindless" actions often results in less efficient behavior (Langer & Weinman, 1981). Readers who have spoken into a public address system in a stadium or very large auditorium and suddenly become aware of their own voices have probably experienced verbal disruptions due to overattention to one's speech. Recently, Schwartz (1976) presented evidence that stuttering results from a dilation reflex in the throat that is exacerbated under conditions of stress.

Since loss of poise is evaluated negatively in our society, anxious individuals will usually attempt to hide overt indices of their nervousness. However, it is often difficult to control arousal-mediated responses, particularly as anxiety increases. Unfortunately, the failure to hide one's nervousness creates additional difficulties for the socially anxious person. Pilkonis (1977b) found that shy people who regarded behavioral manifestations as a major component of their shyness were more bothered by being shy than were shy people who manifested little overt evidence of their inner distress. One's social problems are compounded when one's internal discomfort is obvious to everyone.

Disaffiliative Behaviors

Disaffiliative behaviors are actions that serve to reduce the amount of social contact one individual has with another. When people feel socially anxious, they initiate conversations less frequently, participate less fully in ongoing conversations, talk a lower percentage of the time, allow more silences to develop in the conversation, are less likely to break silences, and speak for shorter periods of time when addressing an audience (e.g., Cheek & Buss, 1981; Borkovec, Fleishman, & Caputo, 1973; Glasgow & Arkowitz, 1975; Leary, 1980; Natale, Entin, & Jaffe, 1979; Murray, 1971). They also tend to avoid those social settings in which they expect to feel nervous, and they prematurely withdraw from those which cause anxiety (Cheek & Buss, 1981; Pilkonis, 1977b; Twentyman & McFall, 1975; Zimbardo, 1977). Once they feel anxious in an interpersonal encounter, people tend to give less eye contact to others (Cheek & Buss, 1981; Modigliani, 1971; Pilkonis, 1977b) and disclose less about themselves (Zimbardo, 1977). All of these responses effectively function to reduce the individual's level of social contact with others, either by keeping them out of anxiety-arousing social settings altogether or by minimizing the length and depth of their involvement in ongoing encounters. As a result of these kinds of responses, shy people are more likely to report feeling lonely and have greater difficulty overcoming their loneliness in new situations (Cheek & Busch, 1981).

Behaviors such as these have generally been regarded as consequences of social anxiety. However, it is better to regard social anxiety and disaffiliative behaviors as *coeffects* and not as directly causally linked (see Bandura, 1977; Schlenker & Leary, in press). Both social anxiety and disaffiliation appear to result from cognitions about one's ability (or, more precisely, inability) to deal effectively with a particular social encounter. In the terms of the self-presentation model of social anxiety discussed above, when people are motivated to make particular impressions on others, the belief that they will be unsuccessful produces both affective and behavioral consequences. The combination of these two factors causes the individual to feel socially anxious and, at the same time, increases disaffiliative behaviors.

Carver (1979, p. 1264) notes that when people's analysis of a situation leads them to believe there is a small probability of attaining a particular goal or behavioral standard, "the behavioral consequence is withdrawal." Thus, when people perceive they cannot obtain the evaluative reactions they desire from others, they will withdraw as much as possible from further attempts to obtain them. In most cases, full withdrawal from the problematic interaction is not an immediately viable option. Thus, the anxious person uses the disaffiliative responses at his or her disposal, such as reticence and reduced eye contact. Carver (1979) additionally notes that when people can neither continue engaging in goal-directed behaviors (in this case, making desired impressions on others) nor withdraw from the situation, they become locked in a self-assessment stage in which they "repeatedly confront evidence of their own inadequacy" (p. 1266). Although Carver was not writing specifically about social anxiety, his model of self-attention may account for the heightened self-consciousness and self-preoccupation of socially anxious people (Schlenker & Leary, in press).

Disaffiliation also reduces the possibility that the individual's social image will be further damaged by full participation in the problematic encounter. Since anxious persons already believe they are not coming across well to others, they may take steps to assure that things do not get any worse. In addition, avoidance of and withdrawal from anxiety-producing social occasions is, in operant conditioning terms, negatively reinforcing. People disaffiliate in anxiety-arousing social settings because doing so reduces the aversiveness of such situations.

Image Protection

Consider the plight of people who experience social anxiety in an interpersonal encounter. They wish to make certain desired impressions on others but think they will be unable to do so effectively. Others are expected to view their self-presentations less positively than they would like and respond in a hedonically unsatisfactory manner. What can be done?

If withdrawal from the encounter is not a viable option, socially anxious individuals might be expected to attempt to enhance and/or protect their social images *as best they can* under the circumstances. Although they do not think they can come across to others as well as they would like, they should attempt to establish as desirable a public self-image as possible (Leary & Schlenker, in press, Zimbardo, 1981). Zimbardo (1981) suggests that the impression management attempts of socially anxious people are likely to involve a "protective" rather than an "acquisitive" self-presentation style. Protective self-presentations are characterized by attempts to avoid losses in social approval and/or avoid receiving social disapproval, as contrasted with acquisitive self-presentations in which the aim is to gain approval (Arkin, 1981). Thus, protective self-presentations are typically conservative, easily defensible (the individual will not make exaggerated claims), and often involve the projection of images that others would be expected to regard as innocuous.

Little research has specifically examined the expressive behaviors or self-presentations of people experiencing social anxiety. Nevertheless, several studies support the hypothesis that protective self-presentations are employed by socially anxious individuals. For example, when socially anxious, people engage in behaviors that would be expected to convey impressions of innocuous sociability without participating fully in the ongoing encounter. Socially anxious people smile and nod more frequently (as in agreement) in face-to-face conversations (Pilkonis, 1977b), interrupt others less often, and engage in more back-channel responding—the sounds people make to indicate they are listening to another, such as "uh-huh" (Natale et al., 1979). These responses may serve to project an image of the person as friendly, agreeable, polite, interested, and even sociable without incurring any social risks.

Another tactic for improving one's chances for acceptance by others is doing favors for them (Jones & Wortman, 1973; Schlenker, 1980). Research on embarrassment—social anxiety precipitated by a self-presentational predicament (Goffman, 1955)—has shown that people who have suffered a loss of face are more likely to comply with others' requests and engage in other helpful behaviors (Apsler, 1975; Miller, 1979). This is juxtaposed to McGovern's (1976) finding that people classified as high in social anxiousness are less likely to engage in prosocial behavior than low socially anxious people. However, in this study, subjects had to disobey the experimenter's instructions in order to help. Apparently, the highly socially anxious individual is less likely to provide help if doing so may incur social disapproval (see Latane & Darley, 1970). It remains to be seen whether favor-doing increases in situations that produce social anxiety when there is no risk associated with being helpful.

People use a wide variety of self-presentational strategies to convey impressions of themselves to others (Arkin, 1981; Schlenker, 1980). The self-presentations of people under conditions of social anxiety warrant future research attention.

Antecedent Versus Consequent Behaviors

The three categories of behaviors just described—arousal-mediated, disaffiliative, and image-protective—occur as the *result* of the kinds of factors that precipitate subjective social anxiety. Thus, they are distinguishable from behaviors that occur *prior* to the onset of social anxiety and that, in many cases, help precipitate it. As noted above, certain kinds of responses may cause social anxiety by creating aversive social situations. Past research on behavioral concomitants of social anxiety has shown few attempts to determine the nature of the relationship between social anxiety and behavior. Future research on the behavior of socially anxious people should direct attention to this question.

SUMMARY AND CONCLUSIONS

This chapter was written to serve three major purposes. First, the construct of social anxiety was critically examined and a definition offered that may help reduce conceptual confusion in the area. Progress in any research area is hampered by inconsistent use of concepts. This has been true of social anxiety research: Imprecise conceptualizations have led to imprecise methodology and measurement and impeded integration of what would seem to be intimately related literatures. Second, an attempt was made to introduce the reader to five major theoretical approaches to social anxiety. Each of these approaches has its merits, but the self-presentation model seems to be the most specific and encompassing. However, this model has not yet been subjected to repeated experimental tests. Finally, the relationship between social anxiety and overt behaviors was examined. Two major points were made regarding this relationship: (a) Not all behavioral manifestations of social anxiety are functionally equivalent; and (b) behavioral concomitants of social anxiety might best be regarded as coeffects rather than as consequences of social anxiety.

Interest in social anxiety has exploded in recent years, partly owing to the topic's intrinsic interest and partly to the awareness that psychologists have neglected this common psychological phenomenon in the past. The continued study of social anxiety is important, not only for its own sake, but because analysis of the experience and its causes tells us something about what people consider important—and, thus, worth worrying about—when they interact with others.

NOTE

1. Scales developed by McCroskey (1970) and Leary (in press) avoid this problem by including scale items assessing subjectively experienced anxiety only.

REFERENCES

Apsler, R. Effects of embarrassment on behavior toward others. *Journal of Personality and Social Psychology,* 1975, *32,* 145-153.

Arkin, R. M. Self-presentation styles. In J. T. Tedeschi (Ed.), *Impression management theory and social psychological research.* New York: Academic Press, 1981.

Arkowitz, H., Lichtenstein, E., McGovern, K., & Hines, P. The behavioral assessment of social competence in males. *Behavior Therapy, 1975, 6,* 3-13.

Bander, K. W., Steinke, G. V., Allen, G. J., & Mosher, D. L. Evaluation of three dating-specific treatment approaches for heterosexual dating anxiety. *Journal of Consulting and Clinical Psychology,* 1975, *43,* 259-265.

Bandura, A. *Principles of behavior modification.* New York: Holt, Rinehart & Winston, 1969.

Bandura, A. Self-efficacy: Toward a unifying theory of behavioral change. *Psychological Review,* 1977, *84,* 191-215.

Bates, H. D. Factorial structure and MMPI correlates of a fear survey in a clinical population. *Behaviour Research and Therapy,* 1971, *9,* 355-360.

Bellack, A. S. Behavioral assessment of social skills. In A. S. Bellack & M. Hersen (Eds.), *Research and practice in social skills training.* New York: Plenum, 1979.

Bellack, A. S., & Hersen, M. *Research and practice in social skills training.* New York: Plenum, 1979.

Borkovec, T. D., Fleischmann, D. J., & Caputo, J. A. The measurement of anxiety in an analogue social situation. *Journal of Consulting and Clinical Psychology,* 1973, *44,* 157-161.

Borkovec, T. D., Stone, N., O'Brien, G., & Kaloupek, D. Identification and measurement of a clinically relevant target behavior for analogue outcome research. *Behavior Therapy,* 1974, *5,* 503-513.

Braun, P. R., & Reynolds, D. J. A factor analysis of a 100 item fear survey inventory. *Behaviour Research and Therapy,* 1969, *7,* 399-402.

Bruskin, J. What are Americans afraid of? *The Bruskin Report: A Market Research Newsletter,* July 1973, No. 53.

Bryant, B., & Trower, P. E. Social difficulty in a student sample. *British Journal of Educational Psychology,* 1974, *44,* 13-21.

Buss, A. H. *Self-consciousness and social anxiety.* San Francisco: W. H. Freeman, 1980.

Cacioppo, J. T., Glass, C. R., & Merluzzi, T. V. Self-statements and self-evaluations: A cognitive response analysis of heterosocial anxiety. *Cognitive Therapy and Research,* 1979, *3,* 249-262.

Carver, C. S. A cybernetic model of self-attention processes. *Journal of Personality and Social Psychology,* 1979, *37,* 125-128.

Catell, R. B. *The scientific analysis of personality.* Harmondsworth: Penguin, 1965.

Catell, R. B. *Personality and mood by questionnaire.* San Francisco: Jossey-Bass, 1973.

Cheek, J. M., & Busch, C. M. The influence of shyness on loneliness in a new situation. *Personality and Social Psychology Bulletin,* 1981, *7,* 572-577.

Cheek, J. M., & Buss, A. H. Shyness and sociability. *Journal of Personality and Social Psychology,* 1981, 41, 330-339.

Clark, J. V., & Arkowitz, H. Social anxiety and self-evaluation of interpersonal performance. *Psychological Reports,* 1975, *36,* 211-221.

Clevinger, T. A synthesis of experimental research in stage fright. *Quarterly Journal of Speech,* 1959, *45,* 134-145.

Comrey, A. L. Scales for measuring compulsion, hostility, neuroticism, and shyness. *Psychological Reports,* 1965, *16,* 697-700.

Comrey, A. L., & Jamison, J. Verification of six personality factors. *Educational and Psychological Measurement,* 1966, *26,* 945-953.

Crozier, W. R. Shyness as a dimension of personality. *British Journal of Social and Clinical Psychology,* 1979, *18,* 121-128.

Curran, J. P. Social skills training and systematic desensitization in reducing dating anxiety. *Behaviour Research and Therapy,* 1975, *13,* 65-68.

Curran, J. P. Skills training as an approach to the treatment of heterosexual-social anxiety. *Psychological Bulletin,* 1977, *84,* 140-157.

Efran, J. S., & Korn, P. R. Measurement of social caution: Self-appraisal, role playing, and discussion behavior. *Journal of Clinical and Consulting Psychology,* 1969, *33,* 78-83.

Endler, N. S., Hunt, J., & Rosenstein, A. J. An S-R inventory of anxiousness. *Psychological Monographs,* 1962, *79* (Whole # 17), 1-33.

Eysenck, H. J., & Eysenck, S.B.G. *Personality structure and measurement.* San Diego: Knapp, 1969.

Farrell, A. D., Mariotto, M. J., Conger, A. J., Curran, J. P., & Wallander, J. L. Self-ratings and judges' ratings of heterosexual social anxiety and skill: A generalizability study. *Journal of Clinical and Consulting Psychology,* 1979, *47,* 164-175.

Fenigstein, A., Scheier, M. F., & Buss, A. H. Public and private self-consciousness: Assessment and theory. *Journal of Consulting and Clinical Psychology,* 1975, *43,* 522-527.

Fischetti, M., Curran, J. P., & Wessberg, H. W. Sense of timing: A skill deficit in heterosexual-socially anxious males. *Behavior Modification,* 1977, *1,* 179-194.

Fremouw, W. J., & Zitter, R. E. A comparison of skills training and cognitive restructuring-relaxation for the treatment of speech anxiety. *Behavior Therapy,* 1978, *9,* 248-259.

Glasgow, R., & Arkowitz, H. The behavioral assessment of male and female social competence in dyadic heterosexual interactions. *Behavior Therapy,* 1975, *6,* 488-498.

Glass, C. R., Gottman, J. M., & Shmurak, S. Response acquisition and cognitive self-statement modification approaches to dating-skills training. *Journal of Counseling Psychology,* 1976, *23,* 520-526.

Glass, C. R., Merluzzi, T. V., Biever, J. L., & Larsen, K. H. Cognitive assessment of social anxiety: Development and validation of a self-statement questionnaire. *Cognitive Therapy and Research,* 1982, *6,* 37-56.

Goffman, E. On facework. *Psychiatry,* 1955, 18, 213-231.

Goffman, E. *The presentation of self in everyday life.* Garden City, NY: Doubleday, 1959.

Jackson, J. M., & Latané, B. All alone in front of all those people: Stage fright as a function of number and type of co-performers and audience. *Journal of Personality and Social Psychology,* 1981, *40,* 73-85.

Jones, E. E., & Wortman, C. *Ingratiation: An attributional analysis.* Morristown, NJ: General Learning Press, 1973.

Kanter, N. J., & Goldfriend, M. R. Relative effectiveness of rational restructuring and self-control desensitization in the reduction of interpersonal anxiety. *Behavior Therapy*, 1979, *10*, 472-490.

Kasl, S. V., & Mahl, G. F. The relationship of disturbances and hesitations in spontaneous speech to anxiety. *Journal of Personality and Social Psychology*, 1965, *1*, 425-433.

Kondas, O. Reduction of examination anxiety and "stage-fright" by group desensitization and relaxation. *Behaviour Research and Therapy*, 1967, *5*, 275-281.

Landy, F. J., & Gaupp, L. A. A factor analysis of the Fear Survey Schedule-III. *Behaviour Research and Therapy*, 1971, *9*, 89-93.

Langer, E. J., & Weinman, C. When thinking disrupts intellectual performance: Mindfulness on an overlearned task. *Personality and Social Psychology Bulletin*, 1981, *7*, 240-243.

Latané, B., & Darley, J. *The unresponsive bystander: Why doesn't he help?* New York: Appleton-Century-Crofts, 1970.

Lawlis, G. F. Response styles of a patient population on the fear survey schedule. *Behaviour Research and Therapy*, 1971, *9*, 95-102.

Layman, E. An item analysis of the adjustment questionnaire. *Journal of Psychology*, 1940, *10*, 87-106.

Leary, M. R. *The social psychology of shyness: Testing a self-presentation model.* Doctoral dissertation, University of Florida, 1980.

Leary, M. R. Social anxiousness: The construct and its measurement. *Journal of Personality Assessment*, in press.

Leary, M. R., & Schlenker, B. R. The social psychology of shyness: A self-presentational model. In J. T. Tedeschi (Ed.), *Impression management theory and social psychological research.* New York: Academic Press, 1981.

MacDonald, M. L., Lindquist, C. U., Kramer, J. A., McGrath, R. A., & Rhyne, L. D. Social skills training: Behavioral rehearsal in groups. *Journal of Counseling Psychology*, 1975, *22*, 224-230.

Mahl, G. F. Disturbances and silences in the patient's speech in psychotherapy. *Journal of Abnormal and Social Psychology*, 1956, *53*, 1-15.

Malkiewich, L. E., & Merluzzi, T. V. Rational restructuring versus desensitization with clients of diverse conceptual level: A test of a client-treatment matching model. *Journal of Counseling Psychology*, 1980, *27*, 453-461.

Mandler, G. & Watson, D. Anxiety and the interruption of behavior. In C. D. Spielberger (Ed.), *Anxiety and behavior.* New York: Academic Press, 1966.

Martinson, W. D., & Zerface, J. P. Comparison of individual counseling and a social program with non-daters. *Journal of Counseling Psychology*, 1970, *17*, 36-40.

McCroskey, J. C. Measures of communication-bound anxiety. *Speech Monographs*, 1970, 37, 269-277.

McGovern, L. P. Dispositional social anxiety and helping behavior under three conditions of threat. *Journal of Personality*, 1976, *44*, 84-97.

Meichenbaum, D. H., Gilmore, J. B., & Fedoravicius, A. Group insight versus group desensitization in treating speech anxiety. *Journal of Clinical and Consulting Psychology*, 1971, *36*, 410-421.

Miller, R. S. *Empathic embarrassment: Reactions to the embarrassment of another.* Paper presented at the meeting of the American Psychological Association, New York, 1979.

Mitchell, K. R., & Orr, T. E. Note on treatment of heterosexual anxiety using short-term massed desensitization. *Psychological Reports,* 1974, *35,* 1093-1094.

Modigliani, A. Embarrassment, facework, and eye-contact: Testing a theory of embarrassment. *Journal of Personality and Social Psychology,* 1971, *17,* 15-24.

Mulac, A., & Sherman, A. R. Relationships among four parameters of speaker evaluation: Speech skill, source credibility, subjective speech anxiety, and behavioral speech anxiety. *Speech Monographs,* 1975, *42,* 302-310.

Murray, D. C. Talk, silence, and anxiety. *Psychological Bulletin,* 1971, *75,* 244-260.

Natale, M., Entin, E., & Jaffe, J. Vocal interruptions in dyadic communication as a function of speech and social anxiety. *Journal of Personality and Social Psychology,* 1979, *37,* 865-878.

Paul, G. L. *Insight versus desensitization in psychotherapy.* Stanford: Stanford University Press, 1966.

Pilkonis, P. A. Shyness, public and private, and its relationship to other measures of social behavior. *Journal of Personality,* 1977, *45,* 585-595 (a).

Pilkonis, P. A. The behavioral consequences of shyness. *Journal of Personality,* 1977, *45,* 596-611 (b).

Porter, H. Studies in the psychology of stuttering: XIV. Stuttering phenomena in relation to size and personnel of audience. *Journal of Speech Disorders,* 1939, *4,* 323-333.

Rehm, L. P., & Marston, A. R. Reduction of social anxiety through modification of self-reinforcement. *Journal of Clinical and Consulting Psychology,* 1968, *32,* 565-574.

Schlenker, B. R. *Impression management: The self-concept, social identity, and interpersonal relations.* Monterey, CA: Brooks/Cole, 1980.

Schlenker, B. R., & Leary, M. R. Social anxiety and self-presentation: A conceptualization and model. *Psychological Bulletin,* in press.

Schwartz, M. F. *Stuttering solved.* Philadelphia: Lippincott, 1976.

Smith, R. E., & Sarason, I. G. Social anxiety and the evaluation of negative interpersonal feedback. *Journal of Consulting and Clinical Psychology,* 1975, *43,* 429.

Snyder, M., Tanke, E. D., & Berscheid, E. Social perception and interpersonal behavior: On the self-fulfilling nature of social stereotypes. *Journal of Personality and Social Psychology,* 1977, *35,* 656-667.

Spielberger, C. D. Theory and research on anxiety. In C. D. Spielberger (Ed.), *Anxiety and behavior.* New York: Academic Press, 1968.

Strahan, R. Situational dimensions of self-reported nervousness. *Journal of Personality Assessment,* 1974, *38,* 341-352.

Twentyman, C. T., & McFall, R. M. Behavioral training of social skills in shy males. *Journal of Consulting and Clinical Psychology,* 1975, *43,* 384-395.

Van Riper, C. G. *Speech correction: Principles and methods.* Englewood Cliffs, NJ: Prentice Hall, 1939.

Watson, D., & Friend, R. Measurement of social-evaluative anxiety. *Journal of Consulting and Clinical Psychology,* 1969, *33,* 448-457.

Wine, J. D. Test anxiety and direction of attention. *Psychological Bulletin,* 1971, *76,* 92-104.

Wolpe, J. *The practice of behavior therapy.* New York: Pergamon, 1973.

Zimbardo, P. G. *Shyness: What it is and what to do about it.* New York: Jove, 1977.

Zimbardo, P. G. *The shy child.* New York: McGraw-Hills, 1981.

5

Exchange and Communal Relationships

JUDSON MILLS

MARGARET S. CLARK

6

Judson Mills is Professor of Psychology at the University of Maryland, College Park.

Margaret S. Clark is Associate Professor of Psychology at Carnegie-Mellon University in Pittsburgh, Pennsylvania.

I magine someone in a crafts shop, searching for a gift for a close friend. Finding something she thinks her friend will like, she looks for the price tag, but it is missing. She points this out to the store owner, who apologizes, finds the tag, and replaces it. She tells the store owner she wishes to buy the item, pays for it, and asks that it be gift-wrapped. As the store owner is wrapping it, she notices that he has not removed the tag from the gift. She calls his attention to the price tag and he apologizes for failing to remove it.

Why does the store owner apologize to the customer twice, first when the price tag is missing and then for failing to remove the tag? The basis for the first apology seems straightforward. The store owner has an obligation to make the conditions of exchange clear to the potential buyer of the item.

121

The point of the second apology is difficult to understand from the perspective of social psychological theories which assume that all social relationships are based on exchange. If all relationships are based on exchange, then leaving the price tag on a gift to a friend would seem to be appropriate and even desirable. It would facilitate the recipient's efforts to maintain equity in the relationship. By knowing the value of the gift, the recipient would know just how much input into the relationship it represents. If the giver had a past debt to the recipient, the extent to which the gift removes that debt is clear. If there was no past debt, the degree of obligation which the recipient now has to the gift-giver is clear.

It might be argued that the reason behind the store owner's need to apologize for leaving the price tag on the gift is the existence of a social norm dictating the removal of price tags from gifts. However, such an explanation is unsatisfying. If social relationships are based on exchange, why should such a norm exist?

In a previous paper (Clark and Mills, 1979) we put forth a distinction between exchange and communal relationships which can provide a theoretical explanation of why price tags are removed from gifts, as well as for a variety of other behaviors.[1] The stimulus for the distinction was the discussion of social and economic exchange by sociologist Erving Goffman (1961, pp. 275-276). Social exchange is, in Goffman's view, quite different from economic exchange. In social exchange, agreement in advance as to what is to be exchanged may be compromising. Something given in a social exchange "need only be returned *if* the relationship calls for it; that is when the putative recipient comes to be in need of a favor or when he is ritually stationed for a ceremonial expression of regard." On the other hand, in an economic exchange, "no amount of mere thanks can presumably satisfy the giver; he must get something of equivalent material value in return."[2]

We used the term "exchange relationship" rather than Goffman's term "economic exchange" because many of the benefits people give to and receive from one another do not involve money or things for which a monetary value can be calculated. A benefit is something one member of a relationship chooses to give to the other that is of use or value to the person receiving it. Benefits are not the same as rewards, when the term "rewards" refers to "the pleasures, satisfactions and gratifications the person enjoys" (Thibaut & Kelley, 1959, p. 12). The receipt of a benefit may not always constitute a reward.[3] Also, rewards may occur for reasons other than the receipt of a benefit. For example, the rewards a parent receives from a newborn infant would not fall within the definition of a benefit, since the infant does not choose to give them to the parent.

In an exchange relationship, the members assume that a benefit is given with the expectation of receiving a benefit in return. The receipt of a benefit incurs a debt or obligation to return a comparable benefit. In exchange relationships, each person is concerned with how much he or she receives in exchange for benefiting the other and how much is owed the other in return for the benefits received.

Since all relationships in which persons give and receive benefits are social, we chose another term to describe relationships in which each person has a concern for the welfare of the other. The term "communal" seemed to be the most appropriate. The relationships which typically exist between romantic partners, family members, and friends exemplify this type of relationship. Although it might appear to an observer that there is an exchange of benefits in such relationships, the rules concerning giving and receiving benefits in communal relationships are different from the rules concerning giving and receiving benefits in exchange relationships.

In a communal relationship, members assume that each is concerned about the welfare of the other. Each person has a positive attitude toward benefiting the other when a need for the benefit exists or when a benefit can be provided which would be especially pleasing to the other. In other words, the members of the relationship follow what Pruitt (1972) has labeled the "norm of mutual responsiveness." This norm may create a pattern which appears to an observer to be an exchange of benefits. However, this rule is distinct from the rule which governs exchange relationships—namely, that the receipt of a benefit is reciprocated by the giving of a comparable benefit. The rules concerning the giving and receiving of benefits are what distinguish communal and exchange relationships, rather than the specific benefits which are given and received.

From the perspective of the participants in a communal relationship, the benefits given and received are not part of an exchange. The attribution of motivation for the giving of benefits is different from that in an exchange relationship. In communal relationships, receipt of a benefit does not create a specific debt or obligation to return a comparable benefit. The general obligation the members have to aid the other when the other has a need is not altered by the receipt of a specific benefit.

In communal relationships there is a tendency to maintain what we might call "equality of affect." At any given point in time the members of a communal relationship should be experiencing about the same affect. If one person experiences good fortune and, consequently, positive affect, the other person should feel good as well. Similarly, if one person experiences misfortune and feels bad, the other should feel bad also.

The norm that in a communal relationship one responds to the other's needs has the effect of maintaining equality of affect. As Walster, Walster, and Berscheid (1978) point out, intimates come to define themselves as a unit. We would emphasize that the members tend to feel the same way. Walster et al. provide the following examples of this: "the joy and pride a parent feels at the success and happiness of his child ('That's my boy!'), the distress a wife experiences when her husband has been denied a hoped for opportunity, the intense pleasure a lover feels while working to make his beloved happy" (p. 153).

The idea that a specific benefit is given in exchange for past or future benefits is inappropriate in a communal relationship because it calls into question the assumption that each member responds to the needs of the other. A benefit which appears to be a response to a prior benefit implies that the person giving the benefit does not desire a communal relationship with the other. This has implications for the rules people who wish to maintain or develop communal relationships with another person follow when giving benefits to the other. For instance, if one does not want a benefit to appear as though it was given in response to a prior benefit, one should not give the benefit to the other soon after receiving a benefit from that other; rather, one should allow some time to pass before benefiting the other.

Another restriction on the giving of benefits to which members of communal relationships adhere is that they refrain from giving benefits which are directly comparable to benefits received from the other in the recent past. The less comparable a benefit is to a benefit previously received, the less likely it is to appear as though it was given in response to that prior benefit.

An illustration of both restrictions is provided by the following quotation from Walster et al. (1978): "We all know how disconcerting it is when, for example, we give of our time to help a neighbor and are offered cash in return. We would be far more comfortable if our neighbor offered to help us sometime when we were in a similar situation" (p. 151). In a communal relationship we do not want benefits to appear as though they are repayments.

The restrictions that one should avoid benefiting another immediately following a prior benefit and that one should not provide a benefit which is directly comparable to a prior benefit may be violated if the need of the other for an immediate and/or comparable benefit is compelling. For instance, if we help our neighbor push his car out of the snow so that he can go to work, and if we are in immediate need of the same service, then it is appropriate for him to offer to perform that service for us, since it will be taken as a response to our need. Indeed, not offering to help in such a situation would indicate a lack of concern for our needs.

In an exchange relationship, giving a benefit immediately after receiving a prior benefit should be more appropriate than giving a benefit after a delay. Also, in an exchange relationship, it should be more appropriate to give comparable rather than noncomparable benefits. The greater the comparability of a benefit to one received in the past, the easier it is to determine the extent to which the benefit eliminates the debt incurred by the receipt of the earlier benefit. If someone with whom you have an exchange relationship buys you lunch, you should be more confident that the resultant debt is eliminated if you buy him lunch at the same place than if you give him advice about some professional problem.

While we assume that the distinction between communal and exchange relationships is made implicitly by most people in their interactions with others, we do not assume that people are explicitly aware of the distinction or are able to describe how it affects their reactions. Certainly they do not use the terms "communal" and "exchange" to describe relationships. We also do not assume that everyone makes the distinction in the same way. Some people restrict their communal relationships to only a very few persons, while others have communal relationships with a wide circle of others. There are some people who do not make the distinction at all. Some people treat every relationship, even relationships with members of their own immediate family, in terms of exchange.

Communal relationships seem to vary in strength in a way that exchange relationships do not. People either have or do not have exchange relationships with others. One exchange relationship is no stronger than another. However, people may have very strong communal relationships with some persons and weaker ones with others. For example, a woman may have a very strong communal relationship with her husband and a weaker communal relationship with her friend. Responding to the needs of a person with whom one has a strong communal relationship takes precedence over responding to the needs of someone with whom one has a weaker communal relationship. For example, if the woman's friend is very sick and has no one to look after her, the woman will respond to her friend's needs by looking after her. However, if that woman's husband is also sick, taking care of her husband will take precedence over taking care of her friend.

We believe that most people consider themselves to have weak communal relationships with everyone. If another person has a need which is great relative to the cost of the benefit we could provide to eliminate that need, we feel obligated and willing to benefit them. For instance, if a stranger is lost and asks us for directions, we are willing to give those directions. Or if someone's car breaks down in front of our house and that person asks us to call the local garage for a tow truck, we will provide that service. A benefit given under such circumstances does not incur a specific debt.

Greetings which often occur between strangers also seem to indicate that people have weak communal relationships with just about everyone. For instance, as a person checks out at a grocery store, the clerk may say, "How are you today?" Expressing a concern about the other person's well being is something appropriate to a communal relationship.

Religious groups typically encourage their members to treat everyone according to the rules of communal relationships. Members of religious groups are expected to respond to the needs of others without expecting anything specific in return from those others. In light of this, it is not surprising that members of religious orders are often referred to as brothers, sisters, mothers and fathers—terms commonly used for family relationships. Social movements also tend to refer to members as brothers and sisters in order to foster communal relationships.

Both communal and exchange relationships may vary in certainty. People are usually less certain of communal relationships they have with new friends or with someone they are just beginning to date than they are of relationships with old friends or with their husband or wife. The more certain one is of a communal relationship with another, the less careful one has to be about doing something which might be interpreted as indicating a preference for an exchange relationship rather than a communal relationship. Thus, the more certain one is of a communal relationship, the less likely one is to be concerned that a benefit given to the other might look like a repayment for a prior benefit from the other or that a benefit might leave the impression that one feels it should be repaid.

Parents and their children are usually very certain of the communal relationships they have with one another. Most parents can give money as a gift to their children and not worry that the child will misunderstand and think they should pay the money back. On the other hand, in a communal relationship about which one is less certain, giving money as a gift is very awkward.

A person's certainty about having an exchange relationship with another may also vary. For instance, a storeowner may be quite certain he has an exchange relationship with a long-time customer who has always paid his bills on time. However, he may be much less certain of having an exchange relationship with a new customer to whom he has just granted credit. He may have doubts about whether the person will pay his debts, thus adhering to the rules of exchange relationships, or whether the customer will exploit him by failing to pay his debts.

It is possible for a person to have both a communal relationship and an exchange relationship with the same other, as when a person sells something to a friend or hires a family member as an employee. In such instances, a distinction is typically made between what is appropriate for the business (exchange) relationship and what is appropriate for the family or friendship (communal) relationship. Exchange relationships sometimes can develop into communal relationships, such as when a merchant and a customer become close friends or when an employer and employee marry.

Communal relationships involve an expectation of a long-term relationship, while exchange relationships need not be long term. However, the variables of communal versus exchange relationship and expected length of the relationship are conceptually independent. Exchange relationships may continue over a long period. The relationship between a storeowner and a long-term customer or the relationship between a boss and a secretary often are examples of long-term exchange relationships.

EFFECTS ON INTERPERSONAL ATTRACTION
OF RECEIVING A BENEFIT FOLLOWING PRIOR AID

Two studies of interpersonal attraction (Clark and Mills, 1979) lend support to the distinction between communal and exchange relationships. The first study by Clark and Mills dealt with the influence of type of relationship with another on reactions to receiving a benefit from the other after that other has been aided. We were interested in discovering how adherence to or violation of the norms which apply to communal and exchange relationships affects attraction in those relationships.

Based on the ideas about communal and exchange relationships presented above, we hypothesized that a benefit from another after the other has been benefited should reduce attraction for the other if there is a desire for a communal relationship with the other, but increase attraction if an exchange relationship is preferred. We assumed that when a communal relationship does not yet exist but is desired, the receipt of a benefit should have the same effect as when a communal relationship is assumed to exist. These predictions were tested in our first study (Clark & Mills, 1979).

In this study unmarried male students served as subjects. The desire for a communal relationship with another was manipulated by having the part of the other played by an attractive woman whom the subject was led to believe was either married or unmarried. In all cases the subject expected to participate in a second experiment with the woman during which they would have the opportunity to get to know one another by discussing common interests in a relaxed atmosphere. The assumption was that the male subjects would desire a communal relationship with the attractive, unmarried woman but would prefer an exchange relationship with the attractive, married woman.

When the subject reported to the experiment, he was seated at a desk and asked to work on a vocabulary task. A TV monitor in the room showed an attractive woman supposedly waiting to work on a similar task in another room. The experimenter said she suspected that people's approaches to solving this task varied when certain conditions were changed and that, in the condition to which the subject and the other person were assigned, they would be able to see each other over closed-circuit TV but would not be able to talk to each other directly. (What appeared on the monitor was actually the same for every subject.) Subjects were also told that they could send and request letters from one another on simple forms which were provided for this purpose. The experimenter said she would come into the room from time to time to see if the subject wished to send or to request letters.

The subject was then told that there were two tasks the experimenter was interested in studying. One was more difficult than the other and she had flipped a coin to determine who would be working on which task. The subject was assigned the easy task and the woman got the difficult one.

When the subject completed his task, he was awarded one point toward extra credit for finishing on time and he was given the opportunity to send some of his excess materials to the woman, who was still at work on her task (all subjects did). After receiving the aid, the woman completed her more difficult task and was awarded four points toward extra credit. At this point, the subject could see the woman writing a note which she folded and handed to the experimenter. The experimenter reentered the subject's room and handed him a note. Some of the subjects received a note from the other which thanked them (no benefit condition) while some received a note which thanked them and gave them one of her points (benefit conditions).

After the subject received the note, the experimenter manipulated the type of relationship with the other. She mentioned either that the woman was anxious to complete the next part of the experiment because she thought it would be interesting and her husband would be picking her up soon (exchange conditions) or that she was anxious to complete the next part because she thought it would be interesting, was new at the university, and had to be at the administration building soon (communal conditions).

Shortly after this, the subject's liking for the woman was assessed. The experimenter reminded the subject about the second study involving discussion of common interests in which he and the woman were to participate shortly. The subject was told that, before starting this study, it was necessary to get some idea of their first impressions of one another. To do this, she was asking each participant to rate his or her first impressions of the other.

The subject rated the female on eleven traits, including considerate, friendly, insincere, intelligent, irritating, kind, open-minded, sympathetic, understanding, unpleasant, and warm, and also rated his degree of liking for her. A measure of liking for the other was calculated by summing the ratings for each of the eleven traits (ratings for the negative traits were reversed) together with the overall rating of liking.

The results provided support for our hypothesis that when a communal relationship is desired, a benefit following prior aid decreases attraction. When the attractive woman they had aided was unmarried (communal conditions), the unmarried male subjects liked her significantly less when she gave them a benefit than when she did not. When she turned out to be married (exchange conditions), she was liked significantly more when she gave the subject a benefit than when she did not. The results for the married woman are consistent with the hypothesis that when an exchange relationship is preferred, the receipt of a benefit following prior aid leads to greater attraction.

It should be noted that we would not expect to get the same effect in the communal conditions if the other were not attractive to the subject.

People do not desire communal relationships with unattractive people. They prefer to treat such others in terms of exchange.

In our opinion the effect which was obtained in the communal conditions should also occur if the other merely expresses a wish to provide a benefit following prior aid but is prevented in some way from doing so. An offer to provide a benefit following prior aid violates a rule in a communal relationship just as actually providing the benefit does. The same offer to provide a benefit following prior aid is appropriate in an exchange relationship. It indicates that the other at least has the desire to follow the rules, although it is questionable whether it would actually increase liking, since a wish to repay does not eliminate the prior debt.

If the other had not previously been aided by the person, reactions to receiving a benefit from the other in communal and exchange relationships should be opposite to the reactions obtained when the other was aided. If a communal relationship is desired, the receipt of a benefit when the other was not previously aided should increase liking because it indicates the other is treating the relationship as a communal relationship. On the other hand, in an exchange relationship the receipt of a benefit from someone who was not aided previously may decrease liking if the benefit cannot be repaid or if the person does not wish to repay it.

REACTIONS TO A REQUEST FOR A BENEFIT

The distinction between communal and exchange relationships also has implications for reactions to a request for a benefit. If it is true that in an exchange relationship any benefit given by one member to the other creates a debt or obligation to return a comparable benefit, a request for a benefit from another after one has been given aid by that other creates an opportunity to repay the debt. Thus, such a request should be appropriate in an exchange relationship. It should increase liking for the other, since it provides an opportunity to repay the debt and to eliminate any tension caused by the presence of the debt.

The idea that the recipient of a benefit will like his or her benefactor more if he can return the benefit has been expressed before (Mauss, 1954). Several studies have shown that recipients of benefits like the donor more if they are able to repay the benefit than if they are not able to repay, whether the opportunity is provided by the donor specifically requesting that the other repay the benefit (Gergen, Ellsworth, Maslach, & Seipel,

1975) or whether the opportunity to repay is provided but repayment is not specifically asked for (Castro, 1974; Gross & Latané, 1974).

In communal relationships, requesting a benefit after having given another person aid is inappropriate. It implies that the original aid was not given with the intent of satisfying a need but rather with the expectation of receiving something in return, which may be taken as an indication that the other does not desire involvement in a communal relationship. Assuming that beginning or maintaining a communal relationship with another is desirable, such an implication should be frustrating and therefore result in decreased liking.

If one has not been previously aided by another and there is no opportunity to aid the other in the future, a request for a benefit from that other is inappropriate in an exchange relationship. In such a case a person who has not been aided by another should like the other more when he does not ask for a benefit.

In a communal relationship, requesting a benefit in the absence of previously received aid is appropriate. Such a request implies a desire for a communal relationship, and assuming that beginning or maintaining such a relationship is desirable, it should result in increased liking. Jones & Wortman (1973) suggest asking another for a benefit as a way of conveying that we think highly of them: "This tactic is likely to convey that we feel good about our relationship with the target person, since it is not customary to ask people to do favors for us unless our relationship is a relatively good one" (Jones & Wortman, 1973, p. 13).

Specifically, the following hypotheses were tested in our second study (Clark & Mills, 1979): (1) A request for a benefit from another after the person was aided by the other leads to greater attraction when an exchange relationship is expected. (2) When a communal relationship is expected, a request for a benefit after the person was aided by the other decreases attraction. (3) A request for a benefit in the absence of aid from the other decreases attraction when an exchange relationship is expected. (4) When a communal relationship is expected, a request for a benefit in the absence of aid from the other increases attraction.

Unmarried female students served as subjects. The manipulation of the subject's desire for a communal or an exchange relationship took place shortly after the subject arrived. The experimenter mentioned to the subject that the other did not know many people, was looking forward to meeting people, and that she and the other would be discussing common interests later on (communal conditions) or that the other was busy, her husband would be picking her up soon, and that she and the other would be discussing differences in interests later on (exchange conditions).

As in our first study, the subject was seated at a desk and asked to work on a vocabulary task. Again, a TV monitor showed an attractive woman waiting to work on a similar task in another room and subjects believed that they could send and receive letters and notes to each other.

This time the subject was given the more difficult task (actually impossible) and the other woman supposedly had the easier task. The experimenter told the subject to begin and then appeared on the TV monitor telling the other to begin. The attractive woman always finished first, received one point, and either sent her extra letters to the subject (aid conditions) or did not (no aid conditions). The subject continued to work for a short period before being stopped by the experimenter and given four points. The other female then requested a point from the subject or did not request a point. Finally, the subject's liking for the other was assessed in the same manner as in our first study.

In general, the results supported our hypotheses concerning reactions to a request for a benefit in communal and exchange relationships. As expected from the hypothesis that a request for a benefit after the person was aided by the other leads to greater attraction when an exchange relationship is expected, it was found that liking for the other was significantly higher in the exchange/aid/request condition than in the exchange/aid/no request condition. As predicted from the hypothesis that when a communal relationship is expected, a request for a benefit after the person was aided decreases attraction, liking was significantly lower in the communal-aid-request condition than in the communal/aid/no request condition. In line with the hypothesis that a request for a benefit in the absence of aid from the other decreases attraction when an exchange relationship is expected, liking for the other was significantly lower in the exchange/no aid/request condition than in the exchange/no aid/no request condition.

We did not find support for the hypothesis that when a communal relationship is expected, a request for a benefit in the absence of aid from the other increases attraction. There was no difference in liking between the communal/no aid/request condition and the communal/no aid/no request condition. We believe the subjects in the communal/no aid/no request condition might have been somewhat uncertain about the intentions of the other. While the request might have indicated to the subject that the other wanted a communal relationship with her and consequently led the subject to expect such a relationship, it also might have reminded the subject of the fact that the other had not given her aid earlier. This reminder might have raised some doubt on the subject's part as to whether or not the other would behave in an appropriate way for a communal relationship, which could explain why the request did not result in increased liking for the other in the communal/no aid/request condition.

If we are correct in our assumption that treating a communal relationship in terms of exchange compromises the relationship, theories which assume that all relationships are based on exchange may create a misleading impression about the development and breakup of intimate relationships. For example, the recommendation that has been popular in recent years that prior to marriage a contract be drawn up which specifies in detail what each partner expects from the other should, if followed, tend to undermine the relationship.

EFFECTS ON FEELINGS OF EXPLOITATION

The norms which apply to communal and exchange relationships have implications for when people will feel exploited. In exchange relationships, when a benefit is given, the recipient owes the donor a comparable benefit and the donor should feel exploited if he or she believes it will not be repaid. In communal relationships, in contrast, members are not obligated to repay specific benefits. Thus, in communal relationships, failure to repay a particular benefit should not create feelings of exploitation.

Clark and Waddell (1981) conducted two studies concerning feelings of exploitation. The first was designed to test these hypotheses: (1) In an exchange relationship, after granting a request from the other for a benefit, feelings of exploitation will be greater if the other fails to repay than if the other does repay. (2) In a communal relationship, after granting a request from the other for a benefit, lack of repayment will not influence feelings of exploitation.

Upon arrival for the study, the female subjects were told that the other subject had arrived but had gone to the bookstore located in the building for a moment and would be back shortly. The experimenter said she had already explained the study to the other and would now briefly explain it to the subject. It involved how getting to know another person through a discussion improved one's insight into that other. Both subjects would complete measures of insight into the other twice, once before and once after a discussion with the other. One measure of insight, the one they would begin with, consisted of listing their first associations to a list of words and of guessing the other's first associations to the same words. In the communal conditions, the experimenter added, "Then the two of you will have a brief discussion of common interests," while in the exchange conditions she said, "Then the two of you will have a brief discussion of differences in interests." After the discussion they would repeat the first task. At this point the experimenter commented that she was surprised the other had not returned because her husband would be picking her up immediately following the study (exchange conditions) or because she had been looking forward to meeting people (communal conditions).[4] Within a short time, an attractive female confederate, who was unaware of the relationship manipulation, arrived. Both she and the subject began to fill out the first "associations" measure, and the experimenter left the room—presumably to get some additional materials. She told them not to talk during the task, but that they could talk once it was over.

After they had both finished, and prior to the experimenter's return, the confederate mentioned a survey she had to do for a class. She asked the subject to fill out a questionnaire. Following the subject's agreement (all agreed), the confederate either told the subject she would pay her two dollars from class funds for filling out the survey (benefit conditions) or that there had been class funds to pay people but they had run out (no benefit conditions).

About a minute later, the experimenter returned and told the subjects there was one more form to fill out prior to the discussion. She led the subject to another room telling the confederate she would return shortly. She handed the subject an "impression form" on which she was to confidentially rate her first impressions of the other person, which was explained as a second measure of insight into one another that would be filled out both before and after the discussion. On this form the subject rated the other on the following traits: friendly, insincere, intelligent, irritating, exploitative, kind, open-minded, unpleasant, warm, trustworthy, and willing to take advantage of others.

A measure of perceived exploitation was calculated by summing the subject's ratings of the other on exploitativeness and willingness to take advantage of others. As predicted, the difference between the benefit and no benefit conditions was significant in the exchange conditions but not in the communal conditions. Failure to repay had a greater impact on exchange than on communal relationships.

This study also included a measure of attraction which was calculated by summing the subjects' ratings on the following traits: friendly, insincere, intelligent, irritating, kind, open-minded, unpleasant, warm, trustworthy, and on an overall rating of liking. (Ratings for the negative traits were reversed.) The attraction means paralleled those for the measure of exploitation. In the communal conditions feelings of attraction were unaffected by whether or not a benefit was given, whereas failure to give a benefit in return for prior aid significantly reduced attraction in the exchange conditions.

While the findings for attraction in the exchange conditions of this study paralleled those in the exchange conditions of Clark and Mills's Study 1, the attraction results in the communal conditions did not parallel the findings of Clark and Mills, in that the receipt of a benefit did not lower attraction. This discrepancy can be accounted for in terms of differences between the studies. In the Clark and Mills study, the other person did not ask the subject to give her a benefit, while in the Clark and Waddell study she did. When the benefit was given to the other in response to a request from the other, repayment is not as likely to be interpreted as a rebuff of a gesture of friendliness.

In addition, in the benefit conditions of the Clark and Waddell study, the other indicated that she paid everyone who was willing to fill out her questionnaire and thus repayment was not a reflection of her lack of willingness to enter into a communal relationship with the subject. Similarly, in the no benefit conditions the confederate had run out of money and could not repay anyone, so the lack of repayment did not signify something about the other's view of their relationship.

The first Clark and Waddell study supported the idea that failure to repay a benefit will create feelings of exploitation in exchange relationships but not in communal relationships. However, it does not shed light on the conditions under which people in communal relationships will feel exploited. In a second study, Clark and Waddell (1981) investigated the effects of failure to fulfill a need, as well as failure to repay a benefit, on feelings of exploitation.

As in the first study, it was predicted that (1) in an exchange relationship a person will feel more exploited when the other fails to repay a past benefit than when the other does repay, and that (2) failure to repay will not produce feelings of exploitation in communal relationships. Two new hypotheses were also tested: (3) In an established communal relationship a person will feel more exploited when the other fails to fulfill his or her need than when the other does fulfill that need; and (4) failure to fulfill a need will not produce feelings of exploitation in exchange relationships.

It should be noted that Hypothesis 3, that failure to fulfill a need creates feelings of exploitation in established communal relationships, would not be expected to apply in communal relationships about which members are uncertain. In an established communal relationship, members have implicitly accepted the rule that each should be responsive to the other's needs. Under these circumstances, failure to respond to a clear need on the part of the other should be viewed as unjust. However, this may not occur in a relationship which a person simply desires or expects to be communal. In such a case, failure to respond to a need may be disappointing, but it does not violate an established, implicit agreement between the two people.

In the second Clark and Waddell study subjects were asked how they would react in situations involving persons with whom it could be assumed they had existing communal or exchange relationships. Relationships with a parent and a romantic partner were used as examples of communal relationships and relationships with a fellow student/co-worker whom they did not consider a friend and a landlord as examples of exchange relationships. In some cases subjects were asked to imagine they had a particular need the other knew about and in some cases that they had just provided the other with aid. Sometimes the commodity the subject was in need of or had just provided to the other was gasoline and sometimes it was charcoal. After reading each situation subjects rated how exploited and how hurt they would feel if (a) the other did not give them the benefit that would fulfill their need or repay them and (b) the other did give them the benefit. Ratings of exploitation and hurt were summed to provide a measure of feelings of exploitation.

It was found that, as expected, failure to repay a benefit had a significantly greater impact on feelings of exploitation in exchange than in communal relationships. Also, as expected, failure to fulfill a need had a significantly greater impact on feelings of exploitation in communal than in exchange relationships. It should be mentioned that there were some unexpected results. Failure to repay a benefit significantly increased reports of exploitation in the communal conditions, and failure to fulfill a need significantly increased reports of exploitation in the exchange conditions.

The explanation for these unexpected findings could lie in the manipulations of communal and exchange relationships. A manipulation check showed that the subjects' relationships with parents and romantic partners were generally more communal and less exchange oriented than their relationships with landlords and fellow students/co-workers. However, if some of the subjects had communal relationships with their landlords and/or fellow students/co-workers, those subjects should report feeling unjustly treated if those others failed to fulfill their needs. To the extent that some of the subjects had exchange relationships with their parents and/or romantic partners, they should have reported feeling unjustly treated if those others failed to repay them.

THE CONTENT OF COMMUNICATIONS
ACCOMPANYING A BENEFIT

The content of communications accompanying a benefit from the other should influence reactions to benefits in communal and exchange relationships. In general, as Goffman (1961) suggested, discussion of the giving and receiving of benefits tends to be compromising in a communal relationship. It indicates that the other is treating the relationship in terms of exchange.

If the other mentions prior aid from the person when giving the person a benefit, the benefit is likely to be perceived as a payment for the prior aid. In a communal relationship, mention of the prior aid accompanying a benefit should be perceived as inappropriate and should decrease liking. In an exchange relationship, mention of the prior aid should not affect liking.

Another kind of comment accompanying a benefit which is likely to be taken as an indication that the other is treating the benefit as part of an exchange is one which conveys that the giving of the benefit is costly to the other. Emphasizing the cost of the benefit is likely to increase the perception that the other regards the benefit as part of an exchange, which is inappropriate in a communal relationship. This is appropriate in an exchange relationship, but it is certainly inappropriate in a communal relationship. Generally when people give presents they do not emphasize the cost of the present to themselves but rather try to avoid discussing it at all.

We feel that this is the major reason why price tags placed on items for sale in a store are removed when the items are purchased as gifts. Store owners want to make clear what they expect from the customer in exchange for ownership of the items for sale. On the other hand, a gift giver wants to emphasize that the benefit was given to fulfill the receiver's needs in some way or to suit his preference or tastes. He wants to deemphasize the cost to himself. Removing the price tag from a gift helps to accomplish this.

One kind of communication which is appropriate when giving a benefit in a communal relationship is a comment that emphasizes the way in which the benefit meets a need the person has or might have. Such comments should increase liking if a communal relationship is desired.

WHEN BENEFITS ARE GIVEN

As was touched on earlier, the distinction between communal and exchange relationships has implications for when benefits are given. People in exchange relationships should give benefits to one another when they have specific debts to the other and/or when they are confident that the other will repay them for a benefit. They should be most likely to give a benefit in response to a prior benefit when they can provide a comparable benefit. They may avoid giving a benefit in response to a prior benefit when the only benefits they can provide are inadequate for eliminating the debt, or when it is unclear just how adequate a particular benefit is for eliminating a particular debt.

In communal relationships, people should be most likely to provide the other with a benefit when the other has a need for the benefit. Other occasions on which the giving of benefits should be common are when the person locates something that would be particularly pleasing to the other or on festive occasions, such as birthdays and weddings. Members of communal relationships should avoid giving a benefit immediately after receiving one from the other, especially when the benefit to be given is comparable to that received.

As an example of this norm, suppose you have just purchased a present for a friend. Before you have a chance to give your friend the present, he or she gives you the same thing. You probably would like to be able to return the gift you've purchased and get something else.

It should be noted that just how strictly we adhere to the norms regarding when benefits are given in communal relationships depends on the two factors discussed previously. First, the less certain we are of having a communal relationship with the other, the more strictly the norms will be followed. Second, these norms may be violated if the other's need for the particular benefit is compelling.

OUTSIDERS' PERCEPTIONS OF RELATIONSHIPS

How relationships are perceived by outsiders is another topic for which the distinction between communal and exchange relationships has implications. The norms that are followed regarding the giving and receiving of benefits in a relationship may be observed by people outside that relationship. Also, reactions to violations of norms in a relationship may be observed by outsiders. Such information is likely to be used by outside observers to infer the type of relationship which exists between the two persons.

Imagine seeing a car carrying your female next-door neighbor and a handsome male pulling up in front of your neighbor's home. You've never seen the male before and you wonder what his relationship with your next-door neighbor is. If you observe that your neighbor steps out of the car and hands the driver some money, you are likely to infer that their relationship is an exchange relationship, If, however, she simply thanks him as she steps out, you're more likely to perceive that they have a communal relationship.

If one person gives a benefit to another and soon afterwards the second person gives the first a comparable benefit, an observer is likely to infer that the second benefit is a repayment for the first, and that the two people have an exchange relationship. In contrast, if the two people give and receive noncomparable benefits, the observer is likely to assume that the benefits were given to fulfill needs or to please the recipient and that the two people have a communal relationship.

Clark (1981) tested the hypothesis that the comparability of benefits would be used by observers as a cue to the type of relationship existing between two people. In the first study, subjects were given descriptions of brief interactions between two businessmen in which each one gave the other a benefit. In some cases the two benefits were exactly comparable (two rides home or two lunches) and in others the benefits were noncomparable (a ride home and then a lunch or a lunch and then a ride home). Subjects read one description and judged the degree of friendship existing between the two men. The results were as predicted. The mean friendship rating for the noncomparable conditions was significantly greater than the mean friendship rating for the comparable conditions.

Since it seemed possible that giving and receiving of rides might be perceived as a custom which often occurs among people who are not friends (a car pool) and/or that businessmen treating one another to lunch might be perceived to be a similar custom, a second study was conducted using different benefits. In the comparable benefits conditions, pairs of either pens, pads of paper, small jars of coffee, or candy were given and received by two students. In the noncomparable benefits conditions, the same benefits were described as being given and received, but the pairings were changed so that (1) coffee was given first and pens second; (2) pens first, coffee second; (3) candy first, paper second; or (4) paper first, candy second. After reading the descriptions, subjects rated the degree of friendship in the same way as in Study 1. As in the first study, the results were as expected from the hypothesis that noncomparability of benefits given and received would serve as a cue to the existence of a communal relationship. Perceived friendship was significantly greater when the benefits given and received were noncomparable than when they were comparable.

A third study was conducted to test the assumption that noncomparable benefits are a cue to the existence of friendship because the second benefit in a pair of noncomparable benefits is less likely to be seen as a repayment for the first benefit and more likely to be seen as having been given to fulfill a need of the other or to please the other. The stimulus materials were the same as those used in the second study. However, instead of being asked to rate the degree of friendship existing between the two people described, subjects were asked to give a reason why the second benefit was given. The answers were given to two judges who were unaware of the conditions. They classified the answers under one of three categories: exchange, communal, and neither. The exchange category included "as a repayment," "out of obligation," and "as a replacement." The communal category included "as a thank you," "out of appreciation," "to fulfill a need," "to start a friendship," "to please the other," and "out of kindness." The answer, "to return a favor," was considered ambiguous since people may "return a favor" because they feel in debt or because they want to demonstrate appreciation. As predicted, noncomparable benefits were significantly more likely than comparable benefits to be interpreted as having been given for communal reasons, and comparable benefits were more likely to be perceived as having been given for exchange reasons than noncomparable benefits.

IMPLICATIONS FOR AFFECT

The distinction between communal and exchange relationships also has implications for the generation of affect. When someone behaves in a manner which is inappropriate for the type of relationship one has or wants to have with that person, one is likely to experience negative affect. For example, suppose a male desires a communal relationship with a female and has offered her a ride home specifically to demonstrate his concern for her welfare and his desire for a communal relationship. If, upon arrival, she offers him money, he is likely to feel strong negative affect.

The implications of the distinction for positive affect are more complicated. In both communal and exchange relationships, people should experience positive affect when norms appropriate to that relationship are followed. However, just how much positive affect is generated by adherence to these norms may depend on how certain one is of the relationship with the other. The less certain you are of having a communal relationship with another, and the more you desire such a relationship, the more positive affect should be generated when the other behaves in a manner appropriate to such a relationship, thus demonstrating that the other desires the same kind of relationship with you as you want with them. It should generate more positive affect than the same behavior in a well-established communal relationship. This analysis is similar to the analysis by Aronson and Linder (1965) of why receiving a positive evaluation from someone who has negatively evaluated you in the past is more rewarding than receiving a positive evaluation from someone who has given you consistently positive evaluations.

EPILOGUE

A recent newspaper story from *The Washington Post* began as follows:

The doctors gave two alternatives, but for the Dan children there was never really any choice. Their 71-year-old father, paralyzed by a stroke, would not go to a nursing home. He would come back to his own home. The detailed technical knowledge they would need to care for him, nurses could teach them, but as one nurse noted, the main ingredient—love—was already there.

So on March 17, the lives of Connie, Lydia, John and Linda Dan, aged 14 to 28, became a perpetual relay race, built around keeping Chong Dan, who could not speak, eat or move, as comfortable as possible in their modest Silver Spring home. "We canned that nursing home idea right away," 28-year-old Linda said recently. "We wouldn't have felt comfortable if he wasn't home with us," ninth-grader Connie piped in.

Registered nurse Marti Tinsley, who visits the family twice a week and has taught it the technical nursing skills it needs, said the Dans "had to turn their personal lives inside out to care for their father literally 24 hours a day."

It is clear to us that the relationship between the father and his children in this article can be better understood in terms of the norms governing communal relationships than in terms of exchange. These children are caring for their father because they are concerned about his welfare. As the nurse quoted in the story notes, their motivation is their love for their father.

One might argue that the rules of exchange do apply here; the father cared for his children when they were young and therefore his children are repaying him now. However, it is difficult for us to believe that there was an understanding when the children were younger that child care would be exchanged for nursing care later on. Furthermore, we doubt that the parties involved make any attempt to equate the value of child care with a specific amount of nursing care. We believe the relationship between the children and their father is very different from an exchange relationship, such as the kind he would have had with nurses hired to take care of him.

We feel that for most people communal relationships are the relationships that are most important to them. While it is understandable that past research dealing with the giving and receiving of benefits has been done primarily in industrial settings or with persons brought together for a brief time in a laboratory setting, a regrettable side effect has been that it has concentrated on the study of exchange. In view of the importance of communal relationships, we would hope that in the future at least as much research attention will be focused on them as on exchange relationships.

NOTES

1. Another type of relationship exists when one person exploits another. Exploitative relationships are not considered in the present chapter.

2. Boulding has made a similar distinction. He differentiates "simple exchange" from "reciprocity." "Simple exchange" is conditional. If A gives B a benefit, B must benefit A in return. Boulding (1973, p. 25) notes that while "reciprocity" may look very much like exchange "as it usually involves a two-way transfer, sometimes separated by an interval of time, of commodities or exchangeables between two parties," it differs from exchange "in that whereas exchange is conditional and is based essentially on the acceptance of a conditional offer, reciprocity is formally unconditional. . . . A gives something to B out of the sheer goodness of his heart and his benevolence for B, and B gives something to A out of the sheer goodness of his heart and his benevolence towards A, yet the two acts are not being formally related since neither is a formal condition of the other."

3. An instance in which the receipt of a benefit did not constitute a reward occurred in the communal conditions of the first experiment by Clark and Mills (1979) described below.

4. A manipulation check included in this study supported the assumption that the manipulations were effective in producing expectations of communal and exchange relationships.

REFERENCES

Aronson, E., & Linder, D. Gain and loss of esteem as determinants of interpersonal attractiveness. *Journal of Experimental Social Psychology*, 1975, *1*, 156-171.

Boulding, K. E. *The economy of love and fear.* Belmont, CA: Wadsworth, 1973.

Castro, M.A.C. Reactions to receiving aid as a function of cost to donor and opportunity to aid. *Journal of Applied Social Psychology*, 1974, *4*, 194-209.

Clark, M. S. Noncomparability of benefits given and received: A cue to the existence of friendship. *Social Psychology Quarterly*, 1981, *41*, 375-381.

Clark, M. S., & Mills, J. Interpersonal attraction in exchange and communal relationships. *Journal of Personality and Social Psychology*, 1979, *37*, 12-24.

Clark, M. S., & Waddell, B. Feelings of exploitation in communal and exchange relationships. Unpublished manuscript, Carnegie–Mellon University, 1981.

Gergen, K. J., Ellsworth, P., Maslach, C., & Seipel, M. Obligation, donor resources, and reactions to aid in three cultures. *Journal of Personality and Social Psychology*, 1975, *31*, 390-400.

Goffman, E. *Asylums.* Garden City, NY: Doubleday, 1961.

Gross, A., & Latane, B. Receiving help, reciprocation, and interpersonal attraction. *Journal of Applied Social Psychology*, 1974, *4*, 210-233.

Jones, E. E., & Wortman, C. *Ingratiation: An attributional approach.* Morristown, NJ: General Learning Press, 1973.

Mauss, M. *The Gift: Forms and functions of exchange in archaic societies.* New York: Free Press, 1954.

Pruitt, D. G. Methods for resolving differences of interest: A theoretical analysis. *Journal of Social Issues*, 1972, *28*, 133-154.

Saperstein, S. Labor of love: Children nurse stricken father around the clock. *The Washington Post,* June 18, 1979, p. A1.

Thibaut, J. W., & Kelley, H. H. *The social psychology of groups.* New York: John Wiley, 1959.

Walster, E., Walster, G. W., & Berscheid, E. *Equity: Theory and research.* Boston: Allyn & Bacon, 1978.

Heider and Simmel Revisited:

CAUSAL ATTRIBUTION AND THE ANIMATED FILM TECHNIQUE

SAUL M. KASSIN

Saul M. Kassin is Assistant Professor of Psychology at Williams College. His research interests are in social perception—developmental processes and applications to legal decision-making contexts. He is the coeditor (with Sharon S. Brehm and Frederick X. Gibbons) of *Developmental Social Psychology: Theory and Research* (Oxford, 1981).

In 1944, Fritz Heider and Marianne Simmel conducted what many have called the first attribution experiment. Interested in attribution as a perceptual process and in the parallels between object and social perception (Heider & Simmel, 1944; Heider, 1946, 1958, 1959), Heider and Simmel sought to examine how the kinetics of motion, factors such as temporal contiguity, spatial proximity, range, velocity, and direction of movement give rise to impressions about behavior and its causes. Accord-

AUTHOR'S NOTE: This manuscript is based on an invited paper presented at the Midwestern Psychological Association, St. Louis, May 1980. I am indebted to Fritz and Grace Heider for their hours of conversation, their assistance in locating refer-

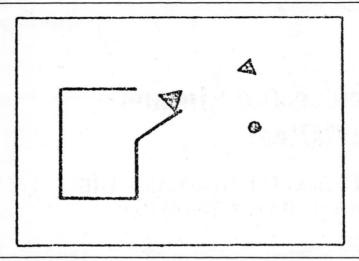

Figure 1: A frame from the Heider and Simmel (1944) film.

ingly, they created a 2½-minute black-and-white cartoon in which three geometrical objects, a large triangle (T), a small triangle (t), and a circle (c), move freely around a rectangular enclosure with a "door" (see Figure 1). The entire event, broken down into scenes, was described by the authors as follows:

> T moves toward the house, opens the door, moves into the house and closes the door. t and c appear and move around near the door. T moves out of the house toward t. T and t fight, T wins; during the fight, c moves into the house. T moves into house and shuts door. T chases c within the house; t moves along the outside of the house and t and c close the door. T seems to try to get out of the house but does not succeed in opening the door; t and c move in circles around outside of the house and touch each other several times. T opens the door and comes out of the house. T chases t and c twice

ences, and their comments on a draft of the manuscript. I would also like to thank John Harvey, James Jaccard, Charles Lowe, Darren Newtson, Thomas Ostrom, and Miron Zuckerman for their helpful comments on earlier versions. Reprint requests should be addressed to the author at the Department of Psychology, Williams College, Williamstown, MA 01267.

around the house. t and c leave the field. T hits the walls of the house several times; the walls break [p. 245].

Subjects watched the film and either answered a series of questions or described the entire event in writing.

A number of interesting findings emerged from this study. For example, when two objects move successively in time and make momentary contact, the first object is perceived to have energized the second, causing it to move forward (see also Michotte, 1963). Unfortunately, the experiment was fairly unsystematic. Isolated scenes within the event differed along a number of dimensions, so the necessary and sufficient stimulus conditions for each impression could not be established. On the response side, the data were coded and analyzed informally so statistically reliable conclusions could not be drawn. In short, Heider and Simmel's (1944) study provided some compelling preliminary insights, and others have since refined its stimulus (Bassili, 1976) and response (Greenberg & Strickland, 1973) components; nevertheless, it had little substantive impact on attribution theory.

Although Heider and Simmel's findings provided, at best, only a basis for speculation, their technique of presenting information through the animated movements of objects did show a good deal of promise for research in social perception. For Heider and Simmel (1944), the technique was advantageous partly because it enabled them to use faceless "actors" while concentrating on the effects of functional relationships in movement among objects. At the same time, their technique was still relevant to the processes of person perception. Subjects readily anthropomorphized, interpreting the objects as people and their movements as behaviors, and attributed all kinds of emotional states, attitudes, motives, and personality traits to these characters. Michotte (1950), who employed a similar method, noted that "subjects did not content themselves with merely describing in an objective fashion what they saw in the apparatus, saying, for example, that they saw 'A pushing B forward,' but they often had an obvious tendency to complete these indications by comparing with human or animal actions. . . . This kind of behavior frequently occurred in quite a spontaneous way" (pp. 115-116). In fact, so compelling is the interpretation of the animated objects as people that subjects (a) cannot avoid anthropomorphizing even when explicitly instructed not to (Hashimoto, 1966) and (b) can readily predict how they would act toward the characters (Marek, 1966). The relevance of objects and their movement as stimuli for social perception research thus seems to be well established. Beyond that, the use of animated film offers a broad range of advantages that will be discussed later in some detail.

CURRENT STATUS

Despite the potential utility of the animated film technique (AFT) and despite renewed interest in person perception *as* perception (e.g., Baron, 1980; McArthur, 1981; Newtson, 1976), the former has aroused relatively little empirical interest. Although several psychologists have used the Heider and Simmel sequence in their research (Dickman, 1956; Greenberg & Strickland, 1973; Hashimoto, 1966; Ihrig, 1953; Marek, 1966; Massad, Hubbard, & Newtson, 1979; Shor, 1957; Sugarman, 1982), only a small number of investigators went on to create their own films or computer-generated graphic displays (Bassili, 1976; Buck & Kates, 1963; Kassin & Lowe, 1979a; Kassin, Lowe, & Gibbons, 1980; Marek, 1963; Tagiuri, 1960; Thayer & Schiff, 1969; Kassin & Lowe, 1979c).[1] Today, Heider and Simmel's "experimental study of apparent behavior" is viewed merely as an intriguing anecdote in the history of attribution theory.

In contrast to Heider's concern for direct, perceptual bases of social perception, contemporary attribution theorists (Jones & Davis, 1965; Jones & McGillis, 1976; Kelley, 1967, 1972) had, until quite recently, focused almost exclusively on the more deliberate, higher-order processes of causal inference (see Baron & Harvey, 1980; Lowe & Kassin, 1980; Weary, Rich, Harvey, & Ickes, 1980). Paralleling this shift in emphasis was a shift in the methods typically used to convey information to "observers." One extensively employed method is the questionnaire in which subjects make attributions from an experimenter's written or oral description of a behavioral event. These second-hand descriptions are often contained in a single sentence to which causally relevant information is appended, or they may consist of more embellished vignettes in which the data about an actor and/or situation are embedded. Alternatively, a number of investigators have employed a second technique, having their subjects observe directly (i.e., first-hand) an action sequence as it unfolds either live or on videotape.

To be sure, the paper-and-pencil technique, exemplified by Asch's classical use of trait words to convey information about fictitious people, can be very efficient for certain types of attribution research. It enables the collection of large amounts of data using a wide range of target behaviors in a relatively short period of time (McArthur, 1972). Likewise, having subjects actually watch instances of behavior has its advantages, such as investigating how perceivers attend to (McArthur & Ginsberg, 1981) and organize (Newtson, 1976) behavioral events, or at how perceptual salience influences attributions and impressions (e.g., McArthur & Post, 1977; Taylor & Fiske, 1975). The theme of this chapter is that the AFT provides an alternative approach for (a) testing the multimethod validity of attributional principles or (b) pursuing certain previously obscured lines of inquiry. Specifically, it will be argued that animated films can be used to broaden the nature of our subject population, control or eliminate extraneous sources of variance, and explore "new" phenomena in social perception.

USES OF THE ANIMATED FILM TECHNIQUE

Before discussing the potential applications of the AFT, it might be instructive to outline its similarities and differences with the two dominant paradigms. Table 1 shows that animated films differ from the verbal description method on four dimensions. It presents information in a visual rather than linguistic (written or oral) mode; it entails dynamic, temporally extended displays rather than static events; it employs as "actors" geometrical objects rather than people; and it portrays physical rather than behavioral events. The similarity between animated films and the behavioral observation method is more evident. Both entail the presentation of dynamic, visual events; but whereas the behavioral observation paradigm has subjects observing people and the vagaries of their behavior, animated films depict objects and their movement. This brief comparative analysis of the three methods carries with it an important implication—that the AFT provides a supplemental and not an alternative approach to the currently popular methods. It will be seen that its strengths are the others' weaknesses and vice versa.

Broadening Our Subject Population

Mainstream attribution research is generally conducted with subjects who are adult, English-speaking, literate, and "normal" in their social and emotional functioning. Accordingly, a method that relies on the presenta-

TABLE 1
A Comparison of Three Information
Presentation Strategies

	Verbal Descriptions	*Behavioral Observations*	*Animated Films*
Mode of Presentation	Linguistic	Visual	Visual
Temporal Features	Static	Dynamic	Dynamic
Types of Actors	People	People	Objects
Types of Events	Interpersonal	Interpersonal	Physical

tion of verbal material or on the direct observation of an individual and his or her interpersonal behavior is appropriate. These methods are restricted somewhat, however, either by their reliance on language as a mediation or on the portrayal of interpersonal behaviors whose sociocultural "meaning" might not be fully comprehended by all subjects. In this respect, animated films have proven useful.

Cross-cultural research. Greenberg and Strickland (1973) suggested that animated films, because they are not language-based and do not require translation, may be appropriate for cross-cultural research. Indeed, Heider and Simmel's (1944) film has been used with Japanese (Hashimoto, 1966) and Australian (Marek, 1966) subjects. In fact, although Hashimoto constructed only a rough duplicate of the original film, his results paralleled Heider and Simmel's very closely. The author concluded that "universals" in social preception might thus be revealed through this technique that relies on objects and their movement as stimulus events.

Clinical research. Some investigators have found animated films useful, for a variety of reasons, in research with "deviant" subject populations. Buck and Kates (1963), for example, were interested in the movement cues that give rise to schizophrenic patients' perceptions of love and anger.

Accordingly, they depicted sequences of nonhuman motion rather than human behavior in order to "eliminate noisy, irrelevant information" (see also Ihrig, 1953). Along somewhat different lines, Kassin and Gibbons (1980) found the technique useful for doing research with intellectually handicapped people. Specifically, they found that mentally retarded subjects made more sophisticated attributions when viewing an animated film than when responding to verbal descriptions of the same event (even when the latter were accompanied by pictures of the characters). The authors concluded that this paradigm can effectively reduce the complexity of the task confronting retarded subjects in addition to enabling them to indicate their judgments nonverbally merely by pointing to an object.

Developmental research. Perhaps the most important application of the AFT for extending our subject population is for investigating the development of attributional processes in young children. A number of psychologists who have employed the films have either speculated about their potential utility in this domain (Greenberg & Strickland, 1973; Michotte, 1950; Tagiuri, 1960) or have actually used children in their research (e.g., Marek, 1963, 1966, looked at the interpretational styles of fifth graders; Olum, 1956, and Lesser, 1977, used Michotte's disk method to study young children's use of spatiotemporal cues for causal attribution). At this point, the developmental implications of the AFT will be illustrated by drawing heavily on examples from my own research.

In a review of the literature on children's attributions, I concluded that "young children are better able to utilize causally relevant information when it is concretized through the use of pictures, dynamic displays, and live events, than when presented through verbal descriptions that make excessive linguistic, memorial, and conceptual demands on the perceiver" (1981, p. 37). Cognitive developmentalists have voiced a related concern about underestimating young children's capacities by operationalizing concepts in complex ways (Gelman, 1978; Shatz, 1977). In this context, the utility of the animated film technique as a "simplification strategy" (see Surber, 1979) is documented in research on the development of two important causal principles—augmentation and discounting.

Kelley (1971) defined the *augmentation principle* as follows: "If, for a given effect, both a plausible *inhibitory* cause and a plausible *facilitative* cause are present, the role of the facilitative cause in producing the effect will be judged greater than if it alone were present" (p. 12). Adults intuitively use this rule all the time (e.g., Enzle, Hansen, & Lowe, 1975). The question posed by developmental investigators is this: At what age do children begin to augment? In the first such test, Shultz, Butkowsky, Pearce, and Shanfield (1975) presented children with descriptions of behaviors that occurred in either the presence or absence of inhibitory causes (e.g., "Johnny is afraid of the dog" was accompanied by either "Johnny is alone" or "Johnny is with his father," the latter statement representing an external factor that should suppress the effect). Subjects were then asked for their inferences about the status of a plausible facilitative cause (e.g., "Is Johnny usually afraid of dogs or is Johnny almost never afraid of dogs?"). As it turned out, eighth graders employed the augmentation principle but kindergarteners and fourth graders did not.

In a later study, Kassin and Lowe (1979a) illustrated the augmentation principle through the AFT. Subjects of various ages watched a brief film of two triangles, one red and the other blue, moving toward a house simultaneously, with equal velocity, and from opposite directions. One triangle overcame an obstacle (a black square that, when contacted, fell with little apparent resistance), en route toward the goal, while the other proceeded without external interference. While the film was in progress, subjects were asked to choose the triangle they thought wanted to go to the house more. In sharp contrast to Shultz et al.'s (1975) findings, children of all ages, including kindergarteners, made the augmentation-consistent choice. In fact, second and fourth graders even understood the more advanced principle that differences in the *magnitude* of inhibition imply correspondent differences in the degree of facilitative cause. This latter version was tested by showing subjects a sequence in which two triangles were inhibited by obstacles of different sizes.

Another attributional rule of thumb people frequently follow (e.g., Thibaut & Riecken, 1955) is Kelley's (1971) *discounting principle,* which asserts: "The role of a given cause in producing a given effect is discounted if other plausible causes are also present" (p. 8). At what age do children discount? Research directed at this question has yielded inconsistent results. For example, intrinsic-extrinsic motivation studies show that pre-schoolers who are rewarded for engaging in an enjoyable activity subsequently manifest a decrease in (presumably because they discount) their intrinsic interest in that activity. At the same time, however, attribution research suggests that young children do not make use of the discounting principle (for recent reviews of the relationship between the two literatures, see Kassin & Lepper, in press; Lepper & Gilovich, 1981). Smith (1975), for example, presented subjects with stories about two children who chose to play with a particular toy—one in the presence of a situational constraint (e.g., reward) and the other without any type of inducement. Subjects then chose the actor who they thought wanted to play with the toy. Overall, fourth graders and adults discounted the "want" of a rewarded actor, but kindergarteners did not. In fact, subsequent studies have consistently shown that kindergarteners often invoke the reverse logic, an additive principle, inferring greater want in the actor who performs in the presence of reward (e.g., Karniol & Ross, 1976).

Paralleling this research, we operationalized the discounting principle by again showing children a film of two triangles approach a house—one is carried to its destination by a square, while the other travels without external assistance. Subjects then indicated either which triangle wanted to go to the house more (Kassin et al., 1980, Experiment 2) or which triangle tried harder (Kassin & Gibbons, 1981). Results showed that second graders readily discounted the facilitated actor's intention (i.e., "want"), and that even kindergarteners discounted the facilitated actors exertion (i.e., "try"). No evidence was found for use of an additive principle.

The above research suggests that young children make more sophisticated judgments when causally relevant information is conveyed through the films than when it is presented in the verbal-story paradigm. How, specifically, do animated films simplify the presentation of material? Three differences between them and the verbal descriptions deserve mention. First, the story-presentation method places severe information-processing demands on the young subject who generally has difficulty with abstract and hypothetical linguistic material (Kail & Siegel, 1977). It also requires that subjects recall successively presented sentences, after which attributions are assessed, a task not easily accomplished by preschoolers (see Bryant & Trabasso, 1971). In contrast, the visual display of animated films is vivid, concrete, and attention-getting; moreover, the relevant information can be presented simultaneously (i.e., where the two target actors' behaviors unfold together) and on-line judgments can be made (i.e., where subjects make attributions while the event unfolds and the characters are still in view), so that recall demands are reduced dramatically.

A second advantage of the animated films is that concepts can be operationalized in their simplest forms—through physical events whose

causal powers are understood by young children who might otherwise lack
an appreciation for the subtleties of human motives and interpersonally
based causes. In the Shultz et al. (1975) example provided earlier (i.e.,
"Johnny is afraid of the dog"), children could not logically demonstrate
their use of the augmentation principle unless they first understand that
the presence of Johnny's father represents a circumstance that inhibits fear
of dogs. In the discounting literature, Karniol and Ross (1979) discovered
a similar limitation. They found that children who do not discount the
intrinsic motivation of a rewarded individual do not interpret the reward
as a bribe offered by a manipulative agent and, thus, do not infer that the
target activity must have been less enjoyable. In contrast, with the animated film technique, the concept of inhibition was conveyed by the
presence of an obstacle in the path of a moving object. Conversely,
facilitation is easily translated into one object carrying or pushing another
toward its destination. Subjects thus need not be equipped with sophisticated theories about human behavior and social conventions in order to
grasp important causal (social or nonsocial) concepts (see Gelman &
Spelke, 1981, and Hoffman, 1981, on the distinctions between knowledge
of inanimate objects, organized around physical laws, and animate objects,
organized as well within an affective framework and according to psychological principles).

Third, the animated film, in contrast to other methods, can readily
portray target "behaviors" that do not evoke strong expectancies that
could disrupt children's "objective" use of information. In the discounting
literature, for example, subjects might not discount the intrinsic motivation of any actor (rewarded or not) who chooses to play with an inherently desirable toy. The Shultz et al. (1975) augmentation study is another
case in point. Not only might subjects of various age levels differ in their
naive expectancies for certain events (e.g., for "Johnny is afraid of the
dog," it is likely that younger children view a fear of dogs as consensual,
while older children do not), but they may differ in the extent to which
they rely on their respective beliefs when responding to the experimenter's
questions. Especially among children who cannot fully recall the verbal
material, questions such as "Is Johnny usually afraid of dogs?" might elicit
responses that are dominated by what subjects already know.[2]

It should also be noted that the AFT is flexible, allowing for multiple
operations of each concept. For example, one could illustrate facilitative
or inhibitory *circumstances* without the use of an external agent. An actor

could thus be portrayed moving in a downhill/uphill path, or even with the help/hindrance of a current. Quantitative causal principles may also be tested by varying the size of the external agent, the steepness of a slope, the force of a current, and so on. In view of concerns that developmental researchers too often define a concept vis-à-vis a specific task, the potential availability of converging manipulations is a valuable asset.[3]

In summary, Heider and Simmel's innovation is an especially attractive tool for testing the attributional competencies of young children. Of course, alternative simplification strategies that overcome the major problems are also tenable.[4] Shultz and Butkowsky (1977), for example, found discounting among preschoolers in a videotaped behavioral observation study. On the other hand, Smith (1978) was less enthusiastic about this method. He showed children of various ages brief, videotaped episodes of an actor's behavior in order to test their perceptions of intention. All substantive findings aside, he concluded that the natural stream of behavior is too complex for young children to focus on "relevant" (i.e., experimental) cues.

Controlling Extraneous Sources of Variance

In this section, it will be argued that animated films provide a way to control or eliminate "extraneous" sources of variance in research with adults. Alternatively, the technique can be used to test these effects systematically. Two "biases" in particular will be discussed—the linguistic bias and the normative expectancy bias.

Linguistic (verbal description) bias. As noted earlier, the written mode of information presentation is frequently employed in attribution research. Although this paradigm reasonably approximates how perceivers often obtain information in the real world, its generalizability to the phenomenon of action perception is suspect (see Massad et al., 1979). There is mounting evidence for the contention that behavioral descriptions are precoded interpretations of behavior and, as such, are not strictly comparable to the phenomenal raw data of an unlabeled sensory event.

In a series of studies on language and attribution, Salancik (1974, 1976; Salancik & Conway, 1975) had subjects causally explain their own behavior in a sentence-completion format and varied the "stem" of each sentence. In one experiment, for example, subjects who completed statements like "I always took notes in class *because I* . . ." provided intrinsic causes for their behavior, while others who responded to equivalent statements such as "I always took notes in class *in order to* . . ." were more likely to cite extrinsic factors in their explanations. Self-attributions were thus influenced significantly by the way the incompleted sentences were structured.

Another line of research suggests that the way a hypothetical behavior is described has a dramatic effect on the way that event is processed and explained. Pryor and Kriss (1977) presented subjects with single-sentence descriptions in either active (e.g., "Sue likes the restaurant") or passive (e.g., "the restaurant is liked by Sue") form and found that the *actor* was more available for recall when it was the grammatical subject than the object of the sentence. Similarly, Kassin and Lowe (1979b) varied sentence structure and found greater stimulus attribution when behaviors were described in passive than active form (i.e., when the target stimulus was the grammatical subject).

The implication of these findings for the verbal description method is disturbing to those who are interested in the *content* of perceivers' attributions. For example, McArthur (1972) and others have found that subjects tend to make a large number of personal attributions and relatively few stimulus attributions. Is this phenomenon a manifestation of the "fundamental attribution error" (Ross, 1977), or does it instead reflect on the suggestive nature of single-sentence stimuli? Indeed, the items are typically structured in the active, person verbs-stimulus mode, so that the person is the more salient grammatical subject of the sentence. The AFT, because it entails a visual mode of presentation, avoids the pitfalls of using prelabeled events.

In order to test for the personal attribution bias in the animated film paradigm, Kassin and Lowe (1979c) had subjects watch a series of films in which distinctiveness and consensus information were "acted out" by geometrical objects. The films depicted aggressive and friendly interactions between three triangles (persons A, B, C) and three squares (stimuli X, Y, Z). In one sequence, for example, target actor B hit target stimulus Y. Consensus was varied through the behaviors of persons A and C toward Y, whereas distinctiveness was illustrated through the actions of B toward stimuli X and Z. In contrast to much previous research, stimulus attributions were more frequent (57%) than person attributions (43%). In fact, this effect was even more pronounced (64% to 36%) when subjects made attributions for a prosocial target interaction.

The AFT thus appears to elicit a different pattern of attributions, at least in the context of Kelley's (1967) person-stimulus dichotomy, than the verbal-description method. If language—that is, the way people describe events—does in fact mediate between observation and causal ascription (see Kanouse, 1971), then the AFT, along with the behavioral observation method, allows us to study that phenomenon by having subjects provide their own "natural" descriptions for visual events before making attributions.[5] Of course, it is questionable whether language even affords an adequate way of describing a perceptual experience.

Normative expectancy (causal theory) bias. Psychologists have long recognized that people tend to see what they expect to see (Bruner, 1957). A general "problem" that is thus inherent in behavioral observation as well as verbal description studies is the presentation of stimulus events that are high/low in their prior probabilities of occurrence. Social perceptions are based not only on new data about a target event per se (e.g., temporal contiguity, covariation) but on perceivers' a priori causal schemata (Kelley, 1972), scripts (Abelson, 1981), theories (Nisbett & Ross, 1980), and behavioral expectancies (Jones & McGillis, 1976). In fact, attributors often rely *exclusively* on their preconceptions even if more diagnostic, logically compelling information is available. This pattern is seen most clearly in the literature on consensus, prediction, and attribution, where some studies have shown that people make relatively little use of sample base rates when called upon to predict category membership (Kahneman & Tversky, 1973), explain their own actions (Nisbett, Borgida, Crandall, & Reed, 1976), or make attributions for another actor's behavior (Nisbett & Borgida, 1975). A review of this literature suggests that sample-based consensus is ineffective either when it is redundant with intuitive expectations and hence uninformative or when it is too discrepant with prior beliefs and hence rejected (Kassin, 1979).

The above analysis implies that for assessing the impact of sample-based consensus (or any "new" information for that matter) or for comparing it to other, theoretically equivalent types of information (e.g., McArthur, 1972, reported that distinctiveness information is more powerful than consensus), a priori beliefs should be neutralized by denying subjects access to expectancy-arousing cues. Toward this end, the AFT is ideally suited. In his research on the perception of causality, Michotte (1963) used objects and their movement as stimuli in order to eliminate the influence of "acquired knowledge" (p. 308). More germane to the present discussion, recall that we (Kassin & Lowe, 1979c) "perceptualized" Kelley's (1967) theory by having consensus and distinctiveness information depicted through the movement of triangles and squares. Subjects were thus unable to generate strong actor-based expectancies (i.e., the "actors" were neither male nor female, attractive nor unattractive, etc.) or situation-based scripts for this novel scenario. Sure enough, consensus and distinctiveness information had an equivalent effect on attributions, predictions, and open-ended explanations.

Obviously, expectancy effects are not mere sources of "error variance"—the relationship between prior beliefs and social perception is worthy of investigation in its own right. Toward this end, animated film stimuli are sufficiently ambiguous to permit subjects' preconceptions to be situationally manipulated (via instructional set or exposure to earlier sequences) and their effects tested systematically. Heider (1958), for example, proposed that perceivers' interpretations of a scene in which one triangle trails another (Heider & Simmel, 1944) depends on their beliefs about the two characters: "the more or less unequivocal impression of T chasing t is produced if the observer considers T the more powerful person. . . . Conversely, if T is seen as inferior, the impression will be that T is following t" (p. 45). Indeed, Shor (1957) confirmed this hypothesis, finding that when one object in the Heider-Simmel film is predefined, the others are evaluated by their behavior toward that character. More recently, Massad et al. (1979) sought to test the hypothesis that people's interpretive sets would affect how they encode or perceptually organize an ongoing action sequence. In need of a meaningful but ambiguous event, they pilot tested a number of stimuli and ultimately chose the Heider-Simmel film. Interestingly, the study revealed that divergent expectancies produced different unitization patterns as well as different impressions of the characters. On a methodological level, the authors heralded the animated film as "rich enough to support either one of the two sets."

Perceiver characteristics may also be tested in the proposed paradigm. Personality theorists commonly acknowledge that individual difference variables affect behavior in novel or ambiguous settings.[6] In social learning terms, an individual's stable, generalized expectancies should theoretically predict behavior only in the absence of clear situationally determined specific expectancies (Rotter, 1954; Mischel, 1973). For that reason,

Michotte (1950) suggested that individual differences among perceivers could conceivably reveal themselves in this paradigm. Marek (1963) found this to be the case, finding a significant relationship between family background and interpretations of film sequences. (Specifically, fifth-grade boys who were either spoiled or neglected at home were more "sensitive towards animation," seeing a wider range of object movements as animate, than were children from a satisfactory background.) More recently, Lowe and Kassin (1980) reported that individual differences on the Personal-Environmental Causal Attribution (PECA) scale (Lowe, Medway, & Beers, 1978), though not predictive of attributional content, were significantly related to the kinds of information subjects claimed to have used in an animated film study. Interestingly, these differences were greater when subjects watched a relatively ambiguous prosocial interaction (i.e., where subjects varied in their descriptions of the event) than an unambiguous instance of aggressive behavior.

In sum, films that depict objects and their movement, precisely because of their inherent ambiguity, can conveniently serve a diversity of purposes. Actor- and situation-based expectancies can be neutralized, thereby permitting a "pure" test of the impact of new information and maximizing the potential for detecting individual differences among perceivers. Alternatively, subjects' expectancies can be situationally manipulated in order to test systematically their effects on social judgments.

Exploration of New Content Areas:
Back to Basics

Reuben Baron (1980) recently commented that "by using static as opposed to dynamic displays, we cut the perceiver off from certain higher order sources of information which are available to the more active perceiver" (p. 8). With this in mind, recall that although Heider and Simmel's (1944) initial concern was for how movement cues affect perceptions of an individual's behavior, attribution psychologists have generally focused on people's use of cues that are extraneous to the target event (e.g., a behavior's expectedness, desirability, consequences, and covariation with other events) while simultaneously ignoring the types of critical information that are conveyed to perceivers by the kinetics of human behavior. Indeed, perhaps the most attractive feature of dynamic, animated films is that they provide a means of exploring these fundamentally important cues in social perception that have previously been overlooked. Social perceivers are thus afforded an opportunity to look not only at *what* an actor does but at *how* the actor does it.

In the literature on event perception, the importance of movement has long been recognized. In a series of provocative studies, Johansson (1973) showed that in an otherwise dark room, less than a dozen spots of light representing the movements of main joints on a human body are sufficient for observers to correctly identify not only the mode of biomechanical movement (i.e., whether the actor is walking, running, climbing, dancing, etc.) but the quality of that movement (i.e., the amount of effort expended) as well. Similarly, Bassili (1978) found that facial movements, as revealed through changes in points of reflected light, are sufficient for subjects to identify actors' emotions. The above research has consistently shown that accurate identification is obtained only when subjects view dynamic rather than posed, static light displays.

In the person perception literature of yesteryear, some prominent theorists wrote about the importance of movement cues. Tagiuri (1960) was impressed with how naturally social perceivers interpret patterns of object movement within their framework of human qualities. In his own research, Tagiuri had subjects watch films of dots traveling from one point to another, varying the *angle* of their movement. He found, for example, that an object that travels a straight, linear path was seen as alert, well-reasoned, persevering, determined, logical, and ambitious; a more erratic path elicited impressions such as drunk, confused, immature, emotional, undependable, and careless; in contrast, an arched path was seen as nonchalant, leisurely, relaxed, and even complacent. Tagiuri (1960) concluded that movement cues provide a critical source of information for social perceivers and lamented the empirical neglect of this important topic.

Michotte (1950) adopted an even stronger position, asserting that "I think the necessary conclusion is that they [movement cues] must be considered as constituting a *fundamental* aspect of human action as it appears to an observer" (p. 122). In fact, Michotte suggested that other cues such as facial expression and speech are merely "additional *refinements* compared with the key factors, which are the simple kinetic structures" (p. 122). Complementing Tagiuri's work, Michotte (1950) focused on the information conveyed by the *speed* of movement. He found, for example, that rapid movement gives the impression of violence, slow movement is characterized by gentleness, a sudden reduction in speed is interpreted as hesitation, and sudden, repeated variations in speed elicit impressions of nervousness and agitation.

Historically, then, Heider and Simmel (1944) were not alone in their concern for how basic spatiotemporal components of movement give rise to various perceptions of actors and behavior. Nor were they alone in their belief that the AFT is well suited for the task.

Animated films and behavioral observations. At this point, it should be apparent that the behavioral observation paradigm shares some of the assets of the AFT. Thus, an obvious question is, why are animated films sometimes (depending on the questions posed by an investigator) more appropriate research stimuli for testing movement cues than real human action? Three arguments can be advanced: First, any such test might require that subjects' prior expectancies be neutralized. Observers often have at their disposal too many culturally transmitted theories about how certain types of people behave in certain types of situations. Second, Tagiuri (1960) argued that the animated film approach brings to the forefront and makes accessible for analysis "rapid" and "unconscious" bases of judgment that might otherwise be buried in the complexities of real life. Thus, "when faced with simple movement the subject may be able to say that the 'person' is afraid 'because' he circles the object instead of going directly to it. In a comparable real-life situation he might be unable to abstract the movement component of his judgment, yet he may have used it" (p. 193).[7] Third, the physical parameters of human movement cannot plausibly or readily be manipulated with the spatial and temporal precision that is afforded by the AFT and its variants.[8]

CONCLUSIONS:
ASSETS AND LIABILITIES OF THE AFT

The thrust of this chapter is that we should take a closer, more serious look at a relatively old, relatively underutilized, but promising research paradigm. It was argued, specifically, that the AFT introduced by Heider and Simmel (1944) provides a convenient way to broaden our subject population, control extraneous sources of variance, and explore new substantive areas in social perception. Its utility in these domains stems largely from four distinguishing characteristics of the films—they are *visual* and *dynamic*, and they portray the *physical* movements of *objects*.

It should be emphasized again that the AFT is being proposed as a supplement and not as a replacement for the verbal description and behavioral observation methods. In this context, it provides an alternative approach to empirical problems that require the use of a highly structured, finely tuned, and precisely controlled event and/or one that is illustrated in its simplest structural form (e.g., in developmental research).

Although potentially useful in certain domains, the AFT has its obvious limitations. The tradeoff is that the gains achieved by the increased precision and control feature of this technique are matched by its loss of ecological validity. Having established people's attributional tendencies under the "theoretically ideal," albeit sterile, setting of the animated film laboratory, one need then confront the performance question of how these findings translate into what perceivers actually do in more "natural" situations. For example, Thayer and Schiff (1969) put faces on their animated film characters and found that the objects' expressions, even though they were fixed, moderated subjects' use of strong spatiotemporal cues.

On the response side, a related drawback is that the AFT, although ideal for assessing people's judgments under minimally sufficient information conditions, is less appropriate (i.e., compared to the verbal description and behavioral observation paradigms) for understanding the kinds of data people naturally select in complex, multicue environments. Of course, animated films need not portray only the bare essentials. Complex arrays could be generated, thereby allowing an investigator to study the data-acquisition stage of social perception while maintaining precise control over the physical parameters of movement.

Perhaps the most serious doubt one might raise about using animated films pertains to their relevance to interpersonal perception. It was noted earlier, however, that subjects of all ages and cultures naturally view the animated objects as people and their movements as behavior. Moreover, there is evidence to suggest that structural principles of attribution remain invariant regardless of the social-nonsocial nature of the task. (Surber, 1980, for example, reported that the development of social discounting parallels the development of Piagetian conservation tasks, both reflecting use of an underlying inverse compensation schema.) As Tagiuri (1960) observed, "the real issue is not one of relevance but of what the investigator does with the information he obtains" (p. 192). Indeed, the AFT, especially if used in conjunction with more traditional methods, could provide a number of interesting preliminary insights into basic but previously obscured phenomena.

NOTES

1. The term "animated film technique" is used in a generic sense to refer to three distinct methods of illustrating object movement—Heider and Simmel's (1944) animated film proper, the disk method (Michotte, 1963), and the computer-generated display (Bassili, 1976).

2. Because the verbal description and AFT studies differ along several important dimensions, it is difficult to make inferences about precisely why the latter has proven more effective. There are, however, some data which suggest that the presentation mode (i.e., verbal versus visual) may be critical. Kassin and Gibbons (1980) found that mentally retarded subjects did *not* use Kelley's augmentation principle when presented with an illustrated (memorial aid) story about a triangle (no prior expectancies) whose movement was obstructed by a square (physical inhibition). Yet intellectually comparable subjects who saw the film did augment, thus suggesting that perhaps there is something "special" about perceiving an event directly.

3. Before creating a film, one should consult the literature on the kinematics of events. For example, to illustrate the concept of facilitative cause by showing an object moving downhill, it would be necessary to simulate the velocity conditions that elicit an impression of natural "sliding down a slope" (Bozzi, 1958, cited in Runeson, 1977).

4. Children's recall of verbal information could be improved by supplementing stories with pictures (e.g., DiVitto & McArthur, 1978) or by having subjects repeat the stories until they are learned (e.g., Karniol & Ross, 1976). The causal comprehension problem could be overcome by *describing* physical events (e.g., Kassin & Gibbons, 1980, described the augmentation film in story format) or using easily understood interpersonal scenarios (e.g., Lepper, Sagotsky, Dafoe, & Greene, 1982, found that preschoolers are intimately familiar with the causal implications of the "dinner table debate" in which dessert is contingent upon completion of the meal). Finally, one could neutralize prior probabilities by pretesting materials and selecting those stimulus stories that do not arouse clear expectancies or preferences.

5. Paralleling the grammatical salience effect in verbal descriptions is the visual salience effect in behavioral observation studies. Observers' interpersonal judgments

are disproportionately influenced by actors who "engulf the field" by virtue of their attention-drawing power. Such visual salience effects, derived from Gestalt object-perception phenomena (McArthur, 1981), are easily controlled or manipulated in animated films.

6. Projective assessment devices are founded on this assumption.

7. Smith (1978) made this point with reference to young children. Having shown them videotapes of actors' behaviors, he concluded that the natural stream of behavior is too complex for young children to focus on a selected set of cues.

8. Of the three variants of the animated film technique—the animated film proper, the desk method, and the computer-generated display—the latter is clearly superior when spatiotemporal precision is critical, and can be achieved by programming sequences on a microcomputer (see Bassili, 1976, for details).

REFERENCES

Abelson, R. P. Psychological status of the script concept. *American Psychologist*, 1981, *36*, 715-729.

Asch, S. Forming impressions of personality. *Journal of Abnormal and Social Psychology*, 1946, *41*, 250-290.

Baron, R. M. Social knowing from an ecological event perspective: A consideration of the relative domains of power for cognitive and perceptual modes of knowing. In J. H. Harvey (Ed.), *Cognition, social behavior and the environment*. Hillsdale, NJ: Lawrence Erlbaum, 1980.

Baron, R. M. & Harvey, J. H. Contrasting perspectives on social knowing: An overview. *Personality and Social Psychology Bulletin*, 1980, *6*, 502-506.

Bassili, J. N. Temporal and spatial contingencies in the perception of social events. *Journal of Personality and Social Psychology*, 1976, *33*, 680-685.

Bassili, J. N. Facial motion in the perception of faces and of emotional expression. *Journal of Experimental Psychology: Human Perception and Performance*, 1978, *4*, 373-379.

Beasley, N. E. The extent of individual differences in the perception of causality. *Canadian Journal of Psychology*, 1968, *22*, 399-407.

Bruner, J. S. On perceptual readiness. *Psychological Review*, 1957, *64*, 123-152.

Bryant, P. E. & Trabasso, T. Transitive inference and memory in young children. *Nature*, 1971, *232*, 456-458.

Buck, L. & Kates, S. L. Perceptual categorizations of love and anger cues in schizophrenics. *Journal of Abnormal and Social Psychology*, 1963, *67*, 480-490.

Dickman, H. B. A developmental investigation of animism and the perception of physical causality. Doctoral dissertation, University of Kansas, 1956.

DiVitto, B., & McArthur, L. Z. Developmental differences in the use of distinctiveness, consensus, and consistency information for making causal attributions. *Developmental Psychology*, 1978, *14*, 474-482.

Enzle, M. E., Hansen, R. D., & Lowe, C. A. Causal attribution in the mixed-motive game: Effects of facilitory and inhibitory environmental forces. *Journal of Personality and Social Psychology*, 1975, *31*, 50-54.

Gelman, R. Cognitive development. *Annual Review of Psychology*, 1978, *29*, 297-332.

Gelman, R., & Spelke, E. The development of thought about animate and inanimate objects: Implications for research on social cognition. In J. H. Flavell & L. Ross (Eds.), *Social cognitive development: Frontiers and possible futures*. Cambridge: Cambridge University Press, 1981.

Greenberg, A. M., & Strickland, L. H. "Apparent Behavior" revisited. *Perceptual and Motor Skills*, 1973, *36*, 227-233.

Hashimoto, H. A phenomenal analysis of social perception. *Journal of Child Development*, 1966, *2*, 1-26.

Heider, F. Environmental determinants in psychological theories. *Psychological Review*, 1939, *46*, 383-410.

Heider, F. Social perception and phenomenal causality. *Psychological Review*, 1944, *51*, 358-374.

Heider, F. *The psychology of interpersonal relations*. New York: John Wiley, 1958.

Heider, F. On perception and event structure, and the psychological environment: Selected papers. *Psychological Issues*, 1959, *1* (Whole No. 3).

Heider, F. & Simmel, M. An experimental study of apparent behavior. *American Journal of Psychology*, 1944, *57*, 243-259.

Hoffman, M. L. Perspectives on the difference between understanding people and understanding things: The role of affect. In J. H. Flavell & L. Ross (Eds.), *Social cognitive development: Frontiers and possible futures*. Cambridge: Cambridge University Press, 1981.

Ihrig, H. Literalism and animism in schizophrenia. Ph.D. thesis, University of Kansas, 1953.

Johansson, G. Visual perception of biological motion and a model for its analysis. *Perception and Psychophysics*, 1973, *14*, 201-211.

Jones, E. E., & Davis, K. E. From acts to dispositions: The attribution process in person perception. In L. Berkowitz (Ed.), *Advances in experimental social psychology* (Vol. 2). New York: Academic Press, 1965.

Jones, E. E., & McGillis, D. Correspondent inferences and the attribution cube: A comparative reappraisal. In J. H. Harvey, W. J. Ickes, & R. F. Kidd (Eds.), *New directions in attribution research* (Vol. 1). Hillsdale, NJ: Lawrence Erlbaum, 1976.

Kail, R. V., & Siegel, A. W. The development of mnemonic encoding in children: From perceptions to abstraction. In R. V. Kail & J. W. Hagen (Eds.), *Perspectives in the development of memory and cognition*. Hillsdale, NJ: Lawrence Erlbaum, 1977.

Kahneman, D., & Tversky, A. On the psychology of prediction. *Psychological Review*, 1973, *80*, 237-251.

Kanouse, D. E. *Language, labeling, and attribution*. Morristown, NJ: General Learning Press, 1971.

Karniol, R., & Ross, M. The development of causal attributions in social perception. *Journal of Personality and Social Psychology*, 1976, *34*, 455-464.

Karniol, R., & Ross, M. Children's use of a causal attribution schema and the influence of manipulative intentions. *Child Development, 1979, 50, 463-468.*

Kassin, S. M. Consensus information, prediction, and causal attribution: A review of the literature and issues. *Journal of Personality and Social Psychology, 1979, 37, 1966-1981.*

Kassin, S. M. From laychild to "layman": Developmental causal attribution. In S. Brehm, S. Kassin, & F. Gibbons (Eds.), *Developmental social psychology: Theory and research.* New York: Oxford University Press, 1981.

Kassin, S. M., & Gibbons, F. X. *The augmentation principle in MR persons: Perceptual versus verbal approaches.* Paper presented at the American Psychological Association, Montreal, Canada, September 1980.

Kassin, S. M., & Gibbons, F. X. Children's use of the discounting principle in their perceptions of exertion. *Child Development, 1981, 52, 741-744.*

Kassin, S. M., & Lepper, M. R. Oversufficient and insufficient justification effects: Cognitive and behavioral development. In J. Nicholls (Ed.). *The development of achievement motivation.* Greenwich, CT: JAI Press, in press.

Kassin, S. M., & Lowe, C. A. On the development of the augmentation principle: A perceptual approach. *Child Development, 1979, 50, 728-734.* (a)

Kassin, S. M., & Lowe, C. A. On the use of single sentence descriptions of behavior in attribution research. *Social Behavior and Personality, 1979, 7, 1-8.* (b)

Kassin, S. M., & Lowe, C. A. *Kelley's attribution theory: a perceptual approach.* Paper presented at the Eastern Psychological Association, Philadelphia, April 1979. (c)

Kassin, S. M., Lowe, C. A., & Gibbons, F. X. Children's use of the discounting principle: A perceptual approach. *Journal of Personality and Social Psychology, 1980, 39, 718-728.*

Kelley, H. H. Attribution theory in social psychology. In D. Levine (Ed.), *Nebraska symposium on motivation.* Lincoln: University of Nebraska Press, 1967.

Kelley, H. H. *Causal schemata and the attribution process.* Morristown, NJ: General Learning Press, 1971.

Kelley, H. H. Attribution in social interaction. In E. E. Jones, D. E. Kanouse, H. H. Kelley, R. E. Nisbett, S. Valins, & B. Weiner (Eds.), *Attribution: Perceiving the causes of behavior.* Morristown, NJ: General Learning Press, 1972.

Lepper, M. R., & Gilovich, T. J. The multiple functions of reward: A social-developmental perspective. In S. Brehm, S. Kassin, & F. Gibbons (Eds.), *Developmental social psychology: Theory and research.* New York: Oxford University Press, 1981.

Lepper, M. R., Sagotsky, G., Dafoe, J. L., & Greene, D. Consequences of superfluous social constraints: Effects on young children's social inferences and subsequent intrinsic interest. *Journal of Personality and Social Psychology, 1982, 42, 51-65.*

Lesser, H. The growth of perceived causality in children. *Journal of Genetic Psychology, 1977, 130, 145-152.*

Lowe, C. A., & Kassin, S. M. A perceptual view of attribution: Theoretical and methodological implications. *Personality and Social Psychology Bulletin, 1980, 6, 532-542.*

Lowe, C. A., Medway, F., & Beers, S. Individual differences in causal attribution: The personal-environmental causal attribution (PECA) scale. Paper presented at the American Psychological Association, 1978.

Marek, J. Information, perception, and social context, I. *Human Relations,* 1963, *16,* 209-231.

Marek, J. Information, perception, and social context, II. *Human Relations,* 1966, *19,* 353-380.

Massad, C. M., Hubbard, M., & Newtson, D. Selective perception of events. *Journal of Experimental Social Psychology,* 1979, *15,* 513-532.

McArthur, L. A. The how and what of why: Some determinants and consequences of causal attribution. *Journal of Personality and Social Psychology,* 1972, *22,* 171-193.

McArthur, L. Z. What grabs you? The role of attention in impression formation and causal attribution. In E. T. Higgins, C. P. Herman, & M. P. Zanna (Eds.), *Social cognition: Cognitive structure and processes underlying person memory and social judgment.* Hillsdale, NJ: Lawrence Erlbaum, 1981.

McArthur, L. Z., & Ginsberg, E. Causal attribution to salient stimuli: An investigation of visual fixation mediators. *Personality and Social Psychology Bulletin,* 1981, *7,* 547-553.

McArthur, L. Z., & Post, D. L. Figural emphasis and person perception. *Journal of Experimental Social Psychology,* 1977, *13,* 520-535.

Michotte, A. E. The emotions regarded as functional connections. In M. L. Reymert (Ed.), *Feelings and emotions.* New York: McGraw-Hill, 1950.

Michotte, A. *The perception of causality.* London: Methuen, 1963.

Mischel, W. Toward a cognitive social learning reconceptualization of personality. *Psychological Review,* 1973, *80,* 252-283.

Newtson, D. Foundations of attribution: The perception of ongoing behavior. In J. H. Harvey, W. J. Ickes, & R. F. Kidd (Eds.), *New directions in attribution research* (Vol. 1). Hillsdale, NJ: Lawrence Erlbaum, 1976.

Nisbett, R. E., & Borgida, E. Attribution and the psychology of prediction. *Journal of Personality and Social Psychology,* 1975, *32,* 932-943.

Nisbett, R. E., Borgida, E., Crandall, R., & Reed, H. Popular induction: Information is not necessarily informative. In J. Carroll & J. Payne (Eds.), *Cognition and social behavior.* Hillsdale, NJ: Lawrence Erlbaum, 1976.

Nisbett, R. E., & Ross, L. *Human inference: Strategies and shortcomings of social judgment.* Englewood Cliffs, NJ: Prentice-Hall, 1980.

Olum, V. Developmental differences in the perception of causality. *American Journal of Psychology,* 1956, *69,* 417-428.

Pryor, J. B., & Kriss, M. The cognitive dynamics of salience and the attribution process. *Journal of Personality and Social Psychology,* 1977, *35,* 49-55.

Ross, L. The intuitive psychologist and his shortcomings: Distortions in the attribution process. In L. Berkowitz (Ed.), *Advances in experimental social psychology* (Vol. 10). New York: Academic Press, 1977.

Rotter, J. B. *Social learning and clinical psychology.* Englewood Cliffs, NJ: Prentice-Hall, 1954.

Runeson, S. On visual perception of dynamic events. Doctoral dissertation, University of Uppsala (Sweden), 1977.

Salancik, G. R. Inference of one's attitude from behavior recalled under linguistically manipulated cognitive sets. *Journal of Experimental Social Psychology,* 1974, *10,* 415-427.

Salancik, G. R. Extrinsic attribution and the use of behavior information to infer attitudes. *Journal of Personality and Social Psychology,* 1976, *34,* 1302-1312.

Salancik, G. R., & Conway, C. Attitude inferences from salient and relevant cognitive content about behavior. *Journal of Personality and Social Psychology,* 1975, *32,* 829-840.

Shatz, M. The relationship between cognitive processes and the development of communication skills. In H. E. Howe & C. B. Keasey (Eds.), *Nebraska symposium on motivation* (Vol. 25). Lincoln: University of Nebraska Press, 1977.

Shor, R. E. Effect of preinformation upon human characteristics attributed to animated geometric figures. *Journal of Abnormal and Social Psychology,* 1957, *54,* 124-126.

Shultz, T. R., & Butkowsky, I. Young children's use of the scheme for multiple sufficient causes in the attribution of real and hypothetical behavior. *Child Development,* 1977, *48,* 464-469.

Shultz, T. R., Butkowsky, I., Pearce, J. W., & Shanfield, H. Development of schemes for the attribution of multiple psychological causes. *Developmental Psychology,* 1975, *11,* 502-510.

Smith, M. C. Children's use of the multiple sufficient cause schema in social perception. *Journal of Personality and Social Psychology,* 1975, *32,* 737-747.

Smith, M. C. Cognizing the behavior stream: The recognition of intentional action. *Child Development,* 1978, *49,* 736-743.

Sugarman, D. B. The development of causal perception and understanding: Differentiation of physical and social causality. Doctoral dissertation, Yeshivah University, 1982.

Surber, C. F. The utility of "simplification" as a developmental research strategy. *Child Development,* 1979, *50,* 571-574.

Surber, C. F. Developmental changes in inverse compensation in social and non-social attributions. In S. Yussen (Ed.), *The growth of reflection.* New York: Academic Press, in press.

Tagiuri, R. Movement as a cue in person perception. In H. P. David & J. C. Brengelmann (Eds.), *Perspective in personality research.* New York: Springer, 1960.

Taylor, S. E., & Fiske, S. T. Point of view and perceptions of causality. *Journal of Personality and Social Psychology,* 1975, *32,* 439-445.

Thayer, S., & Schiff, W. Stimulus factors in observer judgment of social interaction: Facial expression and motion pattern. *American Journal of Psychology,* 1969, *82,* 73-85.

Thibaut, J. W., & Riecken, H. W. Some determinants and consequences of the perception of social causality. *Journal of Personality,* 1955, *24,* 113-133.

Weary, G., Rich, M. C., Harvey, J. H., & Ickes, W. J. Heider's formulation of social perception and attributional processes: Toward further clarification. *Personality and Social Psychology Bulletin,* 1980, *6,* 37-43.

7

Self-Evaluation Through Social Comparison:

A DEVELOPMENTAL ANALYSIS

JERRY SULS

GLENN S. SANDERS

Jerry Suls is Associate Professor of Psychology at the State University of New York at Albany. His major interests are in social comparison, self-evaluation, and social psychological factors involved in physical health. He has edited *Social Comparison Processes* (with R. L. Miller) and *Psychological Perspectives on the Self* (Vol. 1).

Glenn S. Sanders is Associate Professor of Psychology at SUNY/Albany. His research interests include the application of social comparison theory to topics in health, education, and task performance. Dr. Sanders has also edited a forthcoming volume on the *Social Psychology of Health and Illness* (with J. Suls).

For some time it has been appreciated that people often evaluate their abilities, opinions, and emotions through interpersonal or social comparisons. As Festinger (1954) observed, there are many occasions when the

AUTHORS' NOTE: We would like to thank Albert Bandura, Roland Radloff, and David Shaffer for their helpful comments and suggestions.

only way to evaluate one's capabilities or to verify the accuracy of one's opinions is by comparing oneself with others, because objective or physical standards are unavailable or nonexistent. While Festinger's initial statement of comparison processes has inspired a considerable amount of theoretical and empirical attention (e.g., Latane, 1966; Pettigrew, 1967; Suls & Miller, 1977; Wheeler, 1974), questions concerning the *development* of social comparison have received very little attention. Yet a thorough understanding of the process through which children begin to compare themselves with others is important for several reasons. First, we need to know when it is likely that children begin to assess themselves with respect to other people and whether they draw the same conclusions from comparative feedback as do adults. A second interest derives from the use of social comparison, implicitly and explicitly, in the educational system (see Levine, in press). Thus, it is important, both theoretically and practically, to know when and how children begin to define themselves relative to their classmates, and the impact of such comparison on their achievement-striving and goal-setting. Finally, it is widely acknowledged that interpersonal comparisons provide the basis for a wide variety of related behaviors (e.g., decision-making, conformity, pro-social behavior, self-concept). If children differ from adults in significant ways with respect to comparison behavior, then we should also find differences related to comparison behavior between adults and children.

This chapter outlines developmental aspects of social comparison both theoretically and empirically and, by so doing, highlights some important age-related changes in social behavior. Our focus will be on the development of the use of interpersonal comparison for self-evaluation of ability. The reader of Festinger's (1954) original statement is, of course, aware that his theory and its offshoots have other facets as well—including, for example, group communications and deviance. Because virtually all of the developmental data available relate to the self-evaluation of *abilities,* our discussion will focus on the ways in which children assess their performance and underlying capacities with less attention to other areas of self-evaluation, such as the validity of opinions or the appropriateness of behavior.

SOCIAL COMPARISON IN ADULTS

The study of social comparison has been primarily carried out with adult subjects, particularly in the 18-25-year range. We will first describe the comparison behavior of this age group, so we may later contrast it with that of children. Some distinctions are appropriate at this point. First, we should distinguish between comparison *preference* as opposed to comparison *effects* (see Sanders, Gastorf, & Mullen, 1979). The former considers what kinds of people the individual prefers or seeks out when in a state of uncertainty and when lacking objective standards; the latter focuses on what kinds of comparison information have the strongest impact on self-evaluations of ability. With respect to preference, Festinger (1954) proposed that "similar" others are the most desirable, important sources of comparison information. Of course, people can be similar in a variety of ways. Goethals and Darley (1977) have recently refined what aspect of similarity appears to be most important for social comparison. They posit that we should choose for comparison someone who is similar on personal characteristics which are relevant to and, perhaps, predictive of performance. These characteristics they call "related attributes." Thus, to evaluate swimming ability, for example, one should compare oneself with someone who is similar on characteristics, presumably, related to swimming performance such as sex, age, weight, and so on.

Empirical support for the hypothesis that others with related attributes are preferred for comparison can be found in several studies. For instance, Zanna, Goethals, and Hill (1975) administered a bogus test to male and female college-aged subjects on which they received an ambiguous score. Before test administration, half of each group was told that either males or females typically perform better on the test, thus relating gender to performance. After receiving their ambiguous scores, subjects were given the opportunity to see various norms in order to evaluate how well they had done. As predicted, the vast majority preferred to compare with a same-sex reference group. More recent work on comparison choice preference also supports the similarity hypothesis (e.g., Suls, Gastorf, & Lawhorn, 1978; Suls, Gaes, & Gastorf, 1979; Wheeler, Koestner, & Driver, in press).

With respect to the *effects* of comparison, Festinger's theory posits that information from similar others provides the greatest evaluative stability and certainty. This prediction has also been supported empirically. For example, Radloff (1966) had Navy recruits perform a pursuit-rotor task over a series of trials. After each trial, subjects were asked to evaluate their performance. Performance feedback about how others were doing on the same task was manipulated in such a way that some subjects thought they were performing similarly to others while other subjects thought they were performing well above or below average. Consistent with comparison theory, subjects exposed to similar others exhibited more stable self-evaluations of ability across trials.

In a more recent study by Gastorf and Suls (1978), college undergraduates performed a reasoning task that measured an ability which they were told increased with age and experience. After receiving an ambiguous and fictitious score, subjects were given information about how either other college students or graduate students performed. Then subjects were asked to evaluate their ability on a series of scales and indicate their confidence or certainty of their judgments. The results showed that subjects had greater certainty after comparing with others similar on related attributes (college students) than after comparing with dissimilar others (graduate students). Sanders et al. (1979) have also reported that comparison with similar others had the greatest impact on self-evaluation. Finally, Tesser (1980) reported evidence suggesting that unfavorable comparisons with similar-aged siblings are particularly upsetting. In contrast, when siblings are separated by several years, their relative standing had little impact.

THEORETICAL BASIS FOR ADULT COMPARISON BEHAVIOR

While the research reviewed above strongly supports Festinger's propositions, it has employed subjects ranging in age from 18 to 25. An important question is whether the same tendencies will be exhibited in younger persons.

As we will argue below, we should not expect adult comparison behavior to be present in early childhood. Rather, it must develop over time and in fact should follow an orderly course before culminating in the form exhibited by adults. To understand this, we must first describe why adults find that similar others are most useful for ability evaluation. An example will be helpful. Suppose you are a jogger and want to know how much running ability you possess. Assume that you compare yourself with someone who is dissimilar in attributes related to performance, such as age and experience. The most likely outcome is that you will be different in performance. But this says very little about your own ability, because either the other person's related attributes and/or his or her ability may be responsible for the performance difference. As Goethals and Darley (1977) point out, the attributional principle of discounting (Kelley, 1973) comes into play here; that is, the influence of any given cause of behavior cannot be determined confidently when there exist two or more plausible causes (in this case, ability versus performance-related attributes of age, sex, and experience). Thus, for example, comparing one's performance with a person who is dissimilar by virtue of his or her advantage on a "related" attribute (i.e., experience) does not allow the individual to confidently determine whether his or her own inferior performance is due to poorer ability, inadequate experience, or both.

In contrast, if one compares oneself with others *similar* in related attributes (matched on experience, age, sex, and any other nonability factors that contribute to performance), then the implication of the comparison is relatively clear. If an individual performs consistently better, he or she can be assumed to possess a comparatively high ability; the related attributes cannot be responsible because the individual is matched with the other person on these characteristics. Consistently poor performance probably means poor ability. Performing consistently at the same level as others indicates an average level of ability.

Several critical concepts must be understood by the person for similar others to have special information value. The first is that the individual must appreciate that ability can only be inferred from performance, since it is a hypothetical entity. Second, it is necessary to understand that any performance or set of performances is the joint result of ability (a relatively stable entity) plus certain related attributes, such as level of practice, effort, fatigue, and the like (Heider, 1958). Also, the individual must have some idea how ability, effort, and other factors work together to result in high or low performance. For example, the individual needs to understand that a high level of effort may compensate for low ability, and vice versa. Lacking this knowledge, he or she could not know how attributes interact with ability to yield different levels of performance. Finally, the individual must understand and employ the discounting principle: that when two or more factors could have produced performance differences, such as different levels of ability and practice, it is not possible to make a clear attribution to any single factor.

While adults possess these cognitive concepts (Kelley, 1973), a variety of theoretical and empirical grounds suggest that young children (under 8 to 9 years of age) do *not*. First, we know it takes some time for the child to appreciate inferred, hypothetical constructs (e.g., Piaget, 1958).

Further, there is ample reason to believe that children cannot distinguish between an abstract concept (like ability) and its concrete examples (like performance). The action-physicalistic thought of the child under four years of age shows little understanding of these subtleties. A similar difficulty is that the relationship between ability and related attributes such as effort has been demonstrated to be poorly understood by children before the age of eight or nine (Kun, 1977; Nicholls, 1978). Finally, the discounting principle, which is thought to underlie the choice of similar others as comparison sources, is typically not well appreciated until age eight or nine (Karniol & Ross, 1976; Kassin, Lowe, & Gibbons, 1980). Given these considerations, we should not expect young children to have an appreciation for the subtleties of ability evaluation or for the greater information value of similar others.

A DEVELOPMENTAL MODEL

In this section, we describe a model for the development of social comparison. The theoretical foundation for the model is based on recent work on the development of cognitive mediators of achievement and attributions (Nicholls, 1978; Weiner & Kun, in press), as well as Goethals and Darley's (1977) attributional treatment of social comparison processes. Specifically, we are concerned with outlining the progression of stages that finally culminates in the social comparison behavior of adults described earlier. After outlining the model, we will review the available empirical evidence.

Before introducing the model, a couple of points are worth mentioning. First, we use the term "stage" as a matter of convenience. We recognize that changes are probably more quantitative than qualitative, gradual rather than abrupt. The reader may prefer to think of the scheme that follows as a set of phases rather than stages, since the latter implies homogeneity and qualitative transformation (Flavell, 1977). A second point is that we will describe the developmental progression in terms of particular ages. We recognize, though, that there may be considerable variability among children in the initial appearance of a particular comparison orientation. Our major proposition is that children exhibit a series of changes in comparison orientation in an invariant sequence, but they may differ in the specific age of onset.

The model proposes four stages. The first stage is thought to begin at birth and extend to approximately age three. During this time, the child has a primitive concept of self which depends only minimally on his or her abilities. Although these years represent a period of notable physical achievements, the child lacks the cognitive skills to gain perspective on his or her abilities, successes, and failures. At best the child responds positively or negatively depending on when a limited physical goal (e.g., walking, reaching) is achieved. While the child relies *exclusively* on the use of physical standards to evaluate performance at this stage, such standards continue to be used throughout the life span.

At approximately the age of three, the child should have developed sufficient perceptual, memory, and motor skills to permit a primitive cognitive appraisal of his or her skills: He or she is capable of making judgments of more than or less than, at least in simple situations (Iijima, 1965, 1966, 1967). However, children under age four or five are too egocentric to appreciate the "self" as a member of a large group whose identity is determined by relative standing rather than absolute characteristics (Selman & Byrne, 1974).

In addition, children between the ages of three and six exhibit preoperational thinking (Piaget, 1958, 1965) and have difficulty with concepts that are unobservable and inferred (Piaget, 1965). Concepts like motive and ability fall within this realm. It is highly unlikely that preschoolers and children in the first years of elementary school have an understanding of the distinction between performance and ability and that they infer any enduring internal trait like ability from overt performance. Therefore, it seems unlikely that young children use social comparison to evaluate their abilities. However, social comparisons of overt physical characteristics and rewards may be exhibited at a young age (Masters, 1971). For instance, Masters (1968) reported that nurseryschool children increased their self-reinforcing behavior by distributing reward tokens to themselves, when they had previously received fewer rewards than their peers. Analogously, they curtailed their self-reinforcements when reward dispensations had been equal. In the same way, preschoolers may imitate the behavior of similar models (e.g., Grusec & Brinker, 1972), but modeling concerns the acquisition and performance of overt behavior, not self-evaluations of ability.

One indication that preschoolers do not infer ability from performance is that they often exhibit positive reactions and unrealistically high expectations of success after failure (Ruble, Parsons, & Ross, 1976). There is also evidence that children under five years of age rate themselves as having high ability even when they are aware that they were correct because they guessed rather than because they had special skill or knowledge (Miscione, Marvin, O'Brien, & Greenberg, 1978). Thus, they make the mistake of confusing ability with performance outcome, rather than viewing performance as only one of several clues to their ability level.

Although social comparisons to evaluate one's ability are unlikely to be made (between the ages of three and five), there is another means of assessing one's capabilities which may be more relevant at that age—self-comparisons based on current versus past performance. Comparisons with self are useful because they indicate improvement or deterioration. As noted above, children between the ages of three and five understand the concept of "more than" and "less than" (Iijima, 1965, 1966, 1967) and thus can perceive improvement or deterioration of performance. We contend, therefore, that from ages three to five temporal comparisons are predominant, although again we emphasize that the child is primarily evaluating performance and not ability. Comparisons in the early years are impeded by a limited memory span, so only recent experiences can be used to compare with present performance. However, as recall ability expands (e.g., Brown, 1975) the child should be able to gauge performance with efforts that are temporally more distant.

Use of temporal comparisons, which begins at this phase, continues into later years (see Albert, 1977; Bandura, 1982). Comparisons of present performance with past performance influence feelings of success and failure as well as goal-setting, as demonstrated by studies of level of aspiration in adults (e.g., Hoppe, 1930; Gardner, 1939; Hertzman & Festinger, 1940). At about age five interpersonal comparisons begin to emerge and eventually to predominate. But, as previously noted, young children have not mastered the critical concepts essential to appreciate the information value of similar others, and, as a result, they compare indiscriminately.

Why does social comparison emerge around age five? We posit several independent factors that facilitate the development of social comparison. First, by this age, egocentrism may substantially decline, so the child's attention can now be focused not only on the self but on other people as well. Second, with age the child has more opportunities to compare with other persons. This is encouraged by the child's increased mobility and entrance into nursery school. In addition, the schools themselves probably implicitly and explicitly encourage social over temporal comparisons (Levine, in press). Even though the child may be learning new skills in which he or she can observe proper temporal changes, most schools in their grading and competitive practices emphasize relative, *social* achievement standards. Finally, there is reason to believe that children move to interpersonal comparisons because temporal comparisons become less gratifying. The years between three and five represent a period of rapid advancement in terms of physical and cognitive skills. During this period, temporal comparisons should be gratifying, since they will usually reveal substantial improvement. But as the spurt of development levels off, temporal comparison should reveal smaller levels of improvement and thus bring less satisfaction than earlier ones. Given that the child can no longer as readily obtain satisfying temporal comparisons, attention may turn to bettering the performances of others.

By the time the child has reached kindergarten, he or she also begins to distinguish performance from its component parts—effort, ability, and other related attributes (Karabenick & Heller, 1976; Shaklee, 1976). Some, but not all, of the processes underlying social comparison-based ability evaluation are thus in place. Children's understanding of the relationship between ability and effort (a related attribute) is not fully developed. They are likely to think, for example, that someone has ability only if that person tries hard but not if he or she succeeds with little effort (Nicholls, 1978; Kun, 1977). Misunderstanding how related attributes in conjunction with ability produce a particular level of performance would not allow children to recognize why others should be matched on related attributes (like practice, use, etc.) to make accurate, unambiguous evaluations of ability. Therefore, we proposed that after age five, children will evaluate ability via social comparison but will compare indiscriminately with both similar and dissimilar others.

The indiscriminate phase should continue until the child has acquired the discounting principle and understands the compensatory relationships between performance, ability, and nonability factors such as practice and effort. Evidence reported by Karniol and Ross (1976; see Sedlak & Kurtz, 1981) suggests that the discounting principle does not appear until the middle-elementary school years (eight-nine). The study by Karniol and

Ross used story-pairs, a linguistic presentation mode, to test for the principle. Using a pictorial mode or presentation, Kassin et al. (1980) found a weak tendency for even kindergarteners to use discounting, although they were not yet able to verbalize the principle. It seems, then, that children younger than eight can, under some circumstances, use the discounting principle. But we should recall that for children to be able to make adultlike ability assessments and compare with similar others, they must also understand how ability and nonability-related attributes work together. A liberal estimate is that these fine-tuned analyses do not emerge until age 10 (Karabenick & Heller, 1976; Kun, 1977). By then, children acknowledge that someone getting a higher score with less effort must be more able. We might add, however, that the ability to verbalize their judgments may not emerge until a couple of years later (Nicholls, 1978).

When the discounting principle and the compensatory relationships between performance, ability, and nonability factors are acquired, the child's comparison behavior should resemble that of adults and follow the dynamics outlined by Festinger (1954) and Goethals and Darley (1977). The developmental literature suggests that at approximately age nine these capabilities will be acquired and comparison with similars should be exhibited. This does not mean that temporal or objective comparisons drop out, but we would argue that social-based evaluations take precedence. Some evidence for these suppositions is reviewed in the next section.

Table 1 depicts the four-stage model described above. It should be clear that the age ranges are approximate, since some schools are likely to place greater emphasis on stratification of age levels which would facilitate and reinforce the use and preference for peer (similar) comparisons. The present model has similarities with an analysis by Veroff (1969). Veroff also suggested that temporal (self) comparisons would precede social comparison in development. However, he did not propose an intermediate stage with indiscriminate social comparisons.

EMPIRICAL SUPPORT FOR THE MODEL

In this section we review empirical evidence relevant to the four-stage model. The model posits that children under three years are not concerned with self-evaluation and do not engage in temporal or social comparisons. This proposition is difficult to evaluate inasmuch as it is exceedingly

TABLE 1

Developmental Sequence of Self-Evaluation Processes

Stage	Basis for Evaluation	Age Range	Performance Inferences	Psychological Mediators
1	Objective Standards	0-3	Success-Failure	Goal Setting and Frustration
2	Temporal Comparison with Self*	4-5	Improvement-Retrogression	Concepts of More Than and Less Than
3	Indiscriminate Social Comparison	6-8	Absolute Superior Ability-Absolute Inferior Ability	Performance is distinguished from ability and related attributes like effort. However, the relationship between ability and effort is not well-understood.
4	Social Comparison with Similar Others	9-Adult	Context-Defined Superior Ability-Context-Defined Inferior Ability	Discounting principle and the Relationship between ability and related attribute are understood.

*Temporal comparison continues to be used beyond this phase although social comparison predominates.

problematic to operationalize comparison tendencies in very young children. Dinner's (1976) research with nurseryschool children has some relevance, however. She had these subjects perform a task in the presence of a co-actor (either a peer or an adult). Dinner then observed how much the children looked at the other's work (presumably an index of social comparison). She reported that nurseryschool children were relatively uninterested in the co-actor, suggesting that social comparison was not operating.

Veroff (1969) also examined the development of social comparison behavior in preschool children. Veroff's measure was whether the child would like to try a task that "most boys (girls) your age can do" or a task that "some boys (or girls) your age can do and some cannot," or a task that "most boys (or girls) cannot do." Selecting a task that "some boys (or girls) can do and some cannot" was coded as high social comparison motivation. This coding followed from the assumption that performance on a task of moderate difficulty would be more informative about one's relative standing than would performance on a task most peers either could or could not complete. Consistent with his assertions, Veroff (1969) found that social comparison motivation, as indexed by choice of the moderate challenge task, was virtually absent in preschoolers.

The stage model suggests that while social comparison may not be operative in the years three to five, temporal comparisons should be exhibited. Several recent studies by McClintock and his associates are consistent with this perspective. McClintock and Moskowitz (1976) and McClintock, Moskowitz, and McClintock (1977) studied the choice behaviors of nurseryschool children in three tasks—individualistic, coordinative, and conflictual. Choice options were structured to reveal whether the children were concerned only with their own outcome, regardless of the implications of their actions for the outcomes of others. Of special interest was whether young children would prefer to maximize or improve their own rewards or achieve a competitive advantage. The former can be viewed as a concern for improving temporal comparison; the latter a concern for favorable social comparisons. McClintock et al. (1977) reported that very young children (3-1/2 years of age) were own-gain oriented and relatively unconcerned with how much others received vis-à-vis themselves. Thus, it appears that temporal comparison is operating in three-year-old children but social comparison is not, just as the model suggests.

At approximately age five the child should become increasingly interested in socially defined standards as he or she moves away from egocentric thinking and finds him/herself to be part of a larger social network. We also expect that temporal comparison will take on less importance relative to social comparison, although surely temporal comparisons will not disappear. McClintock et al.'s results also bear on this point. They included in their testing sample older (age five) children who were also offered the same choice options as the 3-1/2-year-olds. The findings conformed to the model. Older children were more willing to forego own gain for a competitive advantage.

In a similar vein, Ruble, Feldman, and Boggiano (1976) tested pairs of kindergarteners and first and second graders. The frequency and duration with which they pushed a button to observe their partner's progress on a monitor served as an index of social comparison interest. Interest in the partner's progress increased from kindergarten (five years) to second grade (seven years). In another set of experiments, Ruble, Boggiano, Feldman, and Loebl (1980) examined the effects of social comparison information on ability evaluations. In Study 1, Ruble et al. had first and second graders perform a task on which they were told they had succeeded or failed. In some conditions the youngsters also received information about whether other children in the same testing succeeded or failed. Ruble et al. (Study 1) concluded from their results that the self-evaluations of the first and second graders were unaffected by social comparison. This seems inconsistent with the present model's contention that children in the five-eight age range should be affected by social comparison information at least to some extent. Actually, a close examination of Ruble et al.'s data suggests that comparison information did have some effect. There was a trend for self-evaluations to be lower when the children were told that others succeeded than when others failed ($p < .20$). Further, this effect was stronger for second than for first graders ($p < .025$) who were told they themselves had failed, a finding consistent with the notion that the impact of comparison information increases with age.

In a second study with kindergarteners and second- and fourth-grade children, Ruble et al. used the same procedure, except that comparison information was presented by hypothetical others (i.e., co-actors were not present). Ruble et al. reported that only the fourth graders were affected by the receipt of the social comparison information (that the unseen others had succeeded or failed). Again, this result seems inconsistent with our proposals, since even second graders should exhibit some impact of the comparison information. Their findings are also internally inconsistent, given that second graders in Study 1 did show some effects of comparison as noted above. One explanation for the discrepancy is that comparison information came from others who were actually present in Study 1 but from hypothetical others in Study 2. It may be that young children have some difficulty appreciating comparisons when co-actors are not physically present. Finally, we should note that the study possesses one more ambiguity. Since children were given information that they had succeeded or failed independent of the social comparison information, (how peers had done), there is a sense in which all children received objective information about their ability from the experimenter. Festinger (1954) makes clear that objective standards make the need for social comparison (and presumably its impact as well) less important. Thus, Ruble et al.'s studies represent a very conservative and at least marginally supportive test of our thesis.

In another investigation Feld, Ruhland, and Gold (1979) employed fantasy measures of achievement motivation (story generating) and temporal comparisons (excelling past performance) to assess comparison interest. They found that social comparison interest increased and temporal comparison decreased with age.

Thus, empirical evidence suggests that social comparison does not begin to appear until age five and increases from that time. However, our model suggests that comparisons in five- and six-year-olds will be indiscriminate because the child lacks the capacity to appreciate the greater information value obtained from comparing with similar others. The aforementioned studies do not permit an assessment of this aspect of the model because only similar others (peers) were available. A study by Dinner (1976), however, did address this issue. This investigation had nurseryschool, first-, second-, and fourth-grade children perform a task on which they either succeeded or failed relative to either peers or adults. They were then asked to evaluate their level of skill on a series of scales specially designed to be appropriate for children. Dinner's results showed that the nursery-school children were unaffected by comparison with adults or peers, which is consistent with the hypothesis that children at this age are uninterested in social comparison. First and second graders were influenced in their evaluations by success or failure with respect to both peers and adults, suggesting that children in these grades do not appreciate the greater information value of comparison with similar others. However, by fourth grade, the youngsters were affected only by comparisons with peers. Age nine is the time at which related attributes and ability are distinguished, when the discounting principle becomes a part of the child's cognitive repertoire according to available evidence and thus the time when the child should cease indiscriminate social comparisons.

One other piece of indirect evidence comes from Nicholls (1978). He asked children in elementary school classrooms to rank their reading attainment among the other children in their class. The children's teachers were asked also to rate their pupil's reading attainment. Nicholls (1978) found that from nine years on the children became more adultlike in evaluating their ranking (correlations between teacher and child ratings of achievement increased with age). It is at nine that we suggested that comparison with one's peers should become predominant in making accurate self-evaluations.

Thus, as one can see from the preceding review, existing evidence provides some support for the proposed four-stage model. Of course, more focused and parametric studies are needed. As Ruble et al. have recently noted, research in this area has tended to involve subjects in novel tasks in unfamiliar settings. "It is possible that children younger than eight years of age do use social comparison information for self-evaluation in more familiar settings where comparative information is repeatedly available" (1980, p. 114). Studies conducted in naturalistic settings would be especially useful in providing more stringent tests of the present model.

IMPLICATIONS

The developmental model of social comparison described above has a number of implications of both a theoretical and applied nature, and it is to these that we now turn. It is widely acknowledged that early feelings of mastery are necessary to lay the foundation for future achievement-striving and an enduring sense of personal competence (e.g., Harter, 1978; White, 1959). An important issue that is rarely addressed (however, see Bandura, 1981) concerns the kinds of standards and performances which create feelings of mastery. The present model suggests some of these specifics and argues that a sense of mastery will be based on different considerations at different ages. For example, the very young child should be pleased or displeased primarily by physical, objective accomplishments (e.g., "I can walk," "I can climb the stairs"). Lacking social comparison and initially temporal comparison as well, it is likely that standards and feedback are obtained principally from parents and caretakers. These responses and appraisals, given the child's unilateral respect for adults (Piaget, 1965; Suls & Kalle, 1978), should have tremendous influence. It is not so surprising, then, that Baumrind (1970) found that children who were most reliant, self-controlled, explorative, and contented had parents who set definite standards against which their children could judge the adequacy of their behavior. Of course, the need for standards continues, but the focus should change with age. At ages three to five, parents and caretakers' standards, praise, and reproof will be important, but the child will gauge capability by temporal comparisons as well (e.g., "Have I gotten better, worse or stayed the same?"). It is only on reaching kindergarten that the child will turn to interpersonal comparisons. At first, these comparisons will be indiscriminate in their focus, which may provide some pain and discomfort, particularly when the child finds him/herself consistently outperformed by someone who is more experienced or older and thus an inappropriate comparison other. By age nine, comparisons should be much more selective, given that the important cognitive concepts essential for the ability-evaluation process emerge. At nine and with increasing age, perceived mastery and self-efficiency should be based primarily on peer comparisons.

The notion that feelings of competence are mediated by different standards depending on the child's developmental level is nicely illustrated by a study reported by Boggiano and Ruble (1979). In that investigation nurseryschool children's interest in an activity was sustained only when they learned that they met an absolute standard of performance; the effects of social comparison information (i.e., others did better or worse) had no effect. In contrast, social comparison information about relative competence sustained interest in the activity among children in higher grades. These data not only support our preceding analysis of the increasing importance of interpersonal comparisons but also point out that different standards of performance may sustain activities, striving, and interest at different ages via feelings of competence and mastery instilled through rewards.

Of course, by and large the schools support social comparison. Most traditional educational systems strongly encourage socially oriented estimates of one's capacities. Witness such practices as seeing who answers a question, spelling bees, drawing contests, show-and-tell exercises, and so forth. Test scores, grade levels, and tracking systems all serve to emphasize the ranking of children on the basis of their performance. It is not surprising, then, that academic achievement relative to others is assumed to be an important influence on the self-concept (Rosenberg, 1979). But there has been a tendency in much past work to overlook the influence of comparisons in the child's immediate local social environment (i.e., his or her classroom). Rogers, Smith, and Coleman (1978) have observed that research has generally reported no relationship or very low correlations between achievement and self-concept. However, Rogers et al. noted that typically information regarding the child's relative academic standing within his or her own classroom has not been collected in previous research. To remedy this situation, Rogers et al. examined the relationship between children's self-concept and math and reading achievement scores on standardized tests while controlling for each child's relative position (high, medium, low) in his or her classroom. The results indicated that achievement scores were highly related to self-concept when the child's relative achievement in the class was incorporated into the analyses. For example, a child with more reading or math ability compared to his or her classmates had a higher self-concept than a child for which the comparison was unfavorable. The relationship between achievement test scores and self-concept were drastically reduced when within-class achievement was not considered. This means that "two children having identical achievement test results but residing in different classrooms [may] have differing self-concepts to the extent that their relative academic standing in each class differed" (Rogers et al., 1978, p. 51).

It is worth emphasizing that a number of the features of the educational system such as tracking and socially oriented estimates of one's capacities can be seen as either a product of independently developing social comparison tendencies in children or as helping to create or stimulate these tendencies. The patterns of cause and effect are not at all clear, although studies of comparison behavior among children in noncompetitive schools, such as open schools where the unique individual potential of the child is stressed (Weiss, Fischer, Musella, & Traub, 1973), would be of help in answering these questions.

In the normative case, it seems clear that formal education as commonly instituted and self-evaluation in social terms are intimately related. This point has special relevance to individual differences in the development of social comparison. Specifically, some children may begin to appreciate the usefulness of social comparison and the significance of similar others earlier than other children. For instance, it is plausible that children of high-achievement-striving parents may enter school with a fully developed comparison orientation (see Matthews & Siegel, in press), whereas other children may arrive at this stage sometime later. This variability suggests that some children will be much more motivated to outperform their peers than will other children, simply because they find relative standing more meaningful. In turn, differential motivation to excel will probably be reflected in actual performances, in the all-important initial formal appraisals of a child's potential, and ultimately in the child's estimate of his or her own capacities. It follows that an important basis for success in school and for a positive self-concept may not be the child's ability per se, but rather the correspondence between the child's method of self-evaluation and the evaluative orientation of the educational system. Given the plausible hypothesis that the greatest variability in comparison behavior among children is likely to be exhibited in the years five to eight where social comparison skills are being refined, a mismatch between the child's and the school's evaluative orientation is likely to be a problem in this time frame.

The present analysis also has implications for precocious or exceptionally gifted children. These children tend to have more personality and adjustment problems than their age-mates (Lewis, 1943). While there are a number of explanations for this finding, one likely possibility is that gifted children pose a threat to their peers' self-concepts. If a child's estimate of his or her own capabilities is largely determined by his or her standing relative to others, the presence of another whose performances are consistently and highly superior must lead to frustration, resentment, and diminished interest in ability development. In turn, the superior other is sure to experience difficulties in interacting with those whose self-concepts he or she is inadvertently threatening, and these difficulties could easily trigger a variety of spiraling and self-fulfilling emotional problems. This reasoning is supported by the fact that adjustment difficulties are not manifested in gifted children until the age of nine or ten (DeHann & Havighurst, 1961; Zorbaugh, Boardman, & Sheldon, 1951). It is just prior to this period that we have placed the full development of the comparison process, particularly the emphasis on comparison with peers. The close sequencing of the use of comparison for ability evaluation and the appearance of adjustment problems in precocious children may be coincidental, but it is certainly consistent with our reasoning. The fact that many gifted children deliberately choose to avoid excellence and work beneath their capacity (Zorbaugh et al., 1951) also suggests that their high performances pose a threat to others, resulting in punishing interactions and pressures for conformity to more typical performances. Given that comparison-based self-concepts may be responsible for adjustment problems and/or underachievement among gifted children, we suggest the value of developing and encouraging other methods of ability evaluation which emphasize self-mastery instead of peer comparison. Some educational contexts have taken strides in this direction. For example, *norm-referenced* achievement tests, where a given child's score is compared with that of a specified group, have been replaced by *criterion-referenced* tests. The latter reveal what the child can do based on what he or she knows, in absolute terms, rather than in comparison with a norm (Popham & Husek, 1969).

Opinion Evaluation

Thus far, the implications we have discussed focus on social comparison and *ability*. This has been done because developmental research has focused on this form of comparison. However, our analysis can also be extended to the evaluation of *opinions* without much difficulty. Initially, the young child is capable of only egocentric perspective-taking (Piaget, 1958; Chandler & Greenspan, 1972; Selman and Byrne, 1974). The child recognizes that he or she is a different entity from others but does not clearly distinguish between one person's perspective and another's. Flavell (1977) suggests that there is "simply an unreflective Piagetian-type egocentric assumption that for example 'toys are fun' and mother, brother and so on will find toys enjoyable also. In the child's mind there is only *the* reality; there are no personal constructions, or interpretations of reality" (p. 132). Given this situation, young children should believe that others share their opinions—that everyone believes as they do—so social comparison should not be operative. As the child acquires the ability to take others' perspectives, he or she should begin to appreciate that other people *may* disagree and often do disagree. That is, with age the child will become increasingly cognizant of the fact that a variety of perspectives and viewpoints are possible on a large number of issues and problems. In addition, it is likely that the child's increased mobility and larger social network will place him or her in circumstances where differences in opinion are more likely to become obvious than in the earlier phases of his or her life. Finding that there are disagreements should be a disturbing state of affairs for the young child. In particular, the child is probably unlikely to discriminate between similar and dissimilar others on such related attributes as needs, biases, and wishes. Thus, as in the ability realm, the child will initially compare him/herself with *both* similar and dissimilar others. Only when children appreciate that related attributes can affect opinion judgments should they focus on others who should have similar opinions.[1] When evaluating a value, something personally relevant, it is most critical to know the feelings of someone matched in background and experience. Knowing whether X likes ice-cream floats may help you to decide whether you would also like them, as long as you and X both like rich desserts. But knowing Y's reaction to ice cream floats yields little information about the appropriateness of your opinion if Y hates rich desserts. This is because Y's negative reaction could be due to a general distaste for rich desserts or to specific properties of ice cream floats. In contrast, if X had a negative reaction, it can be attributed unambiguously to factors residing specifically in ice cream floats.

Essentially then, our model suggests there are three phases of opinion evaluation. Before the age of five, children are relatively uninterested in testing the "validity" of their opinions. From age five to eight children should become increasingly aware of the fact that others may agree or disagree with them but should be indiscriminate with respect to sources of comparison information (e.g., the opinion of a grandparent may have as much influence as the opinion of a peer). After age eight, the child should become appreciative of the greater relevance of similar others and begin to discount disagreement from others with different backgrounds, goals, and so on.

These three phases of opinion evaluation have implications for the development of conformity behavior. The more often the child compares opinions with others, the more likely he or she is to encounter disagreements. The fact that there are disagreements suggests that the child's own opinion may be invalid and also suggests that a change in opinions may be appropriate. If the child's comparisons reveal a consensus for a particular position, then disagreement with that norm should be particularly disturbing and should motivate change—that is, conformity to the perceived norm. Thus, we can see conformity depends on two things: using comparison to evaluate opinions and observation of a consensual or normative position. It follows that conformity to the opinions of others should increase through age eight. Before the age of five, the child is not using comparison to evaluate opinions, and between the ages of five and eight, the use of indiscriminate comparison is unlikely to reveal consensual tendencies given the diversity of comparison sources (e.g., it is unlikely that same-age peers, parents, or TV stars all have the same opinions on a particular topic). After age eight, the child should increasingly focus on the opinions of peers because they are appreciated as the most relevant form of comparison information. It is interesting in this regard that Cohen, Bornstein, and Sherman (1973) found that their youngest subjects conformed approximately equally to same-age and different-age peers. Older children differentiated between the two. This tendency to attend to one's peers should increase the likelihood of observing consensus among others. After all, it is more likely that same-age peers will have a similar outlook than will a combined group of peers and adults. By eliminating dissimilar others from one's attention, group norms become more obvious and homogeneous. Consequently, we expect perceived consensus to reach a peak when comparison with similar others is fully developed. However, it is unlikely that this peak is maintained, since a heavy emphasis on consensus as a guide to valid opinions will eventually encounter contradictions. As the child comes to rely primarily on consensus from his or her peer group, he or she should increasingly find cases where that consensus is demonstrated to be invalid by authority figures or by experience. In short, the heavy use of comparison to evaluate opinions should reveal its weaknesses and lead to some skepticism as to its value. A peak period of opinion conformity via comparison should be followed by some disillusionment and a downturn in the level of adherence to peer group norms. Using visual discrimination items that were of intermediate ambiguity, Hoving, Hamm, and Colvin (1969) found just such a curvilinear function.

On an overall basis, then, we would expect conformity to increase steadily through age eight to reach a high plateau some time after and then to gradually diminish. Although there are some empirical contradictions (Allen & Newtson, 1972), the main weight of the evidence supports this curvilinear hypothesis (Costanzo & Shaw, 1966a; Iscoe, Williams, & Harvey, 1963; Berndt, 1979). It should be noted that other plausible explanations for this curvilinear function have been advanced (see Shaw, 1976); thus age changes in comparison behavior are probably best viewed as contributing factors for this phenomenon rather than a complete account.

CONCLUSION

In the preceding pages we have described a model of the development of social comparison in children and attempted to outline the processes by which children's comparison behavior gradually begins to approximate the behavior of adults. Subsequently, we reviewed the available empirical evidence and found some support for the model's major arguments. Finally, we explored some of the educational and social psychological implications of the model. While obviously more research is needed, our analysis may have heuristic value for educators and developmental psychologists as well as social psychologists. Finally, by drawing from the developmental, educational, and social psychological literatures, our model suggests the desirability of crossing disciplinary lines in order to gain a fuller understanding of how people evaluate their abilities, traits, and opinions.

NOTE

1. Actually, there is an important distinction to be made between two kinds of opinions: values—approval or disapproval of an entity—versus beliefs—potentially verifiable assertions about the true nature of entities, situations, and so on. As

Goethals and Darley (1977) suggest, similar others may be most appropriate to evaluate value-type opinions, but dissimilar others may be more helpful in determining the veridicality of one's beliefs. By virtue of their differences in terms of related attributes, dissimilar others perceive things from a different perspective. If they still agree with the subject's belief, then this offers added support. After all, as Wheeler and Zuckerman (1977) note, "Coming from two different directions and arriving at the same place makes you more confident that you are at the right place than if one person follows the other" (p. 337). Although we see the belief-value distinction as an important one, it is highly unlikely that young children make or use the distinction. The distinction between beliefs and values probably only is developed when the child enters adolescence and is capable of formal operations, can deal with abstract propositions and conjure up strictly hypothetical possibilities (Inhelder & Piaget, 1958). Even in adolescence and adulthood, the difference between beliefs and values may not make for differences in comparison behavior, since it is difficult in some cases to draw a line between the two types of opinions.

REFERENCES

Albert, S. Temporal comparison theory. *Psychological Review*, 1977, *84*, 485-503.

Allen, V., & Newtson, D. Development of conformity and independence. *Journal of Personality and Social Psychology*, 1972, *22*, 18-30.

Bandura, A. Self-referent thought: The development of self-efficacy. In J. H. Flavell & L. D. Ross (Eds.), *Cognitive social development: Frontiers and possible futures.* New York: Cambridge University Press, 1981.

Bandura, A. The self and mechanisms of agency. In J. Suls (Ed.), *Psychological perspectives on the self* (Vol. 1). Hillsdale, NJ: Lawrence Erlbaum, 1982.

Baumrind, D. Socialization and instrumental competence. *Young Children*, 1970, *26*, 104-119.

Berndt, T. Developmental changes in conformity to peers and parents. *Developmental Psychology*, 1979, *15*, 608-617.

Boggiano, A., & Ruble, D. Competence and the overjustification effect: A developmental study. *Journal of Personality and Social Psychology*, 1979, *37*, 1462-1468.

Brown, A. L. The development of memory: Knowing, knowing about knowing, and knowing how to know. In H. W. Reese (Ed.), *Advances in child development and behavior* (Vol. 10). New York: Academic Press, 1975.

Chandler, M., & Greenspan, S. Ersatz egocentrisum: A reply to H. Borke. *Developmental Psychology*, 1972, *7*, 104-106.

Cohen, R., Bornstein, R., & Sherman, R. C. Conformity behavior of children as a function of group makeup and task ambiguity. *Developmental Psychology*, 1973, *9*, 124-131.

Costanzo, P., & Shaw, M. Conformity as a function of age level. *Child Development*, 1966, *35*, 1217-1231.

DeHaan, R. F., & Havighurst, R. J. *Educating gifted children.* Chicago: University of Chicago Press, 1971.

Dinner, S. Social comparison and self-evaluation in children. *Dissertation Abstracts International*, 1976, *37* (4-B), 1968-1969.

Feld, S., Ruhland, D., & Gold, M. Developmental changes in achievement motivation. *Merrill-Palmer Quarterly*, 1979, *25*, 43-60.

Festinger, L. A theory of social comparison processes. *Human Relations*, 1954, *7*, 117-140.

Flavell, J. *Cognitive development.* Englewood Cliffs, NJ: Prentice-Hall, 1977.

Gardner, J. W. Level of aspiration in response to a prearranged sequence of scores. *Journal of Experimental Psychology*, 1939, *25*, 601-621.

Gastorf, J., & Suls, J. Performance evaluation via social comparison: Performance similarity versus related-attribute similarity. *Social Psychology*, 1978, *41*, 297-305.

Goethals, G. R., & Darley, J. Social comparison theory: An attributional perspective. In J. Suls & R. L. Miller (Eds.), *Social comparison processes: Theoretical and empirical perspectives.* Washington, DC: Hemisphere, 1977.

Grusec, J. E., & Brinker, D. B. Reinforcement for imitation as a social learning determinant with implications for sex-role development. *Journal of Personality and Social Psychology*, 1972, *21*, 149-158.

Harter, S. Effectance motivation reconsidered. *Human Development*, 1978, *21*, 34-64.

Heider, F. *The psychology of interpersonal relations.* New York: John Wiley, 1958.

Hertzman, M., & Festinger, L. Shifts in explicit goals in a level of aspiration experiment. *Journal of Experimental Psychology*, 1940, *27*, 439-452.

Hoppe, F. Erfolg and Misserfolg. *Psychologishe Forschungen*, 1930, *14*, 1-62.

Hoving, K., Hamm, N., & Galvin, P. Social influence as a function of stimulus ambiguity at three age levels. *Developmental Psychology*, 1969, *1*, 631-636.

Iijima, T. An experimental study on the child's conception of numbers. *Japanese Journal of Educational Psychology*, 1965, *13*, 220-233.

Iijima, T. The developmental sequences of child's conceptions of numbers. *Japanese Journal of Educational Psychology*, 1966, *14*, 25-36.

Iijima, T. Number concept in six-year old children. *Japanese Psychological Research*, 1967, *4*, 173-185.

Inhelder, B., & Piaget, J. *The growth of logical thinking from childhood and adolescence.* New York: Basic Books, 1958.

Iscoe, I., Williams, M., & Havey, J. Modification of children's judgments by a simulated group technique: A normative developmental study. *Child Development*, 1963, *34*, 963-978.

Karabenick, J. D., & Heller, K. A. A developmental study of effort and ability attributions. *Developmental Psychology*, 1976, *12*, 559-560.

Karniol, R., & Ross, M. The development of causal attributions in social perception. *Journal of Personality and Social Psychology*, 1976, *34*, 455-464.

Kassin, S., Lowe, C., & Gibbons, F. X. Children's use of the discounting principle: A perceptual approach. *Journal of Personality and Social Psychology*, 1980, *39*, 719-728.

Kelley, H. H. The process of causal attributions. *American Psychologist*, 1973, *28*, 107-128.

Kun, A. Development of the magnitude-covariation and compensation schemata in ability and effort attributions of performance. *Child Development*, 1977, *48*, 862-873.

Latané, B. (Ed.). Studies in social comparison. *Journal of Experimental Social Psychology Supplement*, 1966, *1*, 1-5.

Levine, J. M. Social comparison and education. In J. M. Levine & M. C. Wang (Eds.), *Teacher and student perceptions: Implications for learning*. Hillsdale, NJ: Lawrence Erlbaum, in press.

Lewis, W. D. Some characteristics of very superior children. *Journal of Genetic Psychology*, 1943, *62*, 301-309.

McClintock, C. G., & Moskowitz, J. M. Children's preferences for individualistic, cooperative, and competitive outcomes. *Journal of Personality and Social Psychology*, 1976, *34*, 543-555.

McClintock, C. G., Moskowitz, J. M., & McClintock, E. Variations in preferences for individualistic, competitive, and cooperative outcomes as a function of age, game class, and task in nursery school children. *Child Development*, 1977, *48*, 1080-1085.

Masters, J. C. Effects of social comparisons upon subsequent self-reinforcement behavior in children. *Journal of Personality and Social Psychology*, 1968, *10*, 391-401.

Masters, J. C. Social comparison by young children. *Young Children*, 1971, *27*, 37-60.

Matthews, K., & Siegel, J. The Type A behavior pattern in children and adolescents: Assessment, development, and associated coronary-risk. In A. Baum & J. E. Singer (Eds.), *Handbook of health and medical psychology* (Vol. 2). Hillsdale, NJ: Lawrence Erlbaum, in press.

Miscione, J. L., Marvin, R. S., O'Brien, R. G., & Greenberg, M. T. A developmental study of preschool children's understanding of the words "know" and "guess." *Child Development*, 1978, *49*, 1107-1113.

Nicholls, J. G. The development of the concepts of effort and ability, perceptions of academic attainment, and the understanding that difficult tasks acquire more ability. *Child Development*, 1978, *49*, 800-814.

Pettigrew, T. F. Social evaluation theory: Convergences and applications. In D. Levine (Ed.), *Nebraska symposium on motivation*. Lincoln: University of Nebraska Press, 1967.

Piaget, J. *The language and thought of the child*. New York: World, 1958.

Piaget, J. *The moral judgment of the child*. New York: Free Press, 1965.

Popham, W. J., & Husek, T. R. Implication of criterion referenced measurement. *Journal of Educational Measurement*, 1969, *6*, 1-9.

Radloff, R. Social comparison and ability evaluation. *Journal of Experimental Social Psychology Supplement, 1,* 1966, 6-26.

Rogers, C. M., Smith, M. D., & Coleman, J. M. Social comparison in the classroom: The relationship between academic achievement and self-concept. *Journal of Educational Psychology,* 1978, *70,* 50-57.

Rosenberg, M. *Conceiving the self.* New York: Basic Books, 1979.

Ruble, D. N., Boggiano, A. K., Feldman, N., Loebl, J. H. A developmental analysis of social comparison in self-evaluation. *Developmental Psychology,* 1980, *16,* 105-115.

Ruble, D. N., Feldman, N., & Boggiano, A. Social comparison between young children in achievement situations. *Developmental Psychology,* 1976, *12,* 192-197.

Ruble, D. N., Parsons, J. E., & Ross, J. Self-evaluative responses of children in an achievement setting. *Child Development,* 1976, *47,* 990-997.

Sanders, G. S., Gastorf, J. W., & Mullen, B. Selectivity in the use of social comparison information. *Personality and Social Psychology Bulletin,* 1979, *5,* 377-380.

Sedlak, A., & Kurtz, S. T. A review of children's use of causal inference principles. *Child Development,* 1981, *52,* 759-784.

Selman, R., & Byrne, D. F. A structural-developmental analysis of levels of role taking in middle childhood. *Child Development,* 1974, *45,* 803-806.

Shaklee, H. Development in inferences of ability and task difficulty. *Child Development,* 1976, *47,* 1051-1057.

Shaw, M. *Group dynamics* (2nd ed.). New York: McGraw-Hill, 1976.

Suls, J., Gaes, G., & Gastorf, J. W. Evaluating a sex-related ability: Comparison with same-, opposite-, and combined-sex norms. *Journal of Research in Personality,* 1979, *13,* 294-304.

Suls, J., Gastorf, J. W., & Lawhorn, J. Social comparison choices for evaluating a sex- and age-related ability. *Personality and Social Psychology Bulletin,* 1978, *4,* 102-105.

Suls, J., & Kalle, R. J. Intention, damage, and age of transgression as determinants of children's moral judgments. *Child Development,* 1978, *49,* 1270-1273.

Suls, J., & Miller, R. L. (Eds.). *Social comparison processes: Theoretical and empirical perspectives.* Washington, DC: Hemisphere, 1977.

Tesser, A. Self-esteem maintenance in family dynamics. *Journal of Personality and Social Psychology,* 1980, *38,* 77-91.

Veroff, J. Social comparison and the development of achievement motivation. In C. P. Smith (Ed.), *Achievement-related motives in children.* New York: Russell Sage, 1969.

Weiner, B., & Kun, A. The development of causal attributions and the growth of achievement and social motivation. In S. Feldman & D. Bush (Eds.), *Cognitive development and social development.* Hillsdale, NJ: Lawrence Erlbaum, in press.

Weiss, J., Fischer, C. W., Musella, D., & Traub, R. E. Closure and openness in education. Paper presented at the meeting of the American Educational Research Association, New Orleans, February, 1973.

Wheeler, L. Social comparison and selective affiliation. In T. Huston (Ed.), *Foundations of interpersonal attraction.* New York: Academic Press, 1974.

Wheeler, L., Koestner, R., & Driver, R. E. Related attributes in the choice of comparison others: It's there, but it isn't all there is. *Journal of Experimental Social Psychology,* in press.

Wheeler, L., & Zuckerman, M. Commentary. In J. Suls & R. L. Miller (Eds.), *Social comparison processes: Theoretical and empirical perspectives.* Washington, DC: Hemisphere, 1977.

White, R. W. Motivation reconsidered: The concept of competence. *Psychological Review,* 1959, *66,* 297-333.

Zanna, M., Goethals, G. R., & Hill, J. Evaluating a sex-related ability: Social comparison with similar others and standard setters. *Journal of Experimental Social Psychology,* 1975, *17,* 86-93.

Zorbaugh, H., Boardman, R., & Sheldon, P. Some observations of highly gifted children. In P. Witty (Ed.), *The gifted child.* Lexington, MA: D. C. Heath, 1951.

8

Cognitive Style and Social Behavior:

A REVIEW OF CATEGORY WIDTH

THOMAS F. PETTIGREW

Thomas F. Pettigrew is Professor of Social Psychology at the University of California, Santa Cruz. In addition to interests in social perception, his work focuses on the applications of social psychology to race relations and energy conservation.

What human beings believe is real *is* real in its social consequences. This dictum of W. I. Thomas unites the various wings of social psychology in the discipline's common purpose. Whether symbolic interactionists in sociology, experimental social psychologists in psychology, or contextual social psychologists in both fields (House, 1977; Pettigrew, 1981), members of the discipline seek to relate what individuals think with important social phenomena. Little wonder that social psychology leans toward a rational model of human beings and has traditionally viewed cognitive factors as central concerns.

From this perspective, social psychology is at once macropsychology and microsociology. It is the social science that delineates and studies the various mediators between the individual and social levels of analysis. These explanatory mediators range from role to dissonance. Since the dramatic demonstrations of the importance of situation by Milgram (1963) and others, the discipline has placed particular emphasis on the demand characteristics of structured situations. But in its enthusiasm over the situational shaping of social behavior, social psychology has given less attention to individual differences. And when it considers personality factors, current work utilizes just those variables—such as Rotter's (1966) external-internal locus of control—that fit easily into a situational analysis. The reorganization of the *Journal of Personality and Social Psychology* and the establishment of this annual volume attempt to bring personality and social psychology closer together again.

In this spirit, this chapter focuses on one individual difference measure that has received attention over the past generation. As a cognitive style measure, category width reaches back to the Thomas dictum. If how we perceive reality has direct social consequences, then individual differences in a critical cognitive dimension should be reflected in systematic differences in social behavior. It pursues this notion by reviewing the category width concept, its measurement, and the results of over 125 published empirical studies that used the Category Width (C-W) Scale.[1] I then relate this review to the potential use of category width as an individual differences mediator of significant social psychological phenomena—though here directly relevant research is limited.

THE CONCEPT, PHENOMENON, AND MEASUREMENT OF CATEGORY WIDTH

Category width refers to the range of instances included in a cognitive category. Individuals vary sharply in their category widths. Some invoke "table" only for pieces of furniture with a flat top, four legs, and substantial size. Others categorize as "tables" a diversity of objects that allow other objects to be placed on them. The interesting phenomenon is that people reveal marked consistency in the width of their cognitive categories. It is this individual consistency across categories that establishes category width as a cognitive style dimension and an individual difference variable of interest.

Using such laboratory equipment as audio-oscillators and color mixing wheels, Bruner and Rodrigues (cited by Bruner, Goodnow, & Austin,

1956, p. 28) asked their subjects to select the extremes—the darkest and lightest or highest and lowest—of a variety of categories. For such diverse categories as the brightness of an overcast sky and the pitch of a female singing voice, their subjects tended to be consistently broad, medium, or narrow in their category widths relative to the entire sample. Pettigrew (1958) replicated this phenomenon using similar laboratory tests, then used these data as the criteria with which to validate a paper-and-pencil measure (the C-W Scale).[2] This scale contains 20 items, each of which provides the category mean and asks subjects to estimate the extreme instances:

The average number of churches per religious denomination in the United States is estimated to be *511*. What do you think:

a. is the largest number of churches of a single religious denomination in the U.S. . . .

1. 4,833	(2)	3. 1,219	(1)
2. 757	(0)	4. 39,801	(3)

b. is the smallest number of churches of a single religious denomination in the U.S. . . .

1. 313	(0)	3. 1	(3)
2. 146	(1)	4. 23	(2)

The four fixed alternatives provided for each estimate constitute the tenth, thirty-fifth, sixty-fifth, and ninetieth percentiles of the distribution of estimates by hundreds of American college students responding to an earlier open-ended form of the scale. The score assigned to each alternative is shown in parentheses but of course is not shown on the scale itself. The total score represents the sum of the 40 responses (two each for the 20 items). The disadvantage of the scale is its reliance on quantitative judgments. Wallach and Kogan (1965, p. 99) list its advantages: "The Pettigrew instrument does not allow for the operation of acquiescence or criticalness as styles of responding, and hence may well be a more pure index of category breadth than are those procedures calling for acceptance-rejection responses on the part of subjects."

The consistency phenomenon of category width is shown in the significant concordance in rankings (Kendall's W) across subjects and items and in the high reliabilities reported for the scale. Spearman-Brown corrected split-half reliabilities have ranged from + .83 to + .93 for all 20 items (e.g.,

Pettigrew, 1958; Vick & Jackson, 1967) to + .90 for 14 items (Singer & Roby, 1967) and + .80 for 10 items (Eagly, 1969). The only over-time split-half coefficient reported was + .72 for a six-week interval (Pettigrew, 1958). This consistency is maintained across a varied assortment of categories—from the speed of sailing craft to the annual rainfall in Washington, D.C. One feature all items share, however, is their remoteness from the knowledge and experience of most subjects. Special expertise with a category can determine a category width at variance with an individual's typical style of categorization. In addition, the original work on the C-W Scale uncovered two orthogonal factors that have proven important in later investigations. Factor I had its heaviest weights on nondiscrete estimates of time and speed items; Factor II has its heaviest weights on discrete items such as above—an important distinction in linguistic pragmatics (Channell, 1980, p. 473).

Employing the same type of items, Mascaro (1968a) showed that individual consistency of category widths even extends to attitude-relevant categories. Wallach and Caron (1959) replicated the phenomenon among sixth-grade children with a children's form of the C-W Scale.[3] Detweiler (1978) devised a cross-cultural form of the C-W Scale and studied the phenomenon among the Trukese of the Eastern Caroline Islands in the Pacific. Additional research has been conducted using slightly modified versions of the C-W Scale in Australia, Canada, Egypt, France, India, Ireland, Israel, Poland, the United Kingdom, and West Germany.

THE COGNITIVE IMPORTANCE OF CATEGORY WIDTH

Research with the C-W Scale over the past generation has shown that individual differences in category widths are part of a more general difference in information processing strategies. Broad categorizers are superior on tasks that benefit from a more integrated, holistic strategy; narrows are superior when detailed or analytic processing is required. In a multiattribute learning task, for example, extremely broad categorizers, both female and male, recalled double the number of attributes as extreme narrows, though the rate of learning was the same for the two groups (Parsons, 1973). Questioning at the conclusion of the experiment revealed the explanation. The narrows reported having concentrated on just one attribute—the colors, the shapes, or the nonsense syllables. But the broads reported a rich store of imaginative associations in contrast to the rote approach of the narrows. Similarly, Huang (1981) found that broad subjects better remembered the common features of designs, narrows the variable features, under an unintentional learning instruction set. But such differences tap styles and strategies, not capacities. When Huang's subjects were asked directly to attend to the common features of the designs, there were no differences between broad and narrow categorizers.

A paired-associate transfer of training situation uncovers the liabilities of the broad categorizers' information-processing strategy. Though they possessed equal IQ scores and did just as well in learning the first list of paired associates, broad categorizers had significantly fewer correct responses and more errors of intrusion on the second list (Hart, 1974). In another study of relative size judgments of circles using the method of constant stimuli, narrows demonstrated significantly greater accuracy with or without feedback (Huckabee, 1976). Similarly, Messick and Damarin (1964) found narrow categorizers (as determined by the C-W Scale's Factor I) to have significantly better incidental recall of photographed human faces. As expected, broad categorizers were equally capable of identifying old faces as old; but they also more often identified new faces as old. These same narrow categorizers also revealed better recall for abstract designs (Messick & Pritzky, 1963).[4] Johnson (1974) notes these demonstrations of the superior long-term memory for detailed information by narrows and hypothesizes that there may be even greater short-term memory stores for narrows, though no relevant research has been located.

There may even be hemispheric differentiation between those who typically employ wide or narrow categories. Huang (1979; Huang & Byrne, 1978) offers evidence from both lateral eye movements and dichotic listening abilities that broads depend more than narrows on their right hemisphere, narrow more than broads on their left hemisphere.[5] Medical evidence hints, too, at further organic involvement. Buchsbaum and Henkin (1980) found that patients with Turner's syndrome (45,X lacking one sex chromosome) possess unusually narrow categories. Elias, Chandler, and Winn (1979) found for a small sample of untreated adult hypertensives significant correlations between C-W and both systolic and diastolic blood pressure levels.

Five complementary interpretations of these differential information processing strategies have been studied: *equivalence range, risk taking, developmental, unit size, and cognitive filtering.*

Equivalence and Range Interpretation

The equivalence range interpretation views the C-W Scale as a measure of the breadth of subjective similarity. Broad categorizers possess expansive views of similarity. They see "the big picture" and show less concern with minute differences between stimuli. Narrows are just the opposite; they utilize strict definitions of similarity and concentrate on details. The original C-W paper reported significant relationships between C-W and two other equivalence range measures (Pettigrew, 1958). College subjects who grouped all ten of Rokeach's (1951) political and religious labels under one concept scored higher on C-W than others. In addition, the number of adjectives chosen by students as self-descriptive from the Gough Adjective Check List and C-W scores correlated a modest +.30. Fillenbaum (1959) and Thompson (1968) later obtained similar correlations between self-descriptive attitudes and C-W. Murdoch (1969) reported a strong association between C-W scores and an experimental measure of category width introduced by Bruner and Tajfel (1961). Working with sixth graders, Wallach and Caron (1959) found C-W scores related as expected with several similarity measures.

Empirical and conceptual confusions abound, however, around the idea of equivalence range (Tajfel, Richardson, & Everstine, 1964). The problem lies with the use of markedly different behaviors to measure the same or similar concepts. The C-W Scale requires subjects to specify the limits of a labeled category with its mean supplied. The other popular measure of equivalence range involves sorting an array of objects into one or more unspecified categories. It is not surprising that these indicators usually do not relate strongly. For example, Gardner and Schoen (1962) obtained only low and generally insignificant correlations between an object-sorting task and C-W. Gardner (1953) used both sorting tasks and size-constancy perceptual judgments to measure what he labeled "equivalence range." Yet Sloane, Gorlow, and Jackson (1963) found little relationship between these two types of indicators. Their factor analysis of 20 measures (but not C-W), each presumed to tap equivalence range, yielded a principal factor comprising only object-sorting variables. Finally, Huckabee (1973) failed to generate any significant relationships between the Clayton-Jackson Object-Sorting Task, an English-Nonsense Words Test of "bandwidth," and C-W. Mascaro (1968a), however, did find among male undergraduates a -.59 correlation between C-W and the number of categories used in a sorting test.

Messick and Kogan (1963) clarified the problem by showing that the equivalence range score obtained from object-sorting tasks (the number of groups used by the subject) comprises two distinct components—categories containing two or more objects and the number of objects left ungrouped.

These scores are both reliable and relate differently with other personality and cognitive measures. Using this distinction, Gorman and Wessman (1974) obtain the expected negative relationship between C-W and the number of multiple-object categories used in the Clayton-Jackson Object-Sorting Task. But strong relationships among measures presumed to tap "equivalence range" are yet to be consistently demonstrated. Hence, this review considers only the C-W Scale.

Risk-Taking Interpretation

Another initial view of category width involved risk taking. "Broad categorizers seem to have a tolerance for Type I errors: they risk negative instances in an effort to include a maximum of positive instances. By contrast, narrow categorizers are willing to make Type II errors. They exclude many positive instances by restricting their category ranges in order to minimize the number of negative instances" (Pettigrew, 1958, pp. 532-533). A substantial literature has tested and extended this view, though risk taking is also plagued by multiple indicators that often do not strongly interrelate (Slovic, 1962, 1964).

Bruner and Tajfel (1961), using a laboratory procedure highly correlated with C-W, expanded this risk-taking perspective. Their narrow categorizers were more sensitive to stimulus changes. Broad categorizers "held on" longer. Only when the stimulus situation reached a steady state did narrows return to their characteristic stance and broads begin to respond to the change. "The narrow categorizer," concluded Bruner and Tajfel (1961, p. 241), "appears to prefer the risk of *reacting* and possibly being wrong. The broad categorizer prefers the risk of *not reacting* to change and possibly being wrong."

Neither of these formulations held risk taking to be linearly related to category width. Both specified that broad and narrow categorizers were likely to take contrasting types of risks. Nonetheless, there was an early trend toward considering broad categorizers as generally more risk taking. The similarity of the correlates of both C-W and risk taking stimulated this thinking. Thus, males tend to score higher on the C-W Scale and under many conditions assume greater risks (e.g., Wallach & Caron, 1959; Wallach & Kogan, 1959). Likewise, across cultures the two variables appear to covary positively. Indian students, when compared to Canadian students, for example, scored lower on both the C-W and the Dilemmas

Risk Test (Carment & Alcock, 1976). But further research soon complicated the picture.

The most definitive report is Kogan and Wallach's (1964) *Risk Taking*.
They found that consistencies in risk taking across divergent domains were
more related to their motivational (test anxiety and defensiveness) than
their cognitive variables. Only among low-anxiety and high-defensive
women did category width relate strongly to risk taking in their situation.
And this relationship was negative, not positive. The broad categorizers'
aversion to Type II errors of inclusion related to conservatism for this
group, whereas the narrow's aversion to Type I errors of exclusion related
to risk taking. This finding emerged despite the fact the Kogan-Wallach
risk-taking situation equalized the costs of inclusion and exclusion errors.
Kogan and Wallach (1964, p. 196) argued that this occurs because inclu-
sion-defined classes are more salient, that "to know what something *is*
provides information of a more direct, applicable kind than to know what
something is *not*."

By equalizing payoffs, Kogan and Wallach studied risk-taking preferences rather than strategies (Slovic, 1964). Taking up this point, Touhey
and Mason (1972) failed to find any consistent risk-taking strategies on an
estimation task for broad and narrow categorizers over three levels of
reward. Other investigators have tested the relationship between C-W and
the generalization of expectancies after negative or positive outcomes.
Phares and Davis (1966) looked at the effects of negative bogus feedback
on female college subjects. Broad categorizers lowered their performance
estimates for a second test of attitude prediction significantly more than
narrow categorizers after learning they had done less well than anticipated
on the first test.[6] Touhey (1973) replicated these results using the same
task for another female student sample. He also found that the effects of
positive bogus feedback were reversed. Broad categorizers now increased
their estimate significantly less than narrows after being told they had
done better than expected. In both cases, then, the broad categorizers
adopted the more conservative approach. They reacted more to bad news
and less to good news.

Irish graduate students of business participated in a study of related
interest (Hession & McCarthy, 1975) in which they assessed the subjective
probabilities of 55 "uncertain quantities." Overconfidence in assessment
and C-W scores correlated negatively (-.41); again, the narrows showed
greater confidence in their estimates. Similarly, Singer and Roby (1967)
found that narrow categorizers more often chose risky strategies and
extreme odds on winning bets.

Differential requests for information before making a decision offer another relevant dependent variable. Harris (1971), with male high school subjects, found that broad categorizers requested significantly more information under nonpayoff conditions, though there were no differences with payoffs. Yet Driscoll, Lanzetta, and McMichael (1967) obtained no relationship between C-W and large and consistent individual differences in seeking information under a variety of conditions.

In sum, category width often relates to aspects of risk taking, but these relationships are complex. Laboratory findings are conditioned by the subject's sex and motivation as well as the task involved. We do know that the view of broad categorizers as more generally risk taking is too simple. Over a range of laboratory conditions, it is generally narrow categorizers who react more to change, seek less prior information, and are more confident of their performances.

Yet field research suggests situations where broad categorizers are more risk taking. Donnelly and his colleagues (Donnelly & Etzel, 1973; Donnelly, Etzel, & Roeth, 1973) report that broadly tuned housewives were more likely to be early adopters of "genuinely new" products (e.g., coffee bags), narrowly tuned housewives more likely to adopt "artificially new" products (e.g., instant oatmeal). Conceptual and methodological problems, however, mar this work (Ostlund & Tellefsen, 1974). But these field findings are consistent with studies showing that extremely broad categorizers score higher than extremely narrow categorizers on a measure of the search for a variety of experience (Taylor & Levitt, 1967; Farley, Peterson, & Whalen, 1974). Hence, these results deserve rigorous testing and linkage with the conflicting work from the laboratory.

Developmental Interpretation and Sex Differences

Since the C-W Scale requires quantitative judgments, it is unsuitable for use at early ages. But on sorting tasks, equivalence ranges appear to expand with age, consistent with the general developmental shift from a focus on perceptual differences toward conceptually based abstractions and synthesis (Kogan, 1976, chap. 4). But one cross-sectional study using the C-W for children from seven to eleven years of age obtained the opposite trend (Penk, 1969, 1971).

Little is known about families that rear extremely broad and narrow categorizers. Two studies report that high scorers on the C-W have better-educated parents than low scorers (Singer & Roby, 1967; Messick & Kogan, 1966). Another finds that broad college students more often rate their mothers as "cold" and their fathers as less "strict" (Pedersen, 1965).

The important point is that "category breadth may not have the same psychological significance in early childhood, later childhood, and young adulthood" (Kogan, 1976, p. 82). Yet initial results from the Blocks' (1973) longitudinal study are of special interest. The Blocks, using a composite category width measure that did not include the C-W, had teachers rate four-year-olds on classroom behavior. They ranked broad categorizers far more negatively than narrows—for example, reacting poorly to stress, undependable, aggressive, and emotionally labile. The Blocks' category width measure predicted more for female than male subjects. This finding is consistent with the Kogan and Wallach (1964) results on risk taking in which C-W predicted better for women. Later testing of the Blocks' sample includes the C-W Scale.

Such sex differences pervade the C-W literature and are principally responsible for developmental interpretations of category width. Most studies at all ages show appreciably higher C-W scores for males than females. Indeed, Wallach and Kogan (1965, p. 124) describe this finding as "apparently one of the most stable in the cognitive-and-personality literature."[7] Some writers suggest that the mean differences by sex are an artifact of the quantitative nature of the C-W Scale. Others speculate that they accurately reflect differential socialization practices in the culture. One promising explanatory possibility was advanced by Kogan and Wallach (1964, p. 150). They presented evidence to suggest that the C-W Scale: "taps somewhat different dimensions in the two sexes—more strictly cognitive in males, more motivational in females." Later work by Crandall (1965) supports this view. Thus, Crandall showed that male subjects took more risks on a conceptual task, but females took more risks on an evaluative task. Moreover, anxiety operated in opposite ways for the two sexes. Highly anxious men were more conservative than less anxious men, while highly anxious women were less conservative than less anxious women. This line of research deserves further attention.

Unit Size Interpretation and
Quantitative Ability Differences

An ingenious interpretation derives from Upshaw's perspective theory emphasis on the relation between scale range and unit size. Murdoch (1969) asked male college students to estimate line lengths on a numerical scale having only an anchor labeled "200 units." He showed that categorizing broadly reflected a style or response language rather than any motivational deficit or inability to discriminate among the stimuli. Broad categorizers, for Murdoch, consider wider stimulus ranges than narrows and then adopt broader judgmental scales. Upshaw (1970) showed the reverse sequence is also possible—unit size manipulation results in concomitant variation in category width. He devised two-open-ended forms of the C-W Scale containing different size units for the same items. Larger units (months, minutes, gallons) consistently led to broader categories than smaller units (weeks, seconds, quarts). Hence, broad categorizers may view culturally prescribed units as larger than narrows and consequently adopt wider categories.

Such a unit size preference is consistent with the oft-noted relationship between C-W and quantitative test scores. The original C-W paper reported a significant correlation between the ACE quantitative test score (+.26) but none for the ACE linguistic test score (+.07) (Pettigrew, 1958, p. 537). This quantitative relationship was strongest for Factor I. Later studies obtained similar correlations, though they found a larger association with Factor II (Messick & Kogan, 1965; Pedersen, 1965; Vannoy, 1965; Rogers, 1973).[8]

This persistent relationship raises several possibilities. It could be an artifact of the C-W Scale's emphasis on quantitative judgment. It could reflect a genuine phenomenon of highly quantitative individuals categorizing their environment broadly. It could also be a result of multiple-choice tests of quantitative ability that lend themselves to the information-processing strategies of broad categorizers. Messick and Kogan (1965) explored this third possibility by presenting their male college subjects with three different types of quantitative tests: a free response version, a multiple-choice version with widely spaced alternatives, and a multiple-choice version with narrowly spaced alternatives. Indeed, broad categorizers did significantly better on the widely spaced alternative test but no better on the narrowly spaced alternative test. These results suggest that broad categorizers use an "approximation strategy" that benefits them in quantitative tests that employ widely spaced response alternatives. But this factor does not explain the full relationship between C-W and quantitative test scores, for Messick and Kogan obtained the typical relationship (+.29) between C-W's factor II and the free-response test.

Cognitive Filtering Interpretation

Finally, Silverman (1964) has proposed a cognitive filtering interpretation of narrow categorizers. Individuals can form extremely narrow perceptual categories in order to minimize awareness of external threats. And under conditions of profound aversiveness, narrow categorizing can generalize to all classes of stimuli. Silverman (1964) demonstrated in two independent samples that chronic paranoid schizophrenics were significantly narrower than other schizophrenics. Moore (1971) replicated this result and also showed that reactive schizophrenics possessed narrower categories than patients with character disorders. And Silverman, Berg, and Kantor (1966) found that San Quentin prisoners, especially new arrivals, evinced unusually low C-W scores.

FACTORIAL STUDIES USING THE C-W SCALE

Factor analyses are a popular means to seek data reduction and theoretical clarity. Fourteen such studies threw the C-W Scale into their undifferentiated brews. Their results shed some light on both cognitive and personality correlates of category width.

Cognitive Correlates of the C-W Scale

There have been repeated attempts to subsume category width under the larger concept of "cognitive complexity" but with little success (e.g., Vannoy, 1965; Poole, 1978). Only Wiedl (1976), working with West German high school students, has shown a "preference for extreme manifestations" of "complexity" among broad categorizers. Cognitive complexity defies unidimensional scaling; and category width itself is factorially complicated. Once again, sex differences underlie the complications. When Otteson (1980) analyzed an array of cognitive and personality variables, he isolated a separate factor for the C-W scores of male undergraduates. But for female undergraduates, C-W scores possessed significant weights on two factors with other variables—positive on a flexibility factor and negative on a dogmatism factor.[9]

But factorial research has uncovered some cognitive variables with which C-W scores modestly relate. Positive correlates include the Watson-Glaser Critical Thinking Appraisal Test (Singer & Roby, 1967) and a measure of inductive ability (Federico & Landis, 1979, 1980). Negative correlates include three different versions of "cognitive complexity" (Vannoy, 1965; Federico & Landis, 1979, 1980).

Personality Correlates of the C-W Scale

Complications arise here, too. Such obvious possibilities as the MMPI scales apparently do not relate to C-W scores (Cunningham, 1969). The factorial structure once again must be separated by sex. Thus, Messick and Kogan (1966) found that narrow males tended to be somewhat cautious, "rigid," and confident in cognitive judgments. Narrow females, by contrast, tended to be impulsive, flexible, and acquiescent.

Yet there is some consistency across investigations. Narrows generally reflect what Singer and Roby (1967) label "intellectual passivity." They appear to value thinking less than broad categorizers (Pedersen, 1965; Singer & Roby, 1967). Gorman and Wessman (1974) also find that narrows show "a constricted sense of time and temporal perspective"—as tapped by the Calabresi-Cohen Time Attitude Scales. By comparison, broad categorizers show more independence of judgment (Vannoy, 1965), needs for "freedom" (Singer & Roby, 1967), and variety of experience (Taylor & Levitt, 1967; Farley, Peterson, & Whalen, 1974).

CATEGORY WIDTH AND CREATIVITY

Research on creativity has applied the C-W Scale more thoroughly than any other area with straightforward results. Broad categorizing contributes to the creative process in several ways—affective responsiveness, vivid imagery, use of metaphors, and divergent thinking.

For a sample of 100 young children of both sexes, Penk (1969) found a small but significantly positive correlation between C-W scores and color responses to inkblots—an indicator of emotional responsiveness. Richardson (1977) found C-W scores to be positively associated with imagery for female, but not male, British college students. C-W correlated with vivid imagery (+.45) and habitual use of imagery (+.39). Similarly, Kogan and his colleagues (Kogan et al., 1980, chap. 4) obtained significant correlations between C-W and their new Metaphoric Triads Task among both young female (+.27) and male (+.40) adults.

Anderson (1966) proposed a "stop-rule theory" for originality in which category width plays a prominent role. Those who most effectively internalize a culture's "code for processing information in a convergent way" are less likely to engage in divergent thinking. From this view, narrow categorizers have more fully adopted the stop rules, the do's and don'ts of a culture. Broad categorizers use the stop rules less. Anderson's contentions help explain why, for instance, narrows typically achieve more than equally intelligent broads in school—where the stop rules of thought are taught and rewarded—and why broad categorizers typically score higher on tests of divergent thinking. Thus, narrows attain higher academic achievement in elementary and secondary schools than broad categorizers of equivalent IQ (Letteri, 1980)—even in high school science in Australia (Cropley & Field, 1969). Consistent with this are the results from an investigation of Israeli college students using Rokeach's value instrument (Rim, 1970). Narrow categorizes more highly valued "intellectual" and "broadminded" (!) goals, while broad categorizers more highly valued "inner harmony."

Anderson and Cropley (1966) administered convergent (IQ), divergent, and nonintellective (including C-W) measures to 320 Canadian seventh graders. Originality, as gauged by such divergent thinking tests as Torrance's Tin Can procedure, related positively to standard IQ indices and socioeconomic class. But once these factors were controlled, divergent thinking was positively associated with C-W and risk taking. Martindale (1972) tested Harvard University undergraduates with Mednick's Remote Associates Test (RAT). He found that among the top half of RAT scorers (but not among the bottom half) that this measure correlated positively with an array of "indices of primitive thought processes" drawn from the TAT, dream reports, and the C-W Scale (+.39). A cross-cultural replication of this general finding involved male students at Egypt's University of Cairo (Ibrahim, 1976). Three tests of divergent thinking—the Link Together Test, Consequences Test, and Plot Titles—all correlated positively and significantly with C-W scores among men. But no such relationship emerged for the female students.

Wallach and Kogan (1965) conducted the most extensive research on the phenomenon. They individually administered to 151 fifth grade boys and girls three verbal and two visual indicators of "creativity." Basically, their composite creativity index tapped divergent thinking by measuring both the number and the uniqueness of the children's responses to these five "games." Wallach and Kogan crossed this creativity index with an intelligence indicator and tested it against other measures, including the children's C-W Scale. For the boys, C-W related to creativity (p <.08) but not to intelligence. Three of the cells were virtually identical; only the low-intelligent, low-creativity boys were conspicuously narrow in their categorizing. For the girls, C-W significantly related to creativity (p <.05) but, again, not to intelligence. Here both high-creative cells categorized broadly, both low-creative cells narrowly. The lack of association between C-W and measured intelligence is a general finding. But Wallach and Kogan (1965, p. 129) showed further that there is no interaction between creativity and intelligence underlying category width.[10]

APPLICATIONS TO SOCIAL PSYCHOLOGY

Though there are few relevant studies in social psychology, this review suggests many potential applications of category width as a mediator of social phenomena. Three areas particularly suggest themselves—dissonance reduction and conformity, small group effects, and social comparison and evaluation.

Dissonance Reduction and Conformity

Research has routinely uncovered large individual differences in social influence. But social psychology has rarely attempted to explain them. Berkowitz (1960) suggested that category width might afford an explanation; and work by Rosen (1961) supported him. On the first day of class, undergraduates made a choice between taking an essay or an objective examination. They were next presented with an annotated listing of three pro-essay and three pro-objective articles and asked to rank their reading preferences. The combined sample showed the predicted dissonance-reducing desire to read pro-decision articles. And among the male subjects, narrow categorizers significantly more often sought information to support their choice. Rosen's female subjects scored significantly lower on C-W and did not show the phenomenon.

Eagly (1969) obtained similar results with a different design. Undergraduates heard a tape-recorded communication about student responsibility. The communicator was prestigious, the attitudinal discrepancy moderate in size. Eagly found an interaction, not a main effect, in predicting attitude change. Males who were both narrow categorizers and intolerant of inconsistency changed their attitudes toward the communication more than others. There was no difference in attitude change between narrows and broads among males tolerant of inconsistency; but there was a large difference among those intolerant of inconsistency. In another investigation, Eagly and Telaak (1972) varied communication discrepancy on birth control issues. Narrow categorizers once again changed their attitudes more than medium or broad categorizers; indeed, as a group the narrows were the only net changers of attitudes. This time the effects held for females as well as males.

Two complementary explanations have been advanced for this persistent finding—one motivational, the other cognitive. Eagly (1969) holds that narrow categorizers have a greater need to resolve inconsistency and consequently respond more intensely by any available means to reduce discrepancy. Another possibility is that broad categorizers do not perceive the discrepancy as sharply. In Berkowitz'a (1960) terms, the broads "assimilate" differences. Sensing less dissonance, broads may simply have less reason to reduce it.

Two relevant studies by Steiner and his colleagues lend credence to both of these explanations. Broad and narrow categorizers responded quite differently to an experimentally created conflict situation (Steiner & Johnson, 1965). Broads tended to underrecall disagreements with accomplices (+.51); narrows tended to conform by agreeing with the accomplices (−.78). Steiner and Vannoy (1966) tested this conforming trend further with male undergraduates. They distinguished between "renouncers" (conformed in the laboratory, but did not repeat conforming responses later in a private situation) and "reaffirmers" (conformed in both situations). The truly influenced, the reaffirmers, scored significantly lower on the C-W than the renouncers.

A third type of explanation for these findings, based on social judgment theory (Sherif & Hovland, 1961), involves the possible influence of category width on latitudes of acceptance. If one thinks of such latitudes as relatively consistent across issues, then they could "profitably be viewed as a personality trait" systematically related to category width (Miller, 1965, p. 131). Plausible as such a theoretical link appears, research on the topic has not supported it.

In a rough test, Mascaro (1968b) related the C-W scores of male undergraduates to their latitudes of acceptance, indifference, and rejection on attitudes toward the Vietnam war. He found no relationships. Eagly and Telaak (1972) also found no relationship between their subjects' C-W scores and latitudes of acceptance, even though C-W related significantly with attitude change. Indeed, in both this and the Eagly (1969) experiments, it was *narrow* categorizers who over time increasingly assimilated the message and evaluated the communicator more highly—both dissonance-reducing mechanisms that legitimate attitude change and conformity. Eagly and Telaak (1972, p. 396) summed it up:

> Accordingly, latitude width and category width apparently function along rather different lines. While latitude of acceptance width is an issue-specific index of influence-ability, category width has related to response to several issues across widely divergent experimental situations. Category width apparently assesses a very general disposition of the person—the strength of the tendency to resolve inconsist-

ency by whatever responses are salient in a given situation. Thus, latitude of acceptance width and category width have a phenotypic similarity if one thinks of both of them as assessing the range of discriminably different events considered exemplars of a category. But their impact works in opposite directions (since *narrow* category width but a *wide* latitude of acceptance increase attitude change) and arises from different sources.

Small Group Effects

Vidmar (1974) introduced the C-W Scale into the study of "risky shift." He ran two experiments with the standard risky shift design of pregroup, group, and postgroup decisions. For both male and female subjects, C-W scores increased sharply after a group discussion about category width items. These increases were greatest for those who were initially the narrowest categorizers—again showing the narrows' tendencies to conform and to be more attuned to environmental change. The increases in C-W scores were maintained in the postgroup decision. Control groups, working on movie plots, witnessed no such changes. A second experiment failed to support Brown's (1965) social comparison explanation for the risky shift phenomenon. Prior to the discussion subjects tended to view others as broader, not narrower, than themselves. Vidmar's findings shed light on the dynamics of group shifts and suggest that task-oriented groups may exhibit a press toward broad categorizing. Research on how groups process information, categorize agenda items, and handle Type I and Type II errors might utilize the C-W Scale. If shifts toward broad categorizing characterize such groups, Type I errors may be tolerated in favor of minimizing Type II errors.

Other small group phenomena relate to category width. Zeidenross-Kuvat and Rim (1977) used a Hebrew translation of the C-W Scale in Israel to test Fiedler's contingency model of leadership in changing situations. Based on the findings of Bruner and Tajfel (1961) described earlier, they demonstrated that category width is an important personality characteristic in leadership effectiveness in unstable groups.

Social Comparison and Evaluation

An unexplored area of application of the C-W Scale is in social comparison research. The key contention is that under a wide range of conditions similar others will be preferred for comparisons. But since individuals differ widely in their conception of "similar," the C-W Scale could specify more precisely this fundamental perception.

This application extends beyond comparison theory to the entire family of social evaluation conceptions—equity theory, relative deprivation, reference group theory, and so on (Pettigrew, 1967). The practical significance of all these conceptions rests on prior specification of the referent. Were category width to contribute to this specification, it would aid both theory and application. Consider the social psychological dynamics underlying group protest and revolt. Social evaluation considerations hold that initiators of a protest movement must somehow break out of the typical pattern of intragroup comparisons and make comparisons with the outgroup. Militant blacks in the 1960s stopped relying exclusively on black comparisons to judge their rights and opportunities. Instead they began to demand equality defined by new white comparisons (Pettigrew, 1964, 1971).

Our review suggests that category width might mediate this process in interesting ways. Broad categorizers may more readily transfer their comparisons to more distant referents; but narrow categorizers might first detect social changes occurring in intergroup relations around them. To learn how these competing tendencies unfold during the emergence of a social movement will require longitudinal research.

The utility of the C-W Scale extends to the many realms in the discipline where subjectively defined similarity is important—such as altruism, interpersonal attraction, and group formation and cohesiveness. And as the research on consumer acceptance of new products suggests (Donnelly & Etzel, 1973; Donnelly et al., 1973), broad categorizing may be a necessary (but not sufficient) condition for early adopters of innovations (Rogers & Shoemaker, 1971, pp. 176-191).

A FINAL WORD

Emphases on individual differences in the past often obscured the importance of the social context. Attention to differences in authoritarianism as an explanation for racial prejudice, for instance, blinded social psychology during the 1950s to the importance of situation, social structure, and culture (Pettigrew, 1961). But social psychology is now more sophisticated. The argument advanced here does not pit individual differences against structural factors. Rather, it argues that social psychology can benefit from a renewed interest in individual differences by viewing them as one type of mediator of social behavior and processes fully enmeshed in a social context.

Category width is an example of an individual difference variable close to social psychological concerns through its connection with cognition. Applications are cited in dissonance-reduction, conformity, group effects, and social comparison areas. Speculations on further applications of category width could easily be extended. But the point to underline is that category width—as an individual differences variable—could potentially contribute to the specification of such critical links in major theories as the actual perception of dissonance and the selection of the comparison referent.

NOTES

1. The author is preparing a meta-analysis review of the category width research literature, together with a complete bibliography.

2. The rank order correlation between the C-W Scale and the criterion rankings was +.57 (p < .01). Pettigrew (1958) provides the full scale.

3. Wallach and Kogan (1965, pp. 112-115) reprint the children's C-W Scale.

4. Bieri (1969) reports a lone exception to these more general findings. In judging the length of lines in a quiet room, broad categorizers discriminated significantly better than narrows. In a noisy condition, there were no differences. The critical difference is probably that Bieri removed the possibility of intrusive and overinclusive errors that hurt the broads' performance in the three studies cited.

5. The results of these studies were not identical. The dichotic listening experiment (Huang, 1979) found that broad and narrow categorizers recalled equal numbers of words presented to the right ear; but broads recalled more of those presented to the left ear (i.e., right hemisphere). Both broads and narrows, however, favored their right to left ears. In the lateral eye movement (LEM) study (Huang & Byrne, 1978), narrows made significantly more right than left LEMs, but broads were directed equally to the right and left. Two other cautions are in order. Only female subjects were used in both studies. This is an important limitation, for Otteson (1980) obtained a positive association between broad categorizing and left LEMs for female but not male subjects. Finally, the connection between LEMs and hemispheric asymmetry is by no means solidly established (Ehrlichman & Weinberger, 1978).

6. These results may be limited to the particular task and/or female subjects. Huckabee (1976) did not replicate with a perceptual accuracy task and a sample that apparently included males.

7. A few studies with unusually low male averages report no sex differences on C-W (e.g., Penk, 1969; Feather, 1967a, 1967b).

8. Here, too, there are rare studies that have not uncovered the C-W and quantitative correlation (e.g., Kogan & Wallach, 1964).

9. It is unusual to find even a modest association between dogmatism and C-W. Starting with the original paper (Pettigrew, 1958), other researchers have found a surprising absence of any relationship between C-W and dogmatism, authoritarianism, and related syndromes.

10. Cronbach (1968) provides an interesting reanalysis of these data. The significant C-W and creativity correlation remains, however, even after Cronbach pools data from the two sexes. He offers the intriguing suggestion of a C-W factor analysis that attempts to separate realistic from implausible responses by treating each boundary choice as a separate item (rather than combining each item's two choices). Actually, research on C-W variability has been conducted. Higgins, Peterson, and Dolby (1968) have shown that C-W variance scores relate to inconsistency in aesthetic preferences for TAT cards (+.45). C-W variance is negatively associated with intelligence and unrelated to willingness to participate in another psychological experiment.

REFERENCES

Anderson, C. C. A cognitive theory of the nonintellective correlates of originality. *Behavioral Science,* 1966, *11,* 284-294.

Anderson, C. C., & Cropley, A. J. Some correlates of originality. *Australian Journal of Psychology,* 1966, *18,* 218-227.

Berkowitz, L. The judgmental process in personality functioning. *Psychological Review,* 1960, *67,* 130-142.

Bieri, J. Category width as a measure of discrimination. *Journal of Personality,* 1969, *37,* 513-521.

Block, J., & Block, J. H. *Ego development and provenance of thought.* National Institute of Mental Health Progress Report (Grant No. M. H. 16080), University of California, Berkeley, 1973.

Brown, R. *Social psychology.* New York: Free Press, 1965.

Bruner, J. S., Goodnow, J. J., & Austin, G. A. *A study of thinking.* New York: John Wiley, 1956.

Bruner, J. S., & Tajfel, H. Cognitive risk and environmental change. *Journal of Abnormal and Social Psychology,* 1961, *62,* 231-241.

Buchsbaum, M. S., & Henkin, R. I. Perceptual abnormalities in patients with chromatin negative gonadal dysgenesis and hypogonadotropic hypogonadism. *International Journal of Neuroscience,* 1980, *11,* 201-209.

Carment, D. W., & Alcock, J. E. Some psychometric correlates of behavior in India and Canada. *International Journal of Psychology,* 1976, *11,* 57-64.

Channell, J. More on approximations: A reply to Wachtel. *Journal of Pragmatics,* 1980, *4,* 461-476.

Crandall, J. E. Some relationships among sex, anxiety, and conservatism of judgment. *Journal of Personality,* 1965, *33,* 99-107.

Cronbach, L. J. Intelligence? Creativity? A parsimonious reinterpretation of the Wallach-Kogan data. *American Educational Research Journal,* 1968, *5,* 491-511.

Cropley, A. J., & Field, T. W. Achievement in science and intellectual style. *Journal of Applied Psychology,* 1969, *53,* 132-135.

Cunningham, A. P. Cognitive controls and measures of personality. Unpublished doctoral dissertation, University of Kentucky, 1969.

Detweiler, R. A. Culture, category width, and attributions. *Journal of Cross-Cultural Psychology,* 1978, *9,* 259-285.

Donnelly, J. H., Jr., & Etzel, M. J. Degrees of product newness and early trial. *Journal of Marketing Research,*1973, *10,* 295-300.

Donnelly, J. H., Jr., Etzel, M. J., & Roeth, S. The relationship between consumers' category width and trial of new products. *Journal of Applied Psychology,* 1973, *57,* 335-338.

Driscoll, J. M., Lanzetta, J. T., & McMichael, J. S. Preference for information under varying conditions of outcome uncertainty, intensity, and delay. *Psychological Reports,* 1967, *21,* 473-479.

Eagly, A. H. Responses to attitude-discrepant information as a function of intolerance of inconsistency and category width. *Journal of Personality,* 1969, *37,* 601-617.

Eagly, A. E., & Telaak, K. Width of the latitude of acceptance as a determinant of attitude change. *Journal of Personality and Social Psychology,* 1972, *23,* 388-397.

Ehrlichman, H., & Weinberger, A. Lateral eye movements and hemispheric asymmetry: A critical review. *Psychological Bulletin,* 1978, *85,* 1080-1101.

Elias, J. W., Chandler, C. K. & Winn, F. J. Category width as a measure of cognitive style and a personality correlate to hypertension. *Social Science & Medicine,* 1979, *13A,* 343-345.

Farley, F. H., Peterson, J. M., & Whalen, T. J. The stimulation-seeking motive: Relationship to conceptual category width. *Bulletin of the Psychonomic Society,* 1974, *3,* 449-451.

Feather, N. T. Evaluation of religious and neutral arguments in religious and atheist student groups. *Australian Journal of Psychology,* 1967, *19,* 3-12. (a)

Feather, N. T. Level of aspiration and performance variability. *Journal of Personality and Social Psychology,* 1967, *6,* 37-46. (b)

Federico, P., & Landis, D. B. *Discriminating between failures and graduates in a computer-managed course using measures of cognitive styles, abilities, and aptitudes.* San Diego, CA: Navy Personnel Research and Development Center, 1979.

Federico, P., & Landis, D. B. *Relationships among selected measures of cognitive styles, abilities, and aptitudes.* San Diego, CA: Navy Personnel Research and Development Center, 1980.

Fillenbaum, S. Some stylistic aspects of categorizing behavior. *Journal of Personality,* 1959, *27,* 187-195.

Gardner, R. W. Cognitive styles in categorizing behavior. *Journal of Personality*, 1953, *22*, 214-233.

Gardner, R. W., & Schoen, R. A. Differentiation and abstraction in concept formation. *Psychological Monographs*, 1962, *76*, No. 41 (Whole No. 560).

Gorman, B. S., & Wessman, A. E. The relationship of cognitive styles and moods. *Journal of Clinical Psychology*, 1974, *30*, 18-25.

Harris, B. Personality factors and information demand in decision making: The influence of category width, the need to achieve, fear of failure, utility of reward, and payoff on information demand on an expanded judgment task. Unpublished doctoral dissertation, New York University, 1970.

Hart, J. J. Interference in a paired-associate transfer of training paradigm as a function of breadth of categorization. *Psychological Reports*, 1974, *34*, 167-173.

Hession, E., & McCarthy, E. Human performance in assessing subjective probability distributions. *Irish Journal of Psychology*, 1975, *3*, 31-46.

Higgins, J., Peterson, J. C., & Dolby, L. L. Variability in cognitive control. *British Journal of Psychology*, 1968, *59*, 127-129.

House, J. S. The three faces of social psychology. *Sociometry*, 1977, *40*, 161-177.

Huang, M. Hemispheric differentiation and category width. *Cortex*, 1979, *15*, 531-539.

Huang, M. Category width and individual differences in information processing strategies. *Journal of Psychology*, 1981, *108*, 73-79.

Huang, M., & Byrne, B. Cognitive style and lateral eye movements. *British Journal of Psychology*, 1978, *69*, 85-90.

Huckabee, M. W. On non-equivalence of equivalence range measures. *Perceptual and Motor Skills*, 1973, *36*, 541-542.

Huckabee, M. W. Category width, confidence, expectancies, and perceptual accuracy. *Bulletin of the Psychonomic Society*, 1976, *8*, 19-21.

Ibrahim, A. Sex differences, originality, and personality response styles. *Psychological Reports*, 1976, *39*, 859-868.

Johnson, J. H. Memory and personality: An information processing approach. *Journal of Research in Personality*, 1974, *8*, 1-32.

Kogan, N. *Cognitive styles in infancy and early childhood*. Hillsdale, NJ: Lawrence Erlbaum, 1976.

Kogan, N., Connor, K., Gross, A., & Fava, D. Understanding visual metaphor: Developmental and individual differences. *Monographs of the Society for Research in Child Development*, 1980, *45*, No. 1 (Serial No. 183).

Kogan, N., & Wallach, M. A. *Risk taking: A study in cognition and personality*. New York: Holt, Rinehart & Winston, 1964.

Letteri, C. A. Cognitive profile: Basic determinant of academic achievement. *Journal of Educational Research*, 1980, *73*, 195-199.

Martindale, C. Anxiety, intelligence, and access to primitive modes of thought in high and low scorers on The Remote Associates Test. *Perceptual and Motor Skills*, 1972, *35*, 375-381.

Mascaro, G. F. Categorization strategies across different domains. *Perceptual and Motor Skills*, 1968, *26*, 1091-1097. (a)

Mascaro, G. F. Category-width tendencies and acceptance of attitude statements. *Perceptual and Motor Skills,* 1968, *27,* 410. (b)

Messick, S., & Damarin, F. Cognitive styles and memory for faces. *Journal of Abnormal and Social Psychology,* 1964, *69,* 313-318.

Messick, S., & Fritzky, F. J. Dimensions of analytic attitude in cognition and personality. *Journal of Personality,* 1963, *31,* 346-370.

Messick, S., & Kogan, N. Differentiation and compartmentalization in object-sorting measures of categorizing style. *Perceptual and Motor Skills,* 1963, *16,* 47-51.

Messick, S., & Kogan, N. Category width and quantitative aptitude. *Perceptual and Motor Skills,* 1965, *20,* 493-497.

Messick, S., & Kogan, N. Personality consistencies in judgment: Dimensions of role constructs. *Multivariate Behavioral Research,* 1966, *1,* 165-175.

Milgram, S. Behavioral study of obedience. *Journal of Abnormal and Social Psychology,* 1963, *67,* 371-378.

Miller, N. Involvement and dogmatism as inhibitors of attitude change. *Journal of Experimental Social Psychology,* 1965, *1,* 121-132.

Moore, N. I. Cognitive styles and the schizophrenias and character disorders. *Perceptual and Motor Skills,* 1971, *33,* 475-482.

Murdoch, P. Effects of perspective and payment on reference scale formation. *Journal of Experimental Research in Personality,* 1969, *3,* 301-310.

Ostlund, L. E., & Tellefsen, B. Relationship between consumers' category width and trial of new products: A reappraisal. *Journal of Applied Psychology,* 1974, *59,* 759-760.

Otteson, J. P. Stylistic and personality correlates of lateral eye movements: A factor analytic study. *Perceptual and Motor Skills,* 1980, *50,* 995-1010.

Parsons, R. J. Category width and the learning of multiattribute paired associates. *Journal of General Psychology,* 1973, *89,* 133-140.

Pedersen, D. M. The measurement of individual differences in perceived personality-trait relationships and their relation to certain determinants. *Journal of Social Psychology,* 1965, *65,* 233-258.

Penk, W. Two measures of category width: Age, sex, examiner differences and intercorrelations. *Psychological Reports,* 1969, *25,* 859-870.

Penk, W. Developmental patterns of conceptual styles. *Psychological Reports,* 1971, *29,* 635-649.

Pettigrew, T. F. The measurement and correlates of category width as a cognitive variable. *Journal of Personality,* 1958, *26,* 532-544.

Pettigrew, T. F. Social psychology and desegregation research. *American Psychologist,* 1961, *16,* 105-112.

Pettigrew, T. F. *A profile of the Negro American.* New York: Van Nostrand, 1964.

Pettigrew, T. F. Social evaluation theory: Convergences and applications. In D. Levine (Ed.), *Nebraska Symposium on Motivation, 1967.* Lincoln: University of Nebraska Press, 1967.

Pettigrew, T. F. *Racially separate or together?* New York: McGraw-Hill, 1971.

Pettigrew, T. F. Extending the stereotype concept. In D. L. Hamilton (Ed.), *Cognitive processes in stereotyping and intergroup behavior.* Hillsdale, NJ: Lawrence Erlbaum, 1981.

Phares, E. J., & Davis, W. L. Breadth of categorization and the generalization of expectancies. *Journal of Personality and Social Psychology*, 1966, *4*, 461-464.

Poole, M. E. Cognitive style and verbal processing strategies: Interdomain analyses. *Journal of Psychology*, 1978, *98*, 215-223.

Richardson, A. The meaning and measurement of memory imagery. *British Journal of Psychology*, 1977, *68*, 29-43.

Rim, Y. Values, cognitive width, external-internal control and tendency to increase performance. *Psychologia*, 1970, *13*, 223-226.

Rogers, E. M., & Shoemaker, F. F. *Communication of innovations: A cross-cultural approach* (2nd ed.). New York: Free Press, 1971.

Rogers, R. I. Category width and decision making in perception. *Perceptual and Motor Skills*, 1973, *37*, 647-652.

Rokeach, M. A method for studying individual differences in "narrow-mindedness." *Journal of Personality*, 1951, *20*, 219-233.

Rosen, S. Postdecision affinity for incompatible information. *Journal of Abnormal and Social Psychology*, 1961, *63*, 188-190.

Rotter, J. B. Generalized expectancies for internal versus external control of reinforcement. *Psychological Monographs*, 1966, *80*, No. 1 (Whole No. 609).

Sherif, M., & Hovland, C. *Social judgment.* New Haven, CT: Yale University Press, 1961.

Silverman, J. Scanning-control mechanisms and "cognitive filtering" in paranoid and non-paranoid schizophrenia. *Journal of Consulting Psychology*, 1964, *28*, 385-393.

Silverman, J., Berg, P. S., and Kantor, R. Some perceptual correlates of institutionalization. *Journal of Nervous and Mental Disease*, 1966, *141*, 651-657.

Singer, E., & Roby, T. B. Dimensions of decision-making behavior. *Perceptual and Motor Skills*, 1967, *24*, 571-595.

Sloane, H. N., Gorlow, L., & Jackson, D. N. Cognitive styles in equivalence range. *Perceptual and Motor Skills*, 1963, *16*, 389-404.

Slovic, P. Convergent validation of risk taking measures. *Journal of Abnormal and Social Psychology*, 1962, *65*, 68-71.

Slovic, P. Assessment of risk taking behavior. *Psychological Bulletin*, 1964, *61*, 220-233.

Steiner, I. D., & Johnson, H. H. Category width and responses to interpersonal disagreements. *Journal of Personality and Social Psychology*, 1965, *2*, 290-292.

Steiner, I. D., & Vannoy, J. S. Personality correlates of two types of conformity behavior. *Journal of Personality and Social Psychology*, 1966, *4*, 307-315.

Tajfel, H., Richardson, A., & Everstine, L. Individual consistencies in categorizing: A study in judgmental behavior. *Journal of Personality*, 1964, *32*, 90-108.

Taylor, R. L., & Levitt, E. E. Category breadth and the search for variety of experience. *Psychological Record*, 1967, *17*, 349-352.

Thompson, E. A. Complexity of the self concept: Contrast and assimilation effects in the perception and acceptance of strangers. Unpublished doctoral dissertation, University of Deleware, 1968.

Touhey, J. C. Category width and expectancies: Risk conservatism or generalization? *Journal of Research in Personality*, 1973, *7*, 173-178.

Touhey, J. C., & Mason, E. P. Relationship of flexibility and category width to risk-taking strategy. *Journal of Experimental Research in Personality,* 1972, *6,* 259-263.

Upshaw, H. S. The effect of unit size on the range of the reference scale. *Journal of Experimental Social Psychology,* 1970, *6,* 129-139.

Vannoy, J. S. Generality of cognitive complexity-simplicity as a personality construct. *Journal of Personality and Social Psychology,* 1965, *2,* 385-396.

Vick, O. C., & Jackson, D. N. Cognitive styles in the schematizing process: A critical evaluation. *Educational and Psychological Measurement,* 1967, *27,* 267-286.

Vidmar, N. Effects of group discussion on category width judgments. *Journal of Personality and Social Psychology,* 1974, *29,* 187-195.

Wallach, M. A., & Caron, A. J. Attribute criteriality and sex-linked conservatism as determinants of psychological similarity. *Journal of Abnormal and Social Psychology,* 1959, *59,* 43-50.

Wallach, M. A., & Kogan, N. Sex differences and judgment processes. *Journal of Personality,* 1959, *27,* 555-564.

Wallach, M. A., & Kogan, N. *Modes of thinking in young children: A study of the creativity-intelligence distinction.* New York: Holt, Rinehart & Winston, 1965.

Wiedl, K. H. Kognitive korrelate von wohlgefallen an visueller komplexitat. *Archiv für Psychologie,* 1976, *128,* 193-209.

Zeidenross-Kuvat, H., & Rim, Y. Fiedler's contingency model in changing situations. *Megamot,* 1977, *23,* 157-171 (in Hebrew).

9

The Psychobiography Debate:

AN ANALYTICAL REVIEW

WILLIAM McKINLEY RUNYAN

William McKinley Runyan is Assistant Professor, School of Social Welfare, and Assistant Research Psychologist, Institute of Personality Assessment and Research, at the University of California, Berkeley. His primary interests are in the study of lives, personality theory, and philosophy of the social sciences. He is author of *Life Histories and Psychobiography: Explorations in Theory and Method* (Oxford University Press, in press).

Psychobiographical studies which utilize psychological (often psycho-analytic) theory in interpreting the lives of public or historical figures have become increasingly prominent and increasingly controversial in recent years. Advocates of psychobiography (e.g., Langer, 1958; Erikson, 1958, 1969; Mazlish, 1971; Anderson, 1981a, 1981b) see the use of systematic psychology as a significant advance over the informal psychology tradi-tionally used in biography. "Viewed in the light of modern depth psychol-

AUTHOR'S NOTE: This project was facilitated by a grant from the Committee on Research, University of California, Berkeley. I would like to thank James W. Anderson, Faye Crosby, and Alan C. Elms for their incisive comments on an earlier version of this chapter.

225

ogy, the homespun, common-sense psychological interpretations of past
historians, even some of the greatest, seem woefully inadequate, not to say
naive" (Langer, 1957, pp. 286-287). Psychological conceptualizations and
assumptions are inevitably embedded in the description and interpretation
of lives, and even those categorically opposed to systematic psychology are
forced to rely on an implicit psychology (Erikson, 1958). The only
question, according to this view, is not whether to use psychology or not,
but whether the biographer should draw on the discipline of psychology as
well as on common sense and personal experience.

On the other hand, critics of psychobiography (e.g., Barzun, 1974;
Coles, 1975; Stannard, 1980; Stone, 1981) claim that the whole enterprise
has been "disappointing, partly because of the flimsiness of the evidence
of childhood experience, partly because of the speculative nature of the
causal links with adult behavior, partly because of the neglect of the
influence of the great processes of historical change in religion, economics,
politics, society, and so on" (Stone, 1981, pp. 220-221). In one of the
more intemperate critiques of the whole field of psychohistory, including
psychobiography, Stannard (1980) charges that "from the earliest endeavors to write psychohistory to those of the present, individual writings of
would-be psychohistorians have consistently been characterized by a cava-
lier attitude toward fact, a contorted attitude toward logic, an irrespon-
sible attitude toward theory validation, and a myopic attitude toward
cultural difference and anachronism" (p. 147).

This review attempts to confront the charges of the critics and to take
an equally critical look at the claims and methods of practitioners. This
examination of foundations and principles in psychobiography is intended
to be of use in assessing the field's potentials and limitations. (See also the
methodological discussions in Anderson, 1981a, 1981b; Crosby & Crosby,
1981; Elms, 1976; Mack, 1971; Greenstein, 1975a, 1975b; Runyan, 1981,
in press; and Tetlock, Crosby, & Crosby, 1981). The next sections present
a brief historical sketch of work in psychobiography, a sample of three
psychobiographical interpretations, and a definition of the boundaries of
the field. Each of the succeeding sections examines a controversial issue in
the debate over the merits and limitations of psychobiography, including
the problem of inadequate evidence, postdictive reconstructions, reductionism, the importance of childhood experience for adult behavior, and,
finally, the transhistorical and cross-cultural generality of psychological
theory.

HISTORICAL BACKGROUND

The psychobiographical enterprise, initially conceived as applied psychoanalysis, was launched with Freud's *Leonardo Da Vinci and a Memory of His Childhood* (1910). A sample of other early psychoanalytic studies are analyses of Shakespeare (Jones, 1910), the artist Giovanni Segantini (Abraham, 1911 [1956]), Richard Wagner (Graf, 1911), Amenhotep IV (Abraham, 1912 [1935]), Martin Luther (Smith, 1913), and Socrates (Karpas, 1915). A number of these earliest psychobiographical studies are summarized in Dooley's "Psychoanalytic Studies of Genius" (1916) and discussed in Barnes (1919) and Fearing (1927). During the 1920s a large number of psychobiographical works were published, often by those with no formal training in psychoanalysis or psychiatry, with several of the best known (Garraty, 1954) being studies of Margaret Fuller (Anthony, 1920), Samuel Adams (Harlow, 1923), Edgar Allen Poe (Krutch, 1926), and Abraham Lincoln (Clark, 1923, 1933).

This rising tide of psychoanalytic biography led to a number of attacks on the method (e.g., Whilbey, 1924; DeVoto, 1933), but the production of psychobiographies continued through the 1930s. By the end of the decade, there were psychobiographical studies of writers such as Tolstoy, Dostoevsky, Molière, Sand, Goethe, Coleridge, Nietzsche, Poe, and Rousseau and of public figures including Caesar, Lincoln, Napoleon, Darwin, and Alexander the Great (Anderson, 1978). "While the father of psychoanalysis, Sigmund Freud, was studying the behavior of Moses, Leonardo da Vinci, and Woodrow Wilson, he himself was under investigation by another psychohistorian. It seemed that by the end of the 1930's almost no one had escaped—even Houdini had been analyzed" (Anderson, 1978, p. 1). In contrast, the 1940s were a relatively slow period for psychological biography, with exceptions such as Guttmacher's (1941) study of George III and Langer's study, *The Mind of Adolf Hitler,* originally written in 1943 for the Office of Strategic Services but not published until 1972.

The 1950s saw a renewed production of psychobiographies, such as studies of Jonathan Swift and Lewis Carroll (Greenacre, 1955), and Beethoven and his nephew (Sterba & Sterba, 1954). The major turning point, however, in terms of more rigorous and methodologically self-conscious psychobiography was the publication of George and George's *Woodrow Wilson and Colonel House: A Personality Study* (1956) and Erikson's *Young Man Luther: A Study in Psychoanalysis and History*

(1958). In the 1960s and '70s there was an enormous outpouring of psychobiographical analyses of writers, artists, musicians, politicians, religious leaders, scientists, and others.[1]

Prominent examples of recent psychobiographical works are studies of Henry James (Edel, 1953-1970), Isaac Newton (Manuel, 1968), Gandhi (Erikson, 1969), Max Weber (Mitzman, 1969), Emily Dickinson (Cody, 1971), Stalin (Tucker, 1973), James and John Stuart Mill (Mazlish, 1975), Andrew Jackson (Rogin, 1975), T. E. Lawrence (Mack, 1976), Adolf Hitler (Waite, 1977), Beethoven (Solomon, 1977), Samuel Johnson (Bate, 1977), B. F. Skinner (Elms, 1981), and Richard Nixon (Brodie, 1981) and studies of groups of individuals, such as American Presidents (Barber, 1972), revolutionary leaders (Wolfenstein, 1967; Mazlish, 1976), personality theorists (Stolorow & Atwood, 1979), utopians (Manuel & Manuel, 1979), and philosophers (Scharfstein, 1980).

The flavor of the field can be given through a sample of psychobiographical arguments or interpretations. I will briefly present examples drawn from studies of Woodrow Wilson, Emily Dickinson, and Wilhelm Reich. Of necessity, these interpretations are given in barest outline, without the density of detail needed to corroborate or disprove them.

Woodrow Wilson

In three major executive positions, as President of Princeton University, as Governor of New Jersey, and as President of the United States, Woodrow Wilson experienced a similar pattern of impressive early accomplishments, followed by a period of controversy, ending in serious setbacks or defeats. The last and most serious of these unnecessary defeats was his failure to obtain Senate ratification of the Versailles Treaty which would have led to participation of the United States in the League of Nations. Edmund Wilson (1952) observed:

> As President of the United States, he repeated after the War his whole tragedy as president of Princeton—with Lodge in the role of West, the League of Nations in the place of the quad system, and the Senate in the place of the Princeton trustees. It is possible to observe in certain lives, where conspicuously superior abilities are united with serious deficiencies, not the progress in a career or vocation that carries the talented man to a solid position or a definite goal, but a curve plotted over and over again and always dropping from some flight of achievement to a steep descent into failure [p. 322].

How is such a pattern to be explained? George and George's (1964) basic hypothesis, derived from Lasswell (1948), is that Wilson's interest in power, and his means of exercising it, was based on a need to compensate for damaged self-esteem. In the stages of seeking power, he could be flexible and adaptive, but in conflicts which developed in the exercise of power, he often became rigid and self-defeatingly uncompromising. In addition to a personal need for power, Wilson also had a desire for social approval and for feeling virtuous. "His stern Calvinist conscience forbade an unabashed pursuit or use of power for personal gratification. He could express his desire for power only insofar as he convincingly rationalized it in terms of altruistic service, and fused it with laudable social objectives" (George & George, 1964, p. 117).

Once faced with political opposition to a program to which he had committed himself, Wilson painted his own position as the only morally worthy one and refused to compromise. In both the battles with Dean Andrew West at Princeton over the formation of a new graduate school and with the Senate opposition headed by Henry Cabot Lodge over the ratification of the Versailles Treaty, Wilson alienated the moderate elements who could have supported him and drove them into the arms of his opponents. In such situations of conflict, Wilson's desire to achieve a worthwhile political goal

> became of less importance than to maintain equilibrium of [his] personality system. He seems to have experienced opposition to his will in such situations as an unbearable threat to his self-esteem. To compromise in these circumstances was to submit to domination in the very sphere of power and political leadership in which he sought to repair his damaged self-esteem. Opposition to his will, therefore, set into motion disruptive anxieties, and brought to the surface long-smouldering aggressive feelings that, as a child, he had not dared to express [George, 1971, p. 94].

Wilson's behavior was traced back to treatment by his father, a perfectionistic and demanding Presbyterian minister who often ridiculed his son. The child's resentment and rage were never directly expressed toward his father, but remained to influence behavior throughout his adult life.[2]

Emily Dickinson

Emily Dickinson was notorious for seclusiveness in her home town of Amherst, while her poetry was virtually unknown.

As early as her twenty-second year Emily Dickinson was going out
of her way to avoid meeting people. A year later she wrote that she
was going to church early to avoid having 'to go in after all the
people had got there'. By the time she was twenty-eight it was a
fixed 'custom' for her to run whenever the doorbell rang. By the age
of thirty she was retreating to her room when old friends called and
listening to their voices from upstairs. The next year she inaugurated
the habit of dressing exclusively in white that she was to maintain
for the rest of her life. . . . Eventually she retreated indoors altogether, and for the last fifteen years of her life the neighbors knew
she was there by faith alone. . . . On the rare occasions when she
consented to visit with old friends, she and the visitor conversed
from opposite sides of a door left slightly ajar. She would not allow
a physician to examine her during an illness, and he was expected to
arrive at his diagnosis from a glimpse of her, fully clothed, as she
walked past a doorway [Cody, 1971, pp. 19-20].

Her reclusiveness has been variously attributed to a frustrated love
affair, an effort to conserve energy and have time to write, vengefulness
towards her father, or her plain looks. Cody (1971) argues that Emily
Dickinson's disturbance can be attributed in part to a troubled relationship
with her mother. Her mother is revealed in family correspondence as "an
habitually complaining woman, subject to depression and hypochondria.
She appears emotionally shallow, self-centered, ineffectual, conventional,
timid, submissive, and not very bright" (p. 42). Cody argues that it is
likely that Emily Dickinson

experienced what she interpreted as a cruel rejection by her mother.
Many of her statements, her choice of certain recurring metaphors
and symbols, and the entire course of her life, viewed psychoanalytically, argue for the truth of this assumption. However, there exists
no record of any concrete instance in which Mrs. Dickinson took
such an attitude toward her daughter. Nevertheless, knowledge
gained from the clinical study of patients who bear scars similar to
Emily Dickinson's is persuasive evidence for the existence in the
poet's life of damaging experiences comparable to theirs [p. 2].

Emily Dickinson once wrote in a letter that if anything upsetting happened to her, she ran home to her brother. "He was an awful Mother, but I
liked him better than none" (Cody, 1971, p. 42). The case for the

existence of maternal depriviation is based, however, primarily on clinical experience, inferences from psychoanalytic theory, and interpretations of her poetry.

Wilhelm Reich

Certain aspects of the thought of Wilhelm Reich, author of *Character Analysis* (1933), *The Mass Psychology of Fascism* (1933), and *The Function of the Orgasm* (1942) can, Stolorow and Atwood (1979) argue, be traced to a traumatic childhood experience. "Our theis is that Reich's theoretical system reflects and symbolizes a profound personal struggle which is traceable to his childhood experience of his mother's suicide" (p. 111).

Three important themes run through all of Reich's work: "(1) the notion that the expression of sexuality coincides with the expression and functioning of life in general; (2) the notion that the life-sexual functions are being perpetually suppressed and distorted by anti-sexual death forces in the world; and (3) the notion that he, by an inner messianic imperative, be the champion of life and sexuality in their struggle against the forces of death" (Stolorow & Atwood, 1979, pp. 111-112). As a psychotherapist, Reich was concerned with helping patients dissolve the "character armor" or defenses which interfered with the free flow of sexual and life energies. In his political and biological writings, he emphasized a similar theme of supporting these sexual and life energies against oppressive forces.

It seems plausible that these themes running through Reich's work have their origin in a traumatic event that occurred during his fourteenth year. Reich discovered that his mother was having a secret love affair with one of his tutors. He reported this to his jealous and explosively violent father. His mother responded by committing suicide, which seemed to be a direct consequence of his own actions. Stolorow and Atwood (1979) hypothesize that "the circumstances of her death constituted the nuclear situation around which the structure of his representational world crystallized. . . . If it is assumed that in betraying his mother's unfaithfulness the young Reich was acting out of an identification with his father's authoritarian and sexually restrictive values, then the reasons for his subsequent life of struggle against sexual repression begin to become clear. Since in acting on the basis of a narrow code of sexual morality he was responsible for the death of the one person he loved above all others, an immense burden of pain and guilt must have been generated. What could be a better way to atone for his fateful act of betrayal than devoting himself to the eradication of all those values and ways of thinking which had motivated him? This line of reasoning also sheds light on why he regarded the repression of sexuality as such a vicious and deadly force in human affairs. This was because his own attempt to inhibit his beloved mother's sexuality led directly to her suicide. . . . [W]e might interpret his relentless struggle against the death forces as a sustained attempt to undo his act of betrayal and thereby magically restore his mother to life" (pp. 120-122).

These three examples suggest the kinds of arguments and interpretations offered in psychobiography and the kinds of analyses that have aroused so much controversy. Can Wilson's rigid behavior be traced to unconscious hostility in his relationship with his father? Is it legitimate to explain Emily Dickinson's reclusiveness and strange behavior in terms of a postdictive reconstruction of her relationship with her mother? Did a single traumatic event have a life-long impact on the themes of Reich's work? After outlining a more systematic definition of the field of psychobiography, this chapter will examine a number of the specific questions that arise in assessing the validity of such interpretations.

DEFINITION

As a preliminary distinction, psychohistory can be divided into two main branches: psychobiography, dealing with the study of individuals, and group psychohistory, dealing with the psychological characteristics or formative experiences of groups such as the Nazi youth cohort, Hiroshima survivors, or Vietnam veterans (e.g., Lifton, 1967; Loewenberg, 1971). The following discussion is concerned primarily with developing a definition of psychobiography, but it also examines conceptions of psychohistory in general that have implications for the definition of psychobiography.

One apparently sensible approach is to define psychohistory as the application of psychology to history, with an associated definition of psychobiography as the use of psychology in biography. One such definition is offered by Anderson (1978): "The term 'psychohistorian' will be used to include any scholar who uses psychology in an attempt to understand and explain historical behavior" (p. 2).

Although enviably simple, this definition has limitations. Consider the argument of Erikson and others that every biography includes at least the use of an implicit psychology. Does all biography then become psychobiography? It seems necessary to elaborate this definition so that it refers to the explicit use of formal or systematic psychological theory. Thus, the definition could now read: Psychobiography is the explicit use of formal or systematic psychology in biography.

Many have defined psychohistory as the application of psychoanalytic theory to history and, correspondingly, psychobiography as the application of psychoanalytic theory to biography. For example, psychobiography is "in other words, the application of psychoanalytic concepts to biography" (Friedlander, 1978, p. 29). If this definition is used, how is one to define the application of other psychological theories to biography? Clearly, this definition is too restrictive. It seems most sensible to define psychobiography as the use of any explicit or formal psychological theory in biography, not just the application of psychoanalytic theory. There may be psychoanalytic psychobiography, phenomenological psychobiography, behavioral psychobiography, and so on.

A broader definition of psychobiography as biography employing any explict personality theory is endorsed by a number of writers, such as Glad (1973) and Tucker (1977). A definition that encompasses all forms of personality theory is an improvement, but how are we to characterize a biographical study that makes use of social psychology, developmental psychology, or some other branch of psychology? Also, how is one to classify a study making use of conceptual frameworks, or typologies, or data, or methods (such as content analysis, graphology, or personality assessment procedures) but not formal theory per se? A case can be made for defining psychobiography not solely as the application of personality theory to biography, but also as the application of psychological concepts, data, and methods from any branch of psychology to biography.

In light of these considerations, psychobiography may be defined as the explicit use of systematic or formal psychology in biography. Three aspects of this definition should be noted. First, the field is defined by the use of psychology, which may or may not be psychoanalytic. Second, the use must be explicit or visible, in order to distinguish psychobiography from all those biographies which make implicit use of commonsense psychology. Third, the definition refers not to the application of personality theory but to the use of psychology, which is intended to include within psychobiography those works drawing on the full range of resources of the field of psychology, including psychological concepts, data, and methods, as well as theory, from developmental, clinical, social, and personality psychology. Additional considerations may eventually necessi-

tate the revision of the definition offered here, but it seems adequate for
present purposes.

THE QUESTION OF INADEQUATE EVIDENCE

In the controversy over psychobiographical methods and accomplishments, one of the most frequent criticisms is that interpretations are based
on inadequate evidence. "The historian's most serious objection to psychohistory is that sweeping declarations about actions or personalities are
based on sparse evidence" (Anderson, 1978, p. 11). A reviewer of Langer's
The Mind of Adolf Hitler (1972) charges that "some of the most important conclusions of Langer's book are based on non-existent, unreliable, or
misinterpreted evidence" (Gatzke, 1973, p. 400). The issue of inadequate
evidence is frequently raised in regard to psychoanalytic biography in the
form: "You can't put the person on the couch." For example, the
application of psychoanalysis to biography "must proceed without the
central instrument for the investigation of the unconscious: free association" (Kohut, 1960, p. 571).

> The psychoanalyst (or 'psychohistorian') who wishes to use psycho-
> logical materials in an effort to obtain a deeper understanding of a
> historical figure, or in the reconstruction of historical events, is,
> however, confronted with major problems of evidence. In conduct-
> ing a psychoanalysis the investigator has only to wait and he is
> likely, through the processes of free association, interpretation, and
> working through, to obtain systematic data concerning his patient's
> past history, motivations, conflicts, and ego strengths. To be sure,
> resistance and the ego defenses distort, but this very distortion can
> then be the subject of further analysis and validation. . . . When we
> try to apply psychological methods to a historical figure, we have no
> such cooperation and no analogous systematic way to obtain infor-
> mation [Mack, 1971, p. 153].

Finally, there is the criticism that if early childhood experience is particularly influential, this is just the period about which the psychohistorian is
likely to have the least information. "Freudian psychology has not been
much use to the historian, who is usually unable to penetrate the bed-
room, the bathroom or the nursery. If Freud is right, and if these are the
places where the action is, there is not much the historian can do about it"
(Stone, 1981, p. 53).

There are, in sum, claims of insufficient evidence, of evidence of the wrong kind (not enough free associations or dream reports), and not enough evidence from the right period (i.e., childhood). These criticisms need to be taken more seriously than they have been. Both Freud in his study of Leonardo and Erikson in his analysis of Luther have been severely criticized for developing psychological interpretations from inadequate data about early experience. In the absence of sufficient historical evidence, it is not possible to develop credible psychological interpretations of the lives of historical figures.

What are the implications of problems of evidence for the psychobiographical enterprise? They do not mean that psychobiography is impossible, as has sometimes been suggested, but rather that attention is best devoted to historical figures about whom there is sufficient evidence to develop and test psychological explanations. Also, in the absence of evidence about childhood experience, some types of early developmental explanations are best avoided, as psychological theory is not sufficiently determinate to permit accurate retrodictions or reconstructions (a problem to be discussed in the next section). The problems of evidence mean that some types of questions cannot be answered about some individuals, but this in no way impairs the possibility of developing psychological interpretations of the many aspects of behavior and experience of historical individuals for which there is adequate evidence. Third, on a comparative basis, the problems of evidence are not as severe as they may first appear, as there are also a number of evidential advantages the psychobiographer has over the psychotherapist.

It seems undeniable that the psychobiographer typically has less access to material such as free associations, dreams, and transference reactions than does the psychoanalyst. On the other hand, the psychobiographer has the advantage of having information about a person who has lived his or her entire life. The average patient in psychoanalysis is relatively young and has often not yet lived through important life experiences such as the rearing of children, the peak of his or her career, or the death of parents. Reactions to these experiences, which may be revelatory of personality, are thus not available for interpretation. But the usual subject of psychobiography

has lived his entire life and has met death. Not only the development and mid-stages of his life are available for inspection but also its ultimate unfolding and final resolution. This means that in discovering the dominant psychological themes of his subject's emotional evolution the psychoanalytic biographer has at his disposal a broader spectrum of behavior through more decades of life than has the analyst with a living patient [Cody, 1971, p. 5].

Second, the psychobiographer is not limited to information coming from the subject alone, but may draw heavily on "outside sources" (Hofling, 1976, p. 229). He or she is able to learn how a variety of other informants perceived the situations the subject was in, and their reactions to the individual's personality (Anderson, 1981a). For important public figures confidential information about their lives is sometimes not released or available until after their death or the death of their immediate relatives.

Third, if the subject is a literary or creative person, the psychobiographer has a wealth of creative material, perhaps expressing inner psychological states and conflicts, which may, with caution, be drawn upon in interpreting the subject's personality. For example, "Emily Dickinson, surely, possessed a greater capacity for the perception and discrimination of psychological processes and a greater ability to find appropriate words to express her inner experiences than any patient who has ever been psychoanalyzed. From this standpoint she is the psychoanalysand par excellence" (Cody, 1971, p. 6). This may put the point a little too strongly, but some creative individuals have been more articulately expressive of their inner states and experiences than the typical therapy patient.

Fourth, there are sometimes substitutes for a person's dreams or free associations (Anderson, 1981a). For example, Davis (1975) analyzes drawings and caricatures made by Theodore Roosevelt in adolescence when he portrayed himself and members of his family turning into animals. Equivalents to free associations have been found in the "language exercises" of archeologist Heinrich Schliemann in which he revealed dreams and unconscious wishes, and in the conversation book written by Beethoven to cope with his deafness (Bergmann, 1973, p. 842).

A fifth advantage is that the evidence used in psychobiography is available to all, so that original interpretations may be critically examined and alternatives may be proposed and tested. In psychotherapy the data are typically not publicly available, which makes it less likely that such a corrective process can take place. In sum, the psychobiographer often has access to information not available to the psychotherapist, such as information about the person's whole life span, from associates of the individual, and from the analysis of expressive or creative activities.

RECONSTRUCTION

In response to the paucity of evidence on childhood experience and the importance of such experience within psychoanalytic theory, psychobiographers have sometimes used psychoanalytic theory to reconstruct or postdict what must have happened in childhood. Greenacre (1955), for example, argues that childhood wants can be "reconstructed from known characteristics, problems, and repetitive actions supported by memory traces." Indeed, "the experienced psychoanalyst knows just as definitely as the internist observing later sequelae of tuberculosis . . . that the deformity is the result of specific acts upon the growing organism" (p. 107). Such reconstructions have, however, not gone uncriticized, even when executed with considerable sophistication. Erikson, for example, has been criticized for reconstructing Luther's relationship to his mother on the basis of adult behavior.

> In his study of the young Luther, Erikson literally invents little Martin's relation to his mother, using as a basis (as a 'document') the behavior of Luther the man. . . . Erikson does not interpret a repetitive behavior on young Luther's part in terms of an unconscious dynamic; he jumps from a presumed characteristic of the Reformer to the inferential reconstruction of essential data about the latter's family environment [Friedlander, 1978, p. 27].

The reconstruction of specific life events is not as extreme as the practice of hagiographers, who sometimes reconstructed entire lives if information was unavailable. Agnellus, a Bishop of Ravenna in the ninth century, while completing a series of lives of his predecessors in that position, confessed: "In order that there might not be a break in the series, I have composed the life myself, with the help of God and the prayers of the bretheren" (Clifford, 1962, p. x). Some historians are outraged at the more limited psychobiographical practice of reconstructing particular events or relationships and feel that it is no more acceptable than the reconstructive techniques of the Bishop. The practice of retrodiction is especially troubling when an earlier event is retrodicted and then later assumed to have been firmly established. This practice has been roundly criticized both by historians and by some psychoanalysts (e.g., Wyatt, 1956).

Before concluding that retrodiction is never justified in psychobiography, let us consider one of the strongest arguments for reconstruction, and one of its most persuasive examples.

> Psychoanalysis is not alone among sciences in providing a means whereby the existence of what is not directly perceptible can be inferred. Thus, the psychoanalytic interpretation of the life of a historical figure is in certain respects comparable to the reassembling of a fossil skeleton. And when the life under consideration has been rent by a psychological cataclysm, the interpretive reconstruction is not unlike the piecing together of the fragments of an aircraft that has exploded in flight.
>
> In the first instance the paleontologist dovetails the scattered bones according to the laws of comparative anatomy; the progression of vertebrae, for example, have a known and more or less constant relationship to each other throughout the animal kingdom. In the second example, the engineer assembles the shattered metal of the aircraft on a scaffold corresponding to the known dimensions of the type of plane to which the wreckage belongs; when all the available pieces are laid out in this way, a sequence of stresses becomes discernible whose concentric waves lead back to and establish the point of origin of the explosion. In either example, what provides the gestalt and guides the interpretation placed on each discrete particle is a body of general knowledge—the laws of bone structure in the one case, the structure or blueprints in the other [Cody, 1971, pp. 1-2].

Cody then argues that psychoanalytic theory has discovered conflicts and motives believed to be operant to some degree in all lives, and that when many pieces of evidence are available the theory can sometimes be used to perceive the relationships among the authentic bits of evidence and to make inferences about the rough structure of missing pieces of evidence. This is equivalent to making plaster bones in reconstructing a fossil skeleton. "One such 'plaster bone' in the present study is the assumption that early in Emily Dickinson's life she experienced what she interpreted as a cruel rejection by her mother. Many of her statements, her choice of certain recurring metaphors and symbols, and the entire course of her life, viewed psychoanalytically, argue for the truth of this assumption" (Cody, 1971, p. 2).

Is such a practice always to be avoided? Perhaps there are a few cases in which extensive evidence is available and in which a clear and well-supported theoretical structure exists which would justify the tentative reconstruction of the gross features of an unknown event. Even so, biographical reconstruction is extremely risky and in most cases unjustified. In light of the indeterminacy of developmental theory, the lack of empirical support for psychoanalytic genetic theory, and the multiple possible processes leading to any given outcome, the case for banning reconstruction altogether in psychobiography is a fairly strong one. But if retrodiction is to be practiced at all, it is essential that reconstructions clearly be labeled as such and kept distinct from events for which there is documentary evidence.

REDUCTIONISM

Another common charge against psychobiography is that of "reductionism." One form of the reductionist critique is that psychological factors are overemphasized at the expense of external social and historical factors. "In turning to Freud, historians interested in the psychological aspect of their discipline have concentrated upon the internal biographies of individuals to the almost complete exclusion of the society in which the lives of their subjects take place" (Hundert, 1972, pp. 467-468). Or, "unlike economic, social, political or religious influences, the subject's 'psychology' is considered to be the source. His mental state determines all other variables, and then responds to them" (Anderson, 1978, p. 15).

A second version of the reductionist criticism is that psychobiography focuses excessively on psychopathological processes and gives insufficient attention to normality and creativity. Particularly in the early history of psychobiography, works were sometimes called "pathographies," "thereby emphasizing the basic concern with abnormality and leading to the conclusion that what psychoanalysis had to offer to an understanding of the lives of great men consisted mainly in a documentation and explication of their foibles and follies" (Meyer, 1972, p. 373).

A third type of reductionism is to explain adult character and behavior exclusively in terms of early childhood experience while neglecting later formative processes and influences. "What is chiefly wrong with the conventional psychoanalytic biography is its crude unilateralism. It suggests a one-to-one relationship, arguing that the protagonist did this or that because of some painful experience in early childhood" (Hughes, 1964,

p. 58). Erikson (1969) identified this form of reductionism as "origin-ology," or "the habitual effort to find the 'causes' of a man's whole development in his childhood conflicts" (p. 98). Two other reductive fallacies are

> "the critical period fallacy," which attempts to build a study of a man's life around a certain "key" period of development, and "eventism," the discovery in some important episode in a man's life of not only the prototype of his behavior but *the* turning point in his life from which all subsequent events and work are derived. Both these oversimplifications lend artistic grace to a biographical study, but also impose unnatural order, shape, and direction to the often rather amorphous nature and fitful course of a human life, even that of a great man [Mack, 1971, p. 156].

In response to these charges of reductionism, it must be acknowledged that too many psychobiographies have suffered from flaws such as over-emphasizing the psychological, the pathological, or the influence of child-hood conflicts. A number of contemporary psychobiographers (e.g., Bate, 1977; Erikson, 1969; Mack, 1976) are, however, aware of such dangers and are avoiding them by integrating the psychological with the social and historical, by analyzing not just pathology but also strengths and adaptive capacities, and by studying formative influences not just in childhood but throughout the life span.

THE RELATIONSHIP OF CHILDHOOD EXPERIENCE
TO ADULT BEHAVIOR

One of the most complex and difficult issues in the field of psycho-biography is that of assessing the influence of childhood experience on adult character and behavior. In psychoanalytically oriented psychobiog-raphies, aspects of adult behavior are often attributed to circumstances and experiences in childhood. In the worst cases, "hypotheses about early developments are speculatively deduced from adult events and then used to explain those events" (Izenberg, 1975, p. 139). In more fortunate cases, available evidence about childhood experience is interpreted as an impor-tant causal determinant of adult personality and behavior. This practice of attributing important causal influence to early experience is consistent with classical psychoanalytic theories of personality development. Freud (1938 [1969]) stated, for example: "Analytic experience has convinced us of the complete truth of the assertion so often to be heard that the child is psychologically father to the adult and that the events of his first years are of paramount importance for his whole later life" (p. 187).

This practice of interpreting the whole life in terms of early childhood experience has, however, come under attack from a number of different directions. Historians have challenged the causal interpretations provided for particular cases: "I just do not think that such things as the extermination of six million Jews can be explained by the alleged fact that Hitler's mother was killed by treatment given her by a Jewish doctor in an attempt to cure her cancer of the breast; or that Luther's defiance of the Roman church can be explained by the brutal way he was treated by his father or by his chronic constipation" (Stone, 1981, p. 220). Stone's statement exaggerates the issues, though, as there is an important difference between claiming that childhood experience is *the* cause of later events versus arguing that it is a partial or contributing cause of individual behavior. Even psychoanalytically oriented psychobiographers criticize the practice of positing childhood experience as the only cause of later behavior, as in Erikson's (1969) critique of "originology" and Mack's (1971) critique of the critical period fallacy, and of the fallacy of attributing all subsequent development to a single important event.

From another direction, empirical tests of Freudian theory, reviewed in Kline (1972) and Fisher and Greenberg (1977), raise serious questions about aspects of Freud's theories of psychosexual development. Although there is some evidence about clusters of traits consistent with Freud's conception of oral character, and substantial evidence about orderliness, obstinancy, and parsimony clustering together as Freud suggested in the anal or obsessive character, the bulk of quantitative empirical studies do not demonstrate connections between character types and specific childhood experiences associated with feeding or toilet-training. Whether more methodologically sophisticated studies in the future will provide more support for these theories is an open question, but at present, a substantial number of studies do not support them and provide little reason for believing them to be valid.

Even if the specific connections between early psychosexual experience and adult character which Freud suggested are not supported, this does not resolve the more general issue of connections between childhood experience and adult behavior. Clinical experience in some cases seems to provide apparently compelling evidence of connections between childhood experience and adult behavior. This may, of course, be no more than a methodological artifact, but it may also be that such clear-cut connections *do* exist for some individuals, even though not in all. Second, more recent developments in psychoanalytic theory, as in the work of Mahler, Winnicott, or Kohut, provide more complex ways of analyzing childhood experience which may provide sounder foundations for connecting childhood experience to adult behavior. Third, the study of childhood experience may be useful in developing interpretations of adult behavior, or forming hypotheses about the meaning of aspects of an individual's adult behavior, even if a causal connection between the two is not explicitly argued.

The study of childhood experience may be of some importance in psychobiography, but perhaps not in the way suggested by classical Freudian theory. There has, in recent years, been a widespread shift in thinking within developmental and personality psychology about the influence of early childhood experience. In contrast to earlier beliefs about the crucial impact of childhood experience on adult behavior (e.g., Bowlby, 1952; Bloom, 1964; Kelley, 1955), there has been a growing belief that the effects of early deprivation can be substantially modified by later experience and that behavior and personality are shaped and changed throughout the life course (e.g., Brim & Kagan, 1980; Clarke & Clarke, 1976; Mischel, 1968; and Rutter, 1979). The argument is not that early childhood experiences have no effects, but rather that the effects of such experiences are mediated by intervening experiences and contingencies, and that personality and behavior are continuously shaped throughout the life cycle.

Early experience, of whatever form, rarely has a direct impact on adult personality; rather, early experience shapes early personality, which influences the kinds of later environments one is likely to encounter, which in turn influences later experience, which affects personality, and so on in an interactive cycle (Wachtel, 1977). The effects of early experiences are mediated through a chain of behavior-determining, person-determining, and situation-determining processes throughout the life course (Runyan, 1978). Thus, any given event or experience can have a variety of possible effects and meanings, depending on initial personality structure, initial environment, and the causal structure of subsequently encountered environments and experiences. Furthermore, the causal structure of the life course is such that there is usually a variety of alternative paths or processes leading to any given outcome (Runyan, 1980).

What are the implications for psychobiography of this transactional view of human development in which personality is modifiable throughout the life span? First, adult personality cannot be attributed directly to specific childhood experiences, and particularly not to specific experiences with breastfeeding or toilet-training, which empirical evidence indicates are not substantial determinants of adult outcome. Second, if there are alternative paths or processes to any given outcome, then in most instances postdiction is to be avoided. Third, if evidence on early experience is available, the effects of such experience should not be applied directly to adult personality, but rather traced through a sequence of intervening stages and processes.

The following example from Cody's (1971) study of Emily Dickinson illustrates such a sequential-interactional model of analysis in psychobiography:

[O]ne sees a circular process inimical to the woman but kindly to the artist; feelings of rejection by the mother lead to hostility and bitter denunciation of the mother and what she represents. As a result, guilt feelings are engendered that in turn evoke a need for punishment that is partly satisfied through self-inflicted social deprivation brought about by means of neurotic symptoms. The ensuing loneliness and frustration then feed the art in ways that have been mentioned. The art in turn, providing its own compensatory and self-reinforcing gratification, demands further self-denial . . ., which is brought about by the perpetuation of the estrangement from and enmity toward mother, religion, God, and society. These hostile rejections in turn evoke more guilt feelings and further suffering and a continuation of the endless cycle [pp. 498-499].

The study of formative influences throughout the life cycle makes analysis more complicated, but it also has certain advantages for psychobiography in that early childhood experience, for which evidence is usually unavailable, is no longer so predominantly important. Attention can then be directed to those formative periods and processes for which adequate evidence is more often available. One of the advantages of Eriksonian theory, in which character and identity are importantly shaped at later ages, is that the psychobiographer is more likely to have usable evidence on this period of the subject's life (Stone, 1981, p. 53).

There are, in sum, several serious difficulties with psychobiographical analyses that attribute adult patterns of behavior to particular childhood experiences. Those analyses which do so on the basis of psychodynamic theories of psychosexual development are problematic because of the bulk of empirical evidence that does not support such theories. On the other hand, the reciprocal-interactive view of development currently advocated in life span developmental psychology and in personality theory is not far enough advanced to be widely used. What should the psychobiographer do in light of these difficulties? One recommendation is to proceed sparingly with statements attributing adult behavior to childhood experiences, deprivations, or conflicts. In reference to the study of Woodrow Wilson discussed earlier, Brodie (1957) states that the authors "are inevitably on weaker ground when they try to explain the genesis of the Wilsonian neurosis than when they describe the manner in which it expressed itself full-blown. . . . It is one thing to observe compulsive behavior and identify it for what it is; it is quite another to find the original causes" (p. 415).

An extensive evaluative review of work in psychobiography and psychohistory by Crosby and Crosby (1981) reaches a similar conclusion about the limitations of explanations in terms of childhood experience. The Crosbys applied a quantitative rating system to 79 articles and books in political psychobiography, and in light of their criteria (e.g., adequacy of evidence, consideration of plausible rival hypotheses, and references to relevant theoretical and empirical literature), those studies focusing on "coherent whole" or pattern explanations of adult behavior were rated more positively than those relying on causal explanations in terms of childhood experience.

Psychology can be used for many purposes other than drawing causal connections between childhood experience and adult behavior. It can be useful for identifying patterns in current behavior, for providing concepts and categories for analyzing experience, for suggesting hypotheses about the meaning of circumstances or events for an individual, for providing normative or comparative data about phenomena of interest, for providing methods to use in analyzing biographical evidence, and so on. It may be that the greatest contributions of psychology to biography lie in just such areas, in the conceptualization and interpretation of biographical evidence, without always attempting to relate adult behavior to childhood experience.

TRANSHISTORICAL AND CROSS-CULTURAL GENERALITY IN PSYCHOLOGICAL THEORY

Psychobiographers and psychohistorians are often criticized for applying a parochial psychological theory to individuals of other cultures and historical periods. If psychoanalysis was developed to explain the behavior of neurotic middle- and upper-class Viennese at the turn of the twentieth century, how can it be appropriately used to explain the behavior of those in other cultures and historical periods? The problem was clearly formulated in 1938 by historian Lucien Febvre: "How can we as historians make use of psychology which is the product of observation carried out on twentieth-century man, in order to interpret the actions of the man of the past?" (quoted in Gilmore, 1979b, p. 31). It is alleged that many psychohistorians

begin by postulating that there is a theory of human behavior which transcends history. This claim to possess a scientific system of explanation of human behavior based on proven clinical data, which is of universal validity irrespective of time and place, is wholly unacceptable to the historians since it ignores the critical importance of changing context—religious, moral, cultural, economic, social, and political. It is a claim, moreover, that has recently been rejected by many of the more perceptive members of the psychological profession itself [Stone, 1981, p. 40].

One final expression of this critique is that

the psychohistorian employs theoretical models and cognitive assumptions created from the material of the present—and then imposes them on the past. In so doing, he or she must assume that in most fundamental ways all people, at all places, at all times, have viewed themselves and the world about them in substantially the same fashion. If man *qua* man were not always essentially the same, the behavior of many past individuals (to say nothing of whole cultures) would be psychoanalytically unintelligible. Their actions and motives would be operating at a level beyond the reach of psychoanalytic concepts and suppositions, which are products of the direct study of primarily urban, post-industrial, literate, twentieth-century, Western individuals—and mostly "abnormal" and demographically nonrepresentative ones at that. . . . It thus seems clear that even if psychoanalytic theory were an effective technique for understanding the world of the present, it would be a hopeless exercise in intellectual myopia to apply it to the past [Stannard, 1980, pp. 121, 143].

What is the validity of such criticisms? First, it must be acknowledged that some of the charges are true, that psychobiographers have, at times, been unaware of cultural and historical differences, which has biased their interpretations. As one example, Langer (1972) is criticized for seeming "largely unaware of the family's social setting or of the customs of the time. It simply will not do to cite Hitler's addressing his father as 'Herr Vater' (Mr. Father) as evidence of paternal tyranny and oppression. Family formality was widespread in nineteenth-century Europe, and did not necessarily indicate either lack of filial affection or the presence of societal authoritarianism" (Orlow, 1974, p. 135). This problem is common to all biographical and historical writing and is not insurmountable; the psychobiographer simply *must* learn about the cultural and historical context of his or her subject.

It can readily be agreed that ethnocentrism and temporocentrism are to be avoided in interpreting individuals from other cultures and historical periods. Does this, however, cause any insoluble problems for psychobiography? I think not, as there are a variety of effective responses to the problem. As a first step, the psychobiographer must learn enough about the subject's social and historical context to have an adequate frame of reference for interpreting the meaning of specific actions, statements, and practices.

Second, the study of relevant comparison groups and of local contexts within the subject's social and historical world can help in developing understandings of the individual (Anderson, 1981b). However, understandings derived from studies of similar groups are not likely to be sufficient in themselves, because we are often most interested in those individuals who stand out significantly from other Renaissance painters, other nineteenth-century writers, other twentieth-century American Presidents, and so on. It is also important to conduct idiographic studies of the individual in order to reveal aspects of his or her personality, situation, and experience that may differentiate him or her from others in the same social and historical context (Runyan, 1982). Finally, if we accept Kluckhohn and Murray's (1952) classic statement that persons are in some ways like all others, like some others, and like no others, then it follows that at least some psychological conceptualizations and theories will hold universally (see Lonner, 1979; Triandis, 1978) and thus can be appropriately applied to any psychobiographical subject. The context-boundedness of many psychological theories is not unrecognized by psychologists (e.g., Cronbach, 1975; Gergen, 1973), and it is necessary to examine more closely what aspects of psychological conceptualizations and theories can and cannot be applied across different cultures and historical periods. This is a difficult task which requires psychology to become more closely integrated with the other social sciences, particularly with history in testing the transhistorical generality or specificity of its propositions (Simonton, 1981), and with anthropology and sociology in exploring the cross-cultural generality of its theories (Triandis & Lambert, 1979).

In short, errors have sometimes been made in naively assuming that psychoanalytic or other psychological theory could automatically be applied to individuals in any cultural or historical setting, but this does not mean that psychohistory does not work or cannot work. Rather, psychobiographical interpretation is a complex three-tiered intellectual enterprise which needs to draw not just on those theories which hold universally but also on group and context-specific generalizations, and on idiographic studies of the particular individual.

CONCLUSION

This chapter has reviewed a wide range of opinions about psychobiography and examined arguments and examples related to issues including the problem of inadequate evidence, historical reconstruction, reductionism, the influence of childhood experience on adult behavior, and the cross-cultural and transhistorical generality of psychological theory. Due to limitations of space, it has not been possible to discuss a number of other important issues, such as the relationship of the biographer to his or her subject (Anderson, 1981b; Erikson, 1975; Mack, 1971), ethical issues in the study of public figures (American Psychiatric Association, 1976; Elms, 1976; Hofling, 1976; Runyan, in press), and the logic of explanation in psychobiography (Crosby, 1979; Runyan, 1981). Progress in psychobiography will depend on advancements in personality, social, clinical, and developmental psychology, as well as on work within its own borders. In turn, psychobiographical inquiry provides an opportunity for exploring the extent to which the discipline of psychology can or cannot illuminate the life and experience of particular individuals.

NOTES

1. Useful historical reviews are contained in Anderson (1978), Bergmann (1973), Coles (1975), Garraty (1954, 1957), Glad (1973), and Mack (1971), and bibliographies in Cremerius (1971), DeMause (1975), and Gilmore (1976, 1979a, 1979b). There are also now journals devoted to the field with the *Psychohistory Review* and the *Journal of Psychohistory,* with occasional contributions in journals such as *Biography,* the *Journal of Interdisciplinary History,* and a great variety of other journals in history, literature, political science, psychoanalysis, and psychology.

2. This interpretation of Wilson's behavior has been challenged in Weinstein, Anderson, and Link (1978) and Weinstein (1981) with an alternative theory that Wilson suffered from a series of small strokes in his later years, but defended with additional evidence in George and George (1981).

REFERENCES

Abraham, K. Giovanni Segantini: A psychoanalytical study. In *Clinical Papers and Essays.* New York: Basic Books, 1955. (Originally published, 1911.)

Abraham, K. Amenhotep IV (Ikhnaton): A psychoanalytic contribution to the understanding of his personality and the monotheistic cult of Aton. *Psychoanalytic Quarterly,* 1935, *4,* 537-569. (Originally published in *Imago,* 1912.)

American Psychiatric Association. Report of the Task Force on Psychohistory. *The psychiatrist as psychohistorian.* Washington, DC: American Psychiatric Association, 1976.

Anderson, J. W. The methodology of psychological biography. *Journal of Interdisciplinary History,* 1981, *XI,* 455-475. (a)

Anderson, J. W. Psychobiographical methodology: The case of William James. In L. Wheeler (Ed.), *Review of personality and social psychology* (Vol. 2). Beverly Hills, CA: Sage, 1981. (b)

Anderson, T. H. Becoming sane with psychohistory. *The Historian,* 1978, *41,* 1-20.

Anthony, K. *Margaret Fuller: A psychological biography.* New York: Harcourt, Brace, 1920.

Barber, J. D. *The presidential character: Predicting performance in the White House.* Englewood Cliffs, NJ: Prentice-Hall, 1972.

Barnes, H. E. Psychology and history: Some reasons for predicting their more active cooperation in the future. *American Journal of Psychology,* 1919, *30,* 337-376.

Barzun, J. *Clio and the doctors: Psycho-history, quanto-history & history.* Chicago: University of Chicago Press, 1974.

Bate, W. J. *Samuel Johnson.* New York: Harcourt Brace Jovanovich, 1977.

Bergmann, M. S. Limitations of method in psychoanalytic biography: A historical inquiry. *Journal of the American Psychoanalytic Association,* 1973, *21,* 833-850.

Bloom, B. *Stability and change in human characteristics.* New York: John Wiley, 1964.

Bowlby, J. *Maternal care and mental health.* Geneva, Switzerland: World Health Organization, 1952.

Brim, O. G., Jr., & Kagan, J. (Eds.). *Constancy and change in human development.* Cambridge, MA: Harvard University Press, 1980.

Brodie, B. A psychoanalytic interpretation of Woodrow Wilson. *World Politics,* 1957, *9,* 413-422.

Brodie, F. *Richard Nixon: The shaping of his character.* New York: W. W. Norton, 1981.

Chesen, E. *President Nixon's psychiatric profile.* New York: Peter H. Wyden, 1973.

Clark, L. P. Unconscious motives underlying the personalities of great statesmen. I. A psychologic study of Abraham Lincoln. *Psychoanalytic Review,* 1923, *10,* 56-69.

Clark, L. P. *Lincoln: A psychobiography.* New York: Scribner's, 1933.

Clarke, A. M. & Clarke, A.D.B. (Eds.). *Early experience: Myth and evidence.* New York: Free Press, 1976.

Clifford, J. L. (Ed.). *Biography as an art.* New York: Oxford University Press, 1962.

Cody, J. *After great pain: The inner life of Emily Dickinson.* Cambridge: Harvard University Press, 1971.

Coles, R. On psychohistory. In *The Mind's Fate.* Boston: Little, Brown, 1975.

Cremerius, J. (Ed.). *Neurose und genialität: Psychoanalytische biographien.* Frankfurt am Main: S. Fischer, 1971.

Cronbach, L. J. Beyond the two disciplines of scientific psychology. *American Psychologist,* 1975, *30,* 116-127.

Crosby, F. Evaluating psychohistorical explanations. *Psychohistory Review,* 1979, *7,* 6-16.

Crosby, F., & Crosby, T. L. Psychobiography and psychohistory. In S. Long (Ed.), *Handbook of political behavior* (Vol. 1). New York: Plenum, 1981.

Davis, G. The early years of Theodore Roosevelt: A study in character formation. *History of Childhood Quarterly,* 1975, *II,* 461-492.

DeMause, L. (Ed.). *A bibliography of psychohistory.* New York: Garland, 1975.

DeVoto, B. The skeptical biographer. *Harper's Magazine,* 1933, *166,* 181-192.

Dooley, L. Psychoanalytic studies of genius. *American Journal of Psychology,* 1916, *27,* 363-416.

Edel, L. *Henry James* (5 volumes). Philadelphia: Lippincott, 1953-1970.

Elms, A. C. *Personality in politics.* New York: Harcourt Brace Jovanovich, 1976.

Elms, A. C. Skinner's dark year and *Walden Two. American Psychologist,* 1981, *36,* 470-479.

Erikson, E. H. *Young man Luther: A study in psychoanalysis and history.* New York: W. W. Norton, 1958.

Erikson, E. H. *Gandhi's truth.* New York: W. W. Norton, 1969.

Erikson, E. H. *Life history and historical moment.* New York: W. W. Norton, 1975.

Fearing, F. Psychological studies of historical personalities. *Psychological Bulletin,* 1927, *24,* 521-539.

Fisher, S., & Greenberg, R. P. *The scientific credibility of Freud's theories and therapy.* New York: Basic Books, 1977.

Friedlander, S. *History and psychoanalysis.* New York: Holmes & Meier, 1978. (Originally published, 1975.)

Freud, S. *Leonardo da Vinci and a memory of his childhood. Standard Edition 12,* 3-82. London: Hogarth Press, 1957. (Originally published, 1910.)

Freud, S. *An outline of psychoanalysis. Standard Edition, 23,* 141-207. London: Hogarth Press, 1969. (Originally published, 1938.)

Garraty, J. A. The interrelations of psychology and biography. *Psychological Bulletin, 1954, 51,* 569-582.

Garraty, J. A. *The nature of biography.* New York: Vintage, 1957.

Gatzke, H. W. Hitler and psychohistory. *American Historical Review, 1973, 78,* 394-401.

Gedo, J. E. The methodology of psychoanalytic biography. *Journal of the American Psychoanalytic Association, 1972, 20,* 638-649.

George, A. L. Some uses of dynamic psychology in political biography: Case materials on Woodrow Wilson. In F. Greenstein & M. Lerner (Eds.), *A source book for the study of personality and politics.* Chicago: Markham, 1971.

George, A. L., & George, J. L. *Woodrow Wilson and Colonel House: A personality study.* New York: Dover, 1964. (Originally published, 1956.)

George, A. L., & George, J. L. *Woodrow Wilson and Colonel House:* A reply to Weinstein, Anderson and Link. International Society of Political Psychology, Mannheim, Germany, June, 1981.

Gergen, K. J. Social psychology as history. *Journal of Personality and Social Psychology, 1973, 26,* 309-320.

Gilmore, W. The methodology of psychohistory: An annotated bibliography. *The Psychohistory Review, 1976, 5,* 4-33.

Gilmore, W. Paths recently crossed: Alternatives to psychoanalytic psychohistory. *The Psychohistory Review, 1979, 7(3),* 43-49. (a)

Gilmore, W. Paths recently crossed: Alternatives to psychoanalytic psychohistory (continued). *The Psychohistory Review, 1979, 7(4),* 26-42. (b)

Glad, B. Contributions of psychobiography. In J. Knutson (Ed.), *Handbook of political psychology.* San Francisco: Jossey-Bass, 1973.

Graf, M. Richard Wagner in the "Flying Dutchman." A contribution to the psychology of artistic creation (English translation). *Schriften zur angewandten Seelunkunde,* 1911, *IX,* 45 pages.

Greenacre, P. *Swift and Carroll: A psychoanalytic study of two lives.* New York: International Universities Press, 1955.

Greenstein, F. *Personality and politics: Problems of evidence, inference, and conceptualization* (new ed.). New York: W. W. Norton, 1975. (a)

Greenstein, F. Personality and politics. In F. Greenstein & N. Polsby (Eds.), *The handbook of political science,* (Vol. 2). Reading, MA: Addison-Wesley, 1975. (b)

Guttmacher, M. G. *America's last king: An interpretation of the madness of George III.* New York: Scribner's, 1941.

Harlow, R. V. *Samuel Adams.* New York: Holt, 1923.

Hofling, C. K. Current problems in psychohistory. *Comprehensive Psychiatry, 1976, 17,* 227-239.

Hughes, H. S. *History as art and as science.* New York: Harper & Row, 1964.

Hundert, E. J. History, psychology, and the study of deviant behavior. *Journal of Interdisciplinary History,* 1972, *2,* 453-472.

Izenberg, G. Psychohistory and intellectual history. *History and Theory,* 1975, *14,* 139-155.

Jones, E. The Oedipus complex as an explanation of Hamlet's mystery: A study in motive. *American Journal of Psychology,* 1910, *21,* 72-113.

Karpas, M. J. Socrates in the light of modern psychopathology. *Journal of Abnormal Psychology,* 1915, *10,* 185-200.

Kelly, E. L. Consistency of the adult personality. *American Psychologist,* 1955, *10,* 659-681.

Kline, P. *Fact and fantasy in Freudian theory.* London: Methuen, 1972.

Kohut, H. Beyond the bounds of the basic rule. *Journal of the American Psychoanalytic Association,* 1960, *8,* 567-586.

Krutch, J. W. *Edgar Allen Poe.* New York: Knopf, 1926.

Langer, Walter C. *The mind of Adolf Hitler.* New York: Basic Books, 1972.

Langer, William L. The next assignment. *American Historical Review,* 1958, *63* (2), 283-304.

Lasswell, H. D. *Power and personality.* New York: W. W. Norton, 1948.

Lifton, R. J. *Death in life: Survivors of Hiroshima.* New York: Random House, 1967.

Loewenberg, P. The psychohistorical origins of the Nazi youth cohort. *American Historical Review,* 1971, *76,* 1457-1502.

Lonner, W. The search for psychological universals. In H. Triandis & W. Lambert (Eds.), *The handbook of cross-cultural psychology* (Vol. 1). Boston: Allyn & Bacon, 1979.

Mack, J. E. Psychoanalysis and historical biography. *Journal of the American Psychoanalytic Association,* 1971, *19,* 143-179.

Mack, J. E. *A prince of our disorder: The life of T. E. Lawrence.* Boston: Little, Brown, 1976.

Manuel, F. E. *A portrait of Isaac Newton.* Cambridge, MA: Harvard University Press, 1968.

Manuel, F. E., & Manuel, F. P. *Utopian thought in the Western world.* Cambridge, MA: Harvard University Press, 1979.

Mazlish, B. (Ed.). *Psychoanalysis and history* (rev. ed.) New York: Grosset & Dunlap, 1971.

Mazlish, B. *James and John Stuart Mill: Father and son in the nineteenth century.* New York: Basic Books, 1975.

Mazlish, B. *The revolutionary ascetic: Evolution of a political type.* New York: Basic Books, 1976.

Meyer, B. C. Some reflections on the contribution of psychoanalysis to biography. *Psychoanalysis and Contemporary Science,* 1972, *1,* 373-391.

Mischel, W. *Personality & assement.* New York: John Wiley, 1968.

Mitzman, A. *The iron cage: An historical interpretation of Max Weber.* New York: Grosset & Dunlap, 1969.

Orlow, D. The significance of time and place in psychohistory. *Journal of Interdisciplinary History,* 1974, *1,* 131-138.

Reich, W. *Character analysis.* New York: Noonday Press, 1949. (Originally published, 1933.)

Reich, W. *The mass psychology of fascism.* New York: Farrar, Straus and Giroux, 1973. (Originally published, 1933.)

Reich, W. *The function of the orgasm.* New York: World, 1971. (Originally published, 1942.)

Rogin, M. P. *Fathers & children: Andrew Jackson and the subjugation of the American Indian.* New York: Knopf, 1975.

Runyan, W. M. The life course as a theoretical orientation: Sequences of person-situation interaction. *Journal of Personality,* 1978, *46,* 569-593.

Runyan, W. M. A stage-state analysis of the life course. *Journal of Personality and Social Psychology,* 1980, *38,* 951-962.

Runyan, W. M. Why did Van Gogh cut off his ear? The problem of alternative explanations in psychobiography. *Journal of Personality and Social Psychology,* 1981, *40,* 1070-1077.

Runyan, W. M. In defense of the case study method. *American Journal of Orthopsychiatry,* 1982, *52,* 440-446.

Runyan, W. M. *Life histories and psychobiography: Explorations in theory and method.* New York: Oxford University Press, in press.

Rutter, M. Maternal deprivation, 1972-1978: New findings, new concepts, new approaches. *Child Development,* 1979, *50,* 282-305.

Scharfstein, B. *The philosophers: Their lives and the nature of their thought.* New York: Oxford University Press, 1980.

Simonton, D. K. The library laboratory: Archival data in personality and social psychology. In L. Wheeler (Ed.), *Review of personality and social psychology* (Vol. 2). Beverly Hills, CA: Sage, 1981.

Smith, P. Luther's early development in the light of psycho-analysis. *American Journal of Psychology,* 1913, *24,* 360-377.

Solomon, M. *Beethoven.* New York: Schirmer Books, 1977.

Stannard, D. E. *Shrinking history: On Freud and the failure of psychohistory.* New York: Oxford University Press, 1980.

Sterba, E., & Sterba, R. *Beethoven and his nephew: A psychoanalytic study of their relationship.* New York: Pantheon, 1954.

Stolorow, R. D., & Atwood, G. E. *Faces in a cloud: Subjectivity in personality theory.* New York: Jason Aronson, 1979.

Stone, L. *The past and the present.* Boston: Routledge & Kegan Paul, 1981.

Tetlock, P. E., Crosby, F., & Crosby, T. L. Political psychobiography. *Micropolitics,* 1981, *1,* 191-213.

Triandis, H. C. Some universals of social behavior. *Personality and Social Psychology Bulletin,* 1978, *4,* 1-16.

Triandis, H. C., & Lambert, W. W. (Eds.). *The handbook of cross-cultural psychology.* New York: W. W. Norton, 1973.

Tucker, R. C. *Stalin as revolutionary 1879-1929: A study in history and personality.* New York: W. W. Norton, 1973.

Tucker, R. C. The Georges' Wilson reexamined: An essay on psychobiography. *American Political Science Review,* 1977, *71,* 606-618.

Wachtel, P. Interaction cycles, unconscious processes, and the person-situation issue. In D. Magnusson & N. Endler (Eds.), *Personality at the crossroads.* Hillsdale, NJ: Lawrence Erlbaum, 1977.

Waite, R.G.L. *The psychopathic God: Adolf Hitler.* New York: Basic Books, 1977.

Weinstein, E. A. *Woodrow Wilson: A medical and psychological biography.* Princeton: Princeton University Press, 1981.

Weinstein, E. A., Anderson, J. W., & Link, A. S. Woodrow Wilson's political personality: A reappraisal. *Political Science Quarterly,* 1978, *93,* 585-598.

Whilbey, C. The indiscretions of biography. *English Review,* 1924, *39,* 769-772.

Wilson, E. Woodrow Wilson at Princeton. In *Shores of light.* New York: Farrar, Straus and Young, 1952.

Wolfenstein, E. V. *The revolutionary personality: Lenin, Trotsky, Gandhi.* Princeton: Princeton University Press, 1967.

Woods, J. M. Some considerations on psycho-history. *The Historian,* 1974, *36,* 722-735.

Wyatt, F. Psychoanalytic biography. (A review of P. Greenacre, *Swift and Carroll.*) *Contemporary Psychology,* 1956, *1,* 105-107.

10

An Introduction to the Use of Structural Equations:

PROSPECTS AND PROBLEMS

HARRY T. REIS

Harry T. Reis is Associate Professor of Psychology at the University of Rochester, where he tries to teach students that the choice of statistical procedures is never theory-free. He wrote this chapter while on sabbatical leave at the University of Denver. His current research interests include justice motivation and naturalistic studies of social interaction.

Path analysis. Causal modeling. Structural equations. Structural modeling. Latent indicator structural relations. It's enough to drive researchers taught that "correlation is not causality" back to the 2 x 2 factorial experiment. Curiously, though, when Galton first asked mathematician J.D.H. Dickson to help him quantify "regression towards mediocrity in hereditary stature," he thought such an index would be superior to

AUTHOR'S NOTE: I am deeply appreciative to the following people for comments on earlier versions of this chapter: David Kenny, Mark Zanna, and Marilynn Brewer. Thanks are also due to Ladd Wheeler and Ellen Nakhnikian for inspiration. Writing of this chapter was greatly facilitated by sabbatical leave aid and encouragement provided by the Department of Psychology, University of Denver.

statistics requiring the underlying assumption of causality (Galton, 1886, 1894). Notably, this was because correlations assessed causal relationships in addition to all other forms of association that could not properly be called causal. In recent years, most personality and social psychologists have come to see Galton's "superiority" as a debit, since causal relations could not be distinguished from other associations. This limitation had more dire consequences for those social sciences that cannot perform experimental manipulation and random assignment as readily as psychology: sociology, political science, and economics. Consequently, in these fields, a greater premium was placed on the development and advocacy of techniques that did allow the researcher to gain information about causality, somehow, from correlational data. These methods, which were originally titled "path analysis," are now more generally known as structural modeling procedures. They began to have appeal for psychologists when their use became widespread and it became apparent that, under certain conditions, it was in fact possible to test causal connections with correlation coefficients.

Unfortunately, structural modeling has been misappropriated and misunderstood more often than it has been properly used. Chief among the misconceptions is the fact that a simple path diagram of the kind usually found in journal articles does not validate that interpretation of the causal flow of events. Alternatively, many researchers neglect these techniques because they are thought to be difficult. Yet most path analyses are simply a structured series of regression analyses. Properly utilized, structural modeling has a great deal to offer us, particularly because of its versatility for analyzing data collected in naturalistic settings (Reis, in press), and its ability to help uncover underlying processes in experimental work (Taylor & Fiske, 1982). It can greatly enhance our capacity to describe the pattern of interrelationship among a body of variables; it can identify the importance of mediating variables in how one variable influences another variable; and, if applied correctly, it enables researchers to choose between competing theories and causal interpretations. On a slightly different level, because of the necessary close interplay between content and analysis, it can expand our ability to conceptualize substantive relationships among variables. Thus, the promise appears fertile for personality and social psychology.

The purpose of this chapter is to provide a broad introduction to structural equation methods, emphasizing what can and cannot be done.

The stress will be on composing a logical framework for conducting such analyses, rather than providing formulas. Even most elementary presentations are heavily mathematical; this discussion will not be, using only very fundamental algebra to establish the meaning of path coefficients. It is to be emphasized that structural models are merely an extension of statistics that psychologists already know. This extension refers to the conduct of traditional regression analyses within the context of a formal system of logical inference principles. In other words, this discussion is intended to be sufficiently simple to permit most psychologists to become aware of what structural modeling is, to be able to review research using these procedures more intelligently, to perceive new possibilities in their own research, and to know where to turn for elaboration. Because of these goals, complexity will be avoided and references to more detailed sources will be frequent.

THE SIMPLEST CASE:
PARTIAL CORRELATIONS

The concept of apportioning variance among several predictors of a single criterion is certainly not new to social and personality psychology. Most graduate-level statistics sequences include some coverage of partialing techniques such as partial correlations or analysis of covariance. One use of these techniques, it turns out, represents the most basic case of structural modeling as a theory comparison technique. Although many psychologists are familiar with the concept of partialing, usually as a means of statistically equating groups that are not equivalent on control or demographic variables that might obscure the impact of the independent variable, it is vastly underutilized relative to the number of theories and empirical statements that could benefit from such tests. Much of the mathematics and some of the notation is similar to that typically used in the structural modeling literature; more important, the logic of phrasing and evaluating theories in structural terms is identical.

Mediation is a key concept in social-personality research. When we demonstrate an effect, we invariably describe the processes believed to be responsible for its occurrence. Quite often, this requires mediating variables, be they underlying and unmeasured or explicitly incorporated into the research design. This mediating variable is said to be somehow responsible for the impact of the independent variable on the dependent variable.

For example, proximity is thought to influence interpersonal attraction because people who are nearer have more frequent opportunities to reward each other (Newcomb, 1956). The mediating variable herein is, of course, the provision of rewards.

Let me use a more problematic theoretical relationship for illustration. A well-replicated finding in the literature is that physically attractive people are more likable than unattractive people (e.g., Dion, Berscheid, & Walster, 1972). Among the numerous potential explanations for this phenomenon is the contrast between two viable models which, although similar, have decidedly different implications. Both concern the role of social competence. Model I can be referred to as the mediational hypothesis: that due to a history of more favorable social experiences, attractive persons come to be more socially skilled. In turn, these skills make them more likable. In other words, social competence mediates the impact of physical attractiveness on likability, as shown in the top of Figure 1. What is particularly unique about this model is that there is no direct path from attractiveness to likability; no cause-and-effect relationship exists between them except for that mediated by social skills. Model II posits a joint effect: Although physical attractiveness and social competence may both relate to likability (and to each other), attractiveness exerts an influence on likability that is independent of competence. (For example, cultural stereotypes might specify that beauty is socially desirable in and of itself.) Examine the Venn diagrams for each of the models. One can think of each circle as representing the total variance of the scores for each variable. The overlap areas portray the variance shared between two variables, or their covariance (squared). If the variables are standardized, the covariance, and hence the overlap areas, equals the correlation between the variables. Suppose now that all of the variance attributable to social skills is removed from Model I. This is accomplished essentially by holding skills constant and eliminating any areas (that is, variance) it shares with attractiveness or likability. What is left? The two crescents labeled a and b, which clearly do not overlap—they do not correlate with each other. In other words, if Model I depicts the true phenomenon, when social competence is partialed out, no correlation remains between attractiveness and likability. If, however, Model II represents reality, partialing will leave overlap and therefore correlation. This is shown in area c. Substantively, it means that attractiveness and likability are at least partially associated with each other in a manner unrelated to skills.

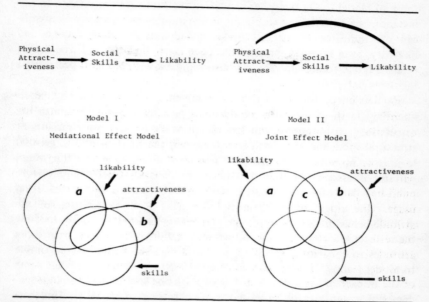

Figure 1: Two hypothetical models of the relationship between physical attractiveness and likability.

Since partial correlations perform this topological juggling mathematically, the value of the partial correlation between attractiveness and likability controlling for skills informs us whether the mediational model is consistent with the actual data[1] (see Cohen & Cohen, 1975, pp. 79-84, for a clear discussion of how equation 1 does this). For example, we might have collected the following hypothetical data: $r_{A,S} = .70$, $r_{A,L} = .50$, and $r_{S,L} = .70$. Since the formula for partial correlation is:

$$pr_{AL.S} = \frac{r_{AL} - r_{AS}r_{SL}}{\sqrt{1 - r_{AS}^2}\ \sqrt{1 - r_{SL}^2}} \qquad [1]$$

we would attain a *pr* of .02. Compare this result to the simple *r* of .50. It indicates that when one controls for social competence, virtually no relationship between appearance and likability remains. Consequently, the diagrams in Model I more nearly reflect the overall pattern of data than those of Model II. On the other hand, imagine that $r_{AS} = r_{SL} = .50$. In this instance, the *pr* obtained would be .33. Assuming this value to be significant, it indicates a substantial relationship between attractiveness and likability, even after competence has been controlled. Model I would then be inadequate to account for the observed data, with Model II providing a relatively better fit.

Readers uncomfortable with these arguments might be helped by experimenting on their own with the diagrams or computations. Although the calculations, assumptions, and specifications of the numerous variants of structural modeling are considerably greater, the fundamental inferential logic is no more complex than that presented above. One tests the overall pattern of association that the theory predicts. A brief example from published data might be useful in demonstrating such a theory-evaluation usage. One aspect of Fishbein and Ajzen's (1975) explanation of the attitude-behavior relationship stipulates that behavioral intentions mediate the effects of attitudes on subsequent actions. No direct path from attitudes to behavior is specified, so that a diagram would be comparable to Model I above. Zuckerman and Reis (1978) speculated that while some of the impact of attitudes on behavior might be so produced, an independent link could also be proposed, similar to that of Model II. Thus, the Fishbein-Ajzen position would predict that partialing intentions from the attitude-behavior relationship should yield a nonsignificant correlation, while the Zuckerman-Reis argument expects that term to remain significant. Using the arena of blood donations, the following correlations were obtained from 189 college students: $r_{AI} = .44$; $r_{AB} = .36$; $r_{IB} = .45$. The partial *r*, removing the effect of intentions, was .20 ($p < .005$). Therefore, the data were more nearly consistent with Model II. Another, simpler way of expressing this result is to note that including a term representing a direct effect of attitudes on behavior that is not mediated by intentions enables the researcher to predict behavior more effectively than from intentions alone.

Before extending these ideas to formal path analysis, a parenthetical note seems in order. Too much research in social and personality psychology falters one step short of providing compelling evidence for hypothesized mediators. By one step short, I refer to those studies that are comprehensive enough to include measures of anticipated mediators and detailed enough to show that these relate to the independent variables in much the same manner that the dependent variable does.[2] Yet this is an incomplete test. Such a variable might merely parallel the actual causal relationship rather than account for it. If a mediator truly serves as an intervening process, then partialing should substantially diminish the primary relationship, if not eradicate it altogether. In regression analyses, this can be done by partial correlations. In the experimental ANOVA framework, the analysis of covariance accomplishes the identical task (since the procedures are one and the same). As an example of an instance in which this could have been done, consider Weary (1980). One purpose of this experiment was to examine the role of affect and egotism as mediators of attributional bias. The author presents three sets of analyses: ANOVAs for attributions, and for the potential mediators, and correlations between them. The conclusion that egotism probably mediates the attributional differences that were found is based on the fact that both were influenced by the independent variables similarly, and that they were correlated with each other (across conditions). While this result might indicate an intervening variable, it might not. A stronger test is available: The analyses for attributions could have been repeated, *controlling for egotism or affect.* If the mediational hypothesis is correct, the once significant effects should now be eliminated. If they are not, then mediation would not be supported.[3]

The point is that partialing provides a strong test of mediational processes and that we ought to be doing this whenever the hypotheses so dictate; for example, in positing that sex-role-related traits mediate the impact of gender on social behavior; that nonverbal cues may be one mechanism by which expectations become reality in self-fulfilling prophecies; or that motivational or informational factors are responsible for situational or personality differences in outcome attributions.

PATH ANALYSIS

The Basic Case

Numerous authors in the structural modeling literature have indicated that although the logic of partial correlation is applicable, regression coefficients are more appropriate for computational purposes. This is for two reasons: first, because regression coefficients provide better estimates of the path between two variables (e.g., Duncan, 1975, pp. 22-24); and second, because the actual value of the partial correlation may be mislead-

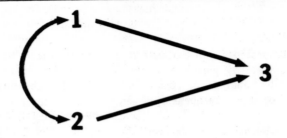

Figure 2: One basic model.

ing when one partials out a variable not directly involved in the flow from cause to effect. For these reasons, as well as many others, it is more useful to think of structural models in terms of regression equations. Since this point is at the heart of the structural modeling approach, it might be more credible to demonstrate this with some basic algebra.

Consider the model in Figure 2. It symbolizes the hypothesis that variable 3 is caused by variables 1 and 2. These latter two variables may be related to each other, as indicated by the curved arrow between them, but their causes are outside this system. Variables whose causes are totally outside the system are usually called *exogenous* (1 and 2); those at least partially determined by variables within the system are called *endogenous* (3). Of course, since none of the relationships are perfect, all three variables are influenced by other, unmeasured factors as well. These are typically called *disturbances* in the path analysis literature, but are better known as error variance in traditional statistical treatments. Disturbance terms do affect the equations that follow, but to focus the argument on the central issue, we will defer discussion of their role until the following section.

An algebraic version of Figure 2 would be as follows. We use the letter z to indicate that these are standardized scores:

$$z_3 = p_{31}z_1 + p_{32}z_2 \tag{2}$$

In English, z_3 is caused by z_2 and z_1 with the degree of impact each has being weighted by p, which we will refer to as a path coefficient. The larger p_{31} is, the more of a change in z_3 a given change in z_1 produces.[4] If p_{31} is zero, then changes in z_1 do not affect z_3 at all.

The path coefficient p appears at first glance to be a new statistical index. Most students would be pleased if this value turned out to be equivalent to a more familiar term. Appendix A presents such a hopeful derivation. It depends entirely on high school algebra, and readers are urged (even exhorted) to follow the equations for themselves. This will make the equivalence of coefficients far more credible, in a "gut belief" sense; it will also engender considerable feelings of mastery, no trivial feat given the mathematical complexity typically used to portray path equations.

As the simple steps of Appendix A demonstrate, p is exactly equal to the standardized regression coefficient, β or:

$$P_{31} = \frac{r_{13} - r_{12} r_{23}}{1 - r_{12}^2} = \beta_{31} \qquad [3]$$

This is the weighting coefficient obtained from simple least-squares regression analysis (see Cohen & Cohen, 1975, pp. 75-78 if this is unclear), so that in most cases a path coefficient is the same as the beta weight with which most psychologists are already familiar.[5] This correspondence is fortunate, because it implies (a) that the path coefficient is *not* a new concept to be mastered and (b) that standard multiple regression computer programs can be used to estimate their value. Readers with any doubt on this point are referred to Appendix A.

An Example

If beta weights and path coefficients are analogous, then any path diagram can be understood in much the same manner as can a regression analysis. Figure 3 presents Helmreich, Spence, Beane, Lucker, and Matthews's (1980) path model of "making it in academic psychology." All of the weights are standardized regression coefficients and may be compared, tested for significance, used to predict outcome scores, and so on. For example, the regression (or path) equation for predicting the number of citations would be:

Citations = .21 Publications − .44 Sex + .31 Graduate Dept. +   [4]
.22 Current Dept. + .33 Mastery-Work X Competitiveness

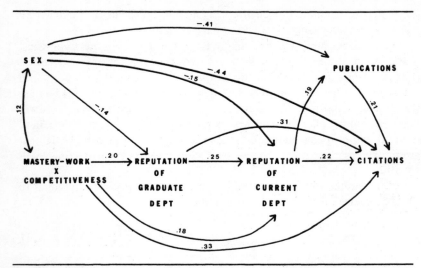

Figure 3: Helmreich et al. (1980) model of success in academic psychology. Copy-
      right 1980 by the American Psychological Association. Reprinted/adapted
      by permission of the publisher and author.

(Mastery-Work X Competitiveness refers to the interaction of these two
components of need achievement.) Once one standardizes the raw scores,
it would be possible to derive the number of citations from this equation.
One z – score unit worth of publication is worth .21 citations, whereas one
z – score unit worth of higher status of one's graduate department is worth
more, .31 citations. What makes the modeling approach interesting is the
proposed sequence of variables and the paths that are missing. For
instance, note that there is no path from the mastery-work x competitiveness interaction to number of publications. Yet these variables are correlated ($r = .13$, $p < .05$). The implication is that the effect is indirect,
mediated by the impact the interaction has on one's graduate and current
departments, which in turn influences publications.

If the reader is tempted to ask "Is that all there is?" at this point, then
the answer must be an unqualified yes and no. Yes, because conceptually,
path analysis can be interpreted and visualized in exactly the same way
one might think of regression equations. Yes, further, because in most
instances the path coefficients will equal the traditional least-squares

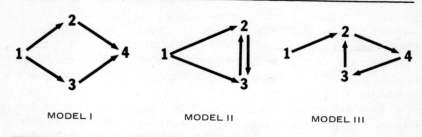

MODEL I   MODEL II   MODEL III

Figure 4: One recursive and two nonrecursive models.

regression weights. But the nos are what lend to structural modeling the exciting potential analysts see for expanding the horizons of psychological research, as well as the complexity that occupies their efforts. Two issues predominate here: less important are the statistical assumptions underlying the previous computations, and more important is the role of theory in guiding structural analyses.

Underlying assumptions. Unfortunately, path coefficients cannot always be estimated by regression weights. There are two necessary (but not sufficient) conditions for this statement to hold. The first is that the models must be recursive; the second is that the various disturbance (error) terms may not be correlated with any predetermined variable in the diagram. The term "recursive" refers to the directional flow in the path model. A recursive model is one which travels only in a single direction, so that the path can never return to a variable it previously included. Model I in Figure 4 is a recursive model; Models II and III are nonrecursive, since in both one can return to variable 2 as an effect subsequent to viewing it as a cause. Such causation is reciprocal, in that variables may be caused ultimately by their effects and consequently require more sophisticated treatment than provided herein. Kenny (1979) presents appropriate techniques for nonrecursive models, as does Duncan (1975). The assumption that disturbances be uncorrelated with predetermined variables is necessary because, were it not the case, the prediction equations would include terms reflecting their impact and, consequently, the ordinary least-squares solution reached in Appendix A would not be correct. This is one among many ways a model can be *underidentified*—that is, have more unknown causal parameters (i.e., path coefficients to be estimated) than observed correlations between actually measured variables. This state of affairs produces more unknowns than equations, an algebraic conundrum. Kenny (1979, chap. 5) and Duncan (1975, chap. 6) offer solutions, but these are not without ambiguity, since they involve adding restrictions, which requires a great deal of theoretical caution or two-stage least-squares procedures.

A final caution concerns the impact of measurement error on the estimation of path coefficients. Regression artifacts attributable to measurement error can have serious (and not always obvious) effects (Cook & Campbell, 1979), and this is especially true in partialing and path-analytic procedures. Greater attention to establishing the reliability of one's measures is one solution; the advent of structural techniques that incorporate confirmatory factor analysis is another (see a later section on the future of structural models).

The role of theory. No statistical technique is ever theory-free *ever*. All statistical applications depend on a meaningful theory of what the relevant variables are and how they ought to be related. Too often, the calculations do not actually test the hypotheses that the theory postulates, rendering results of limited or nil relevance to our fundamental concerns—namely, the concepts. Structural modeling is particularly vulnerable to such matters. It simply cannot be employed in any meaningful way without an a priori understanding of the substantive issues. Moreover, it requires a great deal of sophistication in demanding specification not simply of the fact that variables X and Y ought to be related but the mechanism by which all of the variables in the system relate to all others.

A simultaneous or stepwise regression analysis can be carried out blindly, as existing packaged programs facilitate all too easily: The investigator simply stipulates which variable is the criterion and which are to be predictors. While a path diagram may result, it would likely be theoretically uninteresting: There would be a few exogenous variables that, in one step, lead to the endogenous variables. Further, the linkages that are output might be conceptual nonsense or might not test hypotheses that psychologists care about. Referring to Figure 3, the theoretical advantage of the model is in the ordering of steps and in the direct paths that are omitted. To generate this model, one would first have to indicate which variables are purely exogenous—sex and the mastery-work x competitiveness interaction. Then one would identify the reputation of the graduate department as a first outcome, the reputation of the current department as the second, publications as the third, and citations as the final stage. While sometimes this ordering is temporal, other times no such guidelines are available. Theory must then be the guide. The analyst must also enumerate which prior variables ought to determine each and every outcome, requiring a thorough knowledge of the processes involved. Essentially, these two tasks boil down to the conceptualization and assignment of *direct* and *indirect* paths. Direct paths depict the influence of one variable on another without any intervening variables, at least that have been measured currently. Indirect paths indicate that one variable affects another through the mediation of a third variable. Much of what makes a given structural model intriguing and innovative are the indirect paths: Variables that are correlated with each other, but only because of a crucial intermediary concept. For example, in the first model presented earlier, physical attractiveness was hypothesized to influence likability only because of the mediating role of social skills. I will describe a procedure for determining direct and indirect paths shortly.

An even more compelling argument for the role of theory in structural modeling is its ability to evaluate the relative efficacy of differing theoretical models. Regression analyses do not implicate causality, of course, any more than correlations do. Hence, as will be elaborated below, a structural model, even with a temptingly high R^2, provides no confirmation of causal veridicality. *At all.* (This is one of the most common abuses of path analysis as currently practiced.) However, if there are competing theoretical models in the literature, structural techniques can compare their ability to account for a given data set. Thus, one can validly conclude that the data are more nearly consistent with one set of constructs than another. This does permit causal inference, wholly of the disconfirmation type (Popper, 1959). Obviously, defining and evaluating alternative causal networks requires a strong sense of theory.

It is this crucial interface with substantive theory that renders structural modeling both its delicacy and its promise for social and personality psychology. It threatens to empower the statistician's saw that data analysis cannot be done independent of the content issues.

Description and Evaluation with Structural Models

Now that we have discussed what a structural model is, and the context in which they should be used, it remains to be shown what they buy for us. A basic bifurcation of application exists, distinguishing description versus testing. Kenny (1979) has astutely compared these to descriptive versus inferential statistics, an elementary distinction more widely known. There are two descriptive strategies of note: the articulation of data structures and the determination of direct and indirect influences. A third function is inferential, testing the efficacy of competing models.

Articulation of Data Structures

In its most basic function, a structural model, like its regression analogue, simultaneously details the interrelations of all variables within a system. Most notably, the relative contribution of each of several predictor variables is distinguished, so that proportions of variance that could be attributed to more than one predictor are in fact subdivided among them to avoid redundancy. This is accomplished by incorporating into the mathematics the correlations of the predictors among themselves. The beta weights (and hence path coefficients) that result are called *partial* regression coefficients, because they control for the impact of other predictors.

A structural model is quite useful in articulating these partialed relationships. Assuming the variables are standardized, comparison of the path coefficients discloses the relative role of the various predictors in determining the outcome variable. It also indicates which paths are not necessary, thus encouraging theoretical parsimony and, by contrast with the correlation matrix, can pinpoint the location of mediated or shared effects. In plainer terms, a structural diagram may be worth a thousand words. It simply shows how all the variables are related to each other, within the constraints of the temporal order specified by the researcher.

Figure 5, taken from Bachman and O'Malley's (1977) longitudinal study of the impact of educational and occupational attainment on later self-esteem, exemplifies this approach. For example, it can be seen that high school self-esteem predicts later self-esteem better than does occupational status, or that the effects of socioeconomic background on occupational status and high school self-esteem are largely due to the intervening role of academic ability, performance, and attainment. Figure 5 documents the interrelationships of these variables far more clearly than the correlation matrix in Table 1, even though, of course, they depict the identical data. It goes without saying that very careful examination of Table 1 could have produced the same interpretations. High school self-esteem correlates far higher with later self-esteem than any other predic-

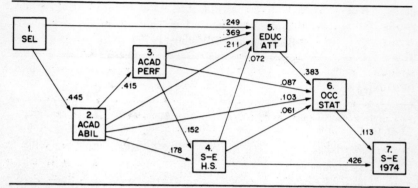

Figure 5: Backman and O'Malley (1977) model of antecedents of self-esteem. Variable 1 = socioeconomic level; variable 2 = academic ability; variable 3 = academic performance; variable 4 = self-esteem; variable 5 = educational attainment; variable 6 = occupational status; variable 7 = self-esteem five years after high school. Copyright 1977 by the American Psychological Association. Reprinted by permission of the publisher and author.

tor, implying that there ought to be a strong, direct path between them. Or take socioeconomic background. It correlates moderately with academic ability (.45), which in turn is correlated with performance (.42). Since background and performance are only weakly correlated (.20), we would anticipate an indirect path, as Figure 5 shows.

Such interocular tests do not meet reasonable standards of rigor, but they are nonetheless helpful in gaining an intuitive grasp of a set of data. A path diagram formalizes and extends what shrewd inspection might discern. But there is a vital caveat to be made here, one which is often (and seriously) at fault in most current journal uses of path analysis. Analyses such as the above do not provide support for the veracity of the model. For one reason, there are undoubtedly numerous other unstated models capable of accounting for the same data equally well or better. Some of these involve different orderings of the same variables; others incorporate variables not measured in the present study. Path coefficients are, as we have shown, regression weights, and regression weights depend not only on how predictors relate to a criterion but on how the set of predictors relate to each other as well. (Suppressor variables supply a convincing demonstration of this inevitable fact.) To make a claim for a given model, it must be

TABLE 1
Product-Moment Correlations Taken from
Bachman and O'Malley (1977)

Variable	Variable					
	2	3	4	5	6	7
1. Family socioeconimic level	.445	.204	.158	.426	.248	.034
2. Academic ability	—	.415	.241	.491	.342	.124
3. Academic performance		—	.226	.523	.344	.099
4. High school self-esteem			—	.245	.199	.448
5. Educational attainment				—	.494	.117
6. Occupational status					—	.198
7. Adult self-esteem						—

Note: N = 1043

shown to be superior to another conceptualization in some fashion. A second reason is that these models are frequently constructed via Heise's (1975) method of theory trimming, a procedure in which nonsignificant paths that have little influence are deleted from the diagram. While this is a desirable step in deriving a parsimonious, efficient model, it is hardly equivalent to evaluating a hypothesized course of events. Minimally, a first study should be used to develop a trimmed model, which is then formally tested for adequacy with a second set of data (see below). For a third reason, path coefficients are based on correlations. If correlations cannot indicate causality by themselves, neither can their heirs.

In short, a path model constructed from available data simply articurates the numerous interconnections possessed by a set of data within the theorist's proposed theoretical framework. This is all that such a "single shot" usage buys us, but it is also quite a lot. The use of structural modeling for theory testing requires other considerations, which will be outlined in the section following the next.

Determination of Direct and Indirect Influences

As mentioned earlier, a variable can influence another directly or indirectly. An *indirect* cause is one mediated by some other measured

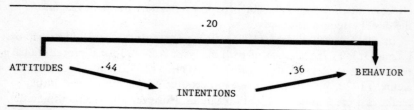

Figure 6: Models testing the mediating role of intentions.

construct, while a *direct* cause proceeds without intervention. (Of course, there is no such thing as a purely direct cause, since any effect is likely to depend on more molecular social, perceptual, and physiological processes. The use of the terms "direct" and "indirect" is to be reserved for the influence of variables assessed in the current research.)

It is probably useful to do more than merely assert the existence of indirect effects. Comparison of the relative magnitude of direct and indirect effects can give researchers clues about the importance of each distinct mechanism influencing the criterion. Consider the Zuckerman-Reis (1978) modification of the Fishbein-Ajzen (1975) attitude-behavior model discussed earlier and now depicted in Figure 6. Extrapolating from equation 6, the correlation between attitudes and behavior can be expressed as:

$$r_{AB} = p_{BA} + p_{BI}r_{IA} \qquad [5]$$

Since there is one and only one predictor for intentions, $r_{IA} = \beta_{IA} = p_{IA}$ and therefore r_{AB} can be written solely as a function of path coefficients.

$$r_{AB} = p_{BA} + p_{BI}p_{IA} \qquad [6]$$

The first term, p_{BA}, represents the direct effect of attitudes on behavior, since it quantifies the path from the former to the latter without any intervening steps. The product term, $p_{BI}p_{IA}$, reflects the indirect effect, as it embodies two shorter direct paths which, when taken together, comprise the mediated impact. Using the path coefficients presented above the arrows in Figure 6, one can see the direct effect (p_{BA}) equals .20, whereas the indirect effect ($p_{BI}p_{IA}$) equals .44 (.36), or .16. Thus the mediated effect of attitudes on behavior is of approximately the same magnitude as the direct effect in this study.

In fact, Sewall Wright (1921) first proposed this multiplication, or tracing, rule as the essence of path analysis. A more formal procedure has recently been devised by Alwin and Hauser (1975) and is clarified by Kenny (1979, pp. 70-73). These procedures are recommended until the reader is more familiar with path diagrams. However, the results will be the same following Wright's heuristics. Given that a model is properly specified, the indirect effect of any variable on another can be estimated by the sum of the products of all coefficients for paths over which one must travel to reach the outcome from the predictor. [This will hold only for recursive models.] Sometimes more than two arrows will be involved. Each step contributes to the total effect. Almost always there will also be multiple indirect effects. For example, there are numerous pathways between academic ability and occupational status in the Bachman-O'Malley data (Figure 5). Academic ability does lead directly to occupation, $p_{62} = .103$, but it also leads to educational attainment, which in turn predicts status, $p_{52}p_{65} = .211 (.383) = .081$. Note that this indirect path is of similar magnitude to the direct effect, implying an important mediation. There are also less consequential two-step paths through performance and self-esteem, $p_{32}p_{63} = .415 (.087) = .036$ and $p_{42}p_{64} = .178 (.061) = .011$, respectively. Finally, there are numerous three-step paths, such as from ability to performance to attainment to status, $p_{32}p_{53}p_{65} = .415 (.369) (.383) = .059$. Assessing direct and indirect influences is no more difficult than this.

Some early popular treatments suggested that the indirect and direct effects will sum to the total effect—that is, the correlation (e.g., Kerlinger & Pedhazur, 1973, pp. 316-317). As Kenny (1979, pp. 70-71) has shown, this assumption is not correct when there are variables that occur earlier in the system. Such a "third variable" might spuriously account for shared variance in both cause and effect, even when they have no path between them. As a result, indirect effects should always be computed either by the multiplication rule or the Alwin-Hauser (1975) procedure. They can, and should, be compared to the correlation coefficients, since the value of r serves as an upper limit for the sum of direct and indirect effects. This is because a regression analysis subdivides the total degree of predictability among components. Obviously, when r and p are equal, there are no mediated effects. It is my opinion that social-personality psychologists will have their theoretical appetities most whetted when r and the direct effect are discrepant—or, in other words, when there are intervening variables on which to feast one's curiosity. This occurred in the previous example, in which academic ability correlated .342 with occupational status, despite the small direct effect, .103. This is the stuff of which interesting theories are made.

Testing Competing Models

The aspect of structural modeling which has aroused the most interest among psychologists is its capacity for evaluating the comparative validity of different causal models. Unfortunately, many researchers have confused this goal with the procedures outlined under the prior two subheadings. A structural model derived to account for a set of data does not, and cannot, prove its accuracy as the one and only true recounting of cause and effect, any more than a simple correlation demonstrates causality. This is true for one simple reason: For every set of data that can be described by a given model, there are a multitude of other models, usually unstated, that can characterize the same data equally well. Thus, proof or confirmation of one interpretation is not possible. What structural modeling can do is disconfirm alternatives and, in so doing, furnish relative support for one conceptualization over explicitly stated others. Even though procedures for such comparisons are readily available, social-personality psychologists have been slow to capitalize on this tool. Of eight articles published in the *Journal of Personality and Social Psychology* during 1980 that utilized structural methods, only one executed some form of model comparison tests—this despite the fact that the plethora of theoretical alternatives within our field would seem to beg for such tests.

Conceptually, the strategy for these procedures is quite elementary. Based on theory, intuition, and common sense, the researcher specifies a priori a series of viable models, every one of which could intelligently account for the phenomenon. Data are then collected and simultaneously fit to each model, to see if the predicted paths could have yielded the relationships that were actually obtained. If the answer is yes, then the data are consistent with that model. If the answer is no, the data are inconsistent with the model. This is the strongest statement that a formal structural analysis can forge: that because the data are consistent with one model and inconsistent with others, it is to be preferred as a formulation of what might be occurring. A finicky conclusion indeed, but one with a great deal of power *when* compelling alternatives that generate meaningfully different understandings are plentiful. A theory cannot be correct if it breeds connections that are not present in a reasonable sample of data.

Of course, the outcome of actual tests is likely to be more uncertain than the above. Unfortunately, rigorous, well-accepted criteria for how well the data fit a given model are not yet apparent in the literature. However, at least four useful and related techniques are available, each of which can be applied for these purposes along with a modicum of reasonability. The first, and simplest, is a version of the theory-trimming method proposed by Heise (1975). For a model to be useful, it should not posit that "everything is directly caused by everything else." (This constraint is also necessary for the model not to be hopelessly underidentified; see Kenny, 1979, p. 261). The test of competing models is then simply whether the paths hypothesized by each model are significant, and whether direct paths omitted by the hypothetical model are in fact dispensable. As an example, refer again to Figure 1. Model I predicts no direct path between physical attractiveness and likability (although, of course, they may still be correlated), whereas Model II does. If, on collecting and analyzing the data, the path coefficient for this path is significant, then the data are more nearly consistent with Model II than I. In other words, the specifications of Model I could not have produced the data we obtained. If the path coefficient was nonsignificant, then Model I more nearly represents the state of affairs. It goes without saying that such reasoning avoids spuriously capitalizing on chance only when the competing models are articulated prior to data collection.

Currently, no benchmarks exist for comparing errors of omission and inclusion across models. However, appropriate models should specify all paths necessary and sufficient for reproducing the data. One approach to this is using a pilot study to predict a model, and subsequent study to cross-validate it. An equally important shortcoming in the literature is the lack of a general standard for when a path is to be included and when it is not. Customarily, significance at $p < .05$ is adopted as the criterion. However, given the problems of power with small samples and triviality with large samples, some authors have suggested using an absolute value, such as $\beta = .05$ (Land, 1969). My recommendation would be to stick with custom, by setting alpha on the basis of the research hypothesis and choosing a suitably powerful sample size. Researchers using this criterion should remember that power can be low even with relatively large samples, due to multicollinearity.

Closely related in spirit to this procedure is the Simon-Blalock technique, which until recent years had been the favored tool of sociologists, political scientists, and economists using structural methods (Simon, 1957, 1971; Blalock, 1971). It is a partialing strategy in which the logical consequences of removing the effects of certain variables is systemically pursued. The central tenet is that by partialing all intervening variables, the remaining correlation between predictor and outcome should be zero. If it is not, the model is in error, since some other unspecified influence must be operative. For example, in the Bachman-O'Malley (1977) data of Figure 5, the correlation between occupational status and family socioeconomic level should be nil, within sampling error, when the effects of academic ability, performance, attainment, and high school self-esteem are partialed out. The systematic aspect of the Simon-Blalock procedure is that all paths identified by a model as being mediated should be tested. Goldberg (1971) provides a nice demonstration of this process, along with the methodical revision of a model in accord with the results. Caution must be stressed in recommending this technique. As Simon (1971), Duncan (1975), and numerous others point out, it is difficult to distinguish intervening cause from spurious cause; that is, from a third variable that affects two others, which are then related only by dint of their common cause. One would do well to become familiar with partialing effects before relying on these tests. Relatedly, one of the beauties of Simon-Blalock is that it requires the researcher to follow through and understand all of the proposed links in the model. While this is performed statistically, it demands a thorough comprehension of the concepts underlying each variable and step.

A third method for evaluating competing models is to utilize χ^2 goodness of fit tests. The data may be matched to an a priori hypothesized model. Lack of fit will appear as a significant value of χ^2. Since this statistic is becoming more frequent in computer packages, it serves as an increasingly valuable statistic. Furthermore, Kenny (1979, chap. 9) shows how systematic tests can be used to identify the location of misfits. For a clear demonstration of the utility of goodness of fit tests in testing competing models, the reader is referred to Bentler and Speckart (1979).

A similar, though less elegant, version of this procedure is simply to compute the R^2 for each endogenous variable in the model, using *only* those variables predicted in advance to be germane. One can then redo the regressions, allowing any predictors to enter the equation. If R^2 increases significantly, then the predicted model is not adequate to account for the data. As noted earlier, such a test does not prove the model; it merely demonstrates that the predicted model accounts for as much variance as any other current possibility. Researchers using this technique would do well to heed Duncan's (1975, pp. 65-66, 166-167) recommendation to down play the actual value of R^2. How much variance is predicted is less important than the correct specification of the variance that is described.

The final procedure for evaluating the confirmatory efficacy of competing models is the method of regenerated correlations. This technique applies only to indirect effects, as any variables directly connected by a path are mathematically constrained to regenerate their simple correlation perfectly. (This limitation on its application has not been recognized by some users.) Fundamentally, the reader has already been acquainted with this procedure in the discussion of partialing. Stipulating that a causal influence is solely indirect implies that all values of the outcome variable in question can be reproduced faithfully without incorporating a direct effect. Once again, consider the Bachman-O'Malley data in Figure 5. According to the model, socioeconomic level (1) and high school self-esteem (4) are correlated by virtue of indirect paths through academic ability (2) and performance (3). Using the identical logic as in Appendix A, it can be shown that since

$$z_4 = p_{43} z_3 + p_{42} z_2 \qquad\qquad [7]$$

$$r^*_{14} = p_{43} r_{13} + p_{42} r_{12} \qquad\qquad [8]$$

(the r^* indicates that this value is a regenerated correlation, rather than one actually computed from the data). This equality will be true only if the paths among variables 1-4 are accurate. Substituting, $r^* = (.152)(.204) + (.178)(.445) = .031 + .079 = .110$. Since the actual r was .158, the model yields a discrepancy of .048. While this difference seems desirably small, the major limitation of this procedure is that no technique exists for evaluating the discrepancies statistically.

This method is useful mainly for comparing across the discrepancies produced by different models, particularly for explaining a relationship between the same variables. Suppose that in Figure 5 we had hypothesized that high school self-esteem was affected only by performance, which in turn was a function of academic ability. In other words, no direct path from ability to esteem existed, an a priori plausible speculation. In this case, equations 7 and 8 would read

$$z_4 = p_{43} z_3 \qquad\qquad\qquad\qquad [9]$$

$$r_{14}^* = p_{43} r_{13} = .226\,(.204) = .046 \qquad\qquad\qquad\qquad [10]$$

Given that the actual r was .158, the discrepancy is now .112, an appreciably greater error than above. Thus, the implication is that the original model can account for the obtained pattern of relationships better than the suggested revision. It is closer to being consistent with the data. In stricter causal terms, the revision could not have led to these data, while the original might have. A more completely documented example of this procedure is given by Kerlinger and Pedhazur (1973, pp. 327-330).

WHAT IS NOT WHAT IN STRUCTURAL MODELING

This seems a suitable place for an exegesis on the nature of causation, even though space limits this discussion to the most superficial details. (Cook & Campbell, 1979, chap. 2, provide an excellent introduction to the problem, as it has been treated in the philosophy of science.) Even though causation and noncausation, the latter in the guise of correlation coefficients, are at the heart of traditional statistical inference, how many statistics courses or texts discuss the logical meaning of the terms with any depth? On the face of it, such understanding would be particularly vital when learning about structural equation methods. While most psychologists were trained to view correlational reports as noncausal in an absolute sense, we are now told that one can extract "causal-like" information from these analyses. So it is essential for researchers to be aware of what can and cannot be done vis-a-vis causal inference before attempting to master the algebraic complexities.

No structural model, no matter how strong the fit of the data or plausible the connections, can prove a given theory as the correct one. At the most global level, this is because no empirical research endeavor can ever confirm a single interpretation—rather, the most that can be accomplished is that inadequate representations can be falsified (Popper, 1959).

The seeming validity of one theoretical account is contingent on numerous weaknesses in the evidence: our failure to generate other equally plausible explanations; the difficulty of identifying all of the necessary preconditions and assumptions for the phenomenon to occur; the sometimes tenuous link between theoretical and operational variables; and the inevitable future discovery of disconfirming instances. These issues, so much at the heart of the philosophy of science, are especially pertinent for structural modelers. To argue for the causal priority of one model over others, it would be minimally necessary to manipulate all of the putative causes and demonstrate their hypothesized effects via the generally accepted standards of Mill's Methods of Agreement and Difference. Furthermore, one would have to postulate and then create conditions under which discriminating predictions between all possible models are made. Clearly, this requirement cannot be fulfilled. As Young (1977) has pointed out, with only three variables, 64 different configurations are possible; with four variables, 4096. While doubtless many of these would be nonsensical, too many are not. Also, the possibility that future researchers will uncover a previously undetected variable or mechanism is always prepotent.

If structural models cannot confirm a model, what can they do? Once again, the distinction between inferential and descriptive methods must be drawn. Inferentially, as was discussed earlier, by comparing the predicted pathways and indirect effects of competing models, important evidence about the relative efficacy of different theories is furnished. Consistent with Popper's (1959) notions, this is achieved primarily through a falsification framework: The data are shown to be inconsistent with certain structural suppositions and assumptions, and, consequently, other mechanisms must be working. When the data are inconsistent with one or more models, this is the strongest conclusion that can be formed. However, it is not to be belittled. Many of the substantive controversies in social and personality psychology focus on alternative explanations for the same phenomenon. Structural models allow for strong choices between them, notably in naturalistic settings as well as in the laboratory. Bear in mind that these models must be posited in advance, or else the test simply capitalizes on chance.

Of course, the question of just what a "cause" is has been problematic in philosophy, science, and law for generations. Hart and Honore's (1959) classic discussion makes this difficulty apparent. Psychologists have traditionally limited their search to what Suppes (1970) called functional relationships, namely variables that, when affected, in turn will reliably produce concomitant changes in other variables. The descriptive use of structural methods highlights Suppes's point. A path diagram, such as that of Figure 3, articulates the general pattern of interrelation among a host of variables (within the very important constraints the researcher introduces by specifying their order). This is useful for a number of reasons: It greatly clarifies the existing data and helps researchers synthesize their import; it can breed models for later critical inferential tests; it can lead to new hypotheses; and, most important, it specifies the nature of the mechanism by which each variable in the system might be related to each other variable. Notable in this regard is the identification of intervening variables and indirect effects. Thirty-four years ago, MacCorquodale and Meehl (1948) suggested that psychological research might be more fruitful if researchers directed their efforts more toward intervening variables than hypothetical constructs. Mediators are, of course, operational measures of proposed mechanisms. Assessment of indirect effects, and their comparison to correlations that require including a direct path for full estimation, can greatly facilitate understanding of why and how certain phenomena happen, particularly if measures of potential intervening factors are included in research more often. To a large extent, mediated effects make a theory interesting. Hence, they should be pursued more actively.

Structural models can also be beneficial for accomplishing such tasks in laboratory experiments. Too often, researchers have assumed that structural techniques were appropriate only for correlational data, in which the absence of manipulation made any quasi-causal methods desirable. Probably, this erroneous assumption stems from the early propagation of path analysis in sociology, political science, and economics, fields in which experimental manipulation of the independent variable is rare. Yet there is nothing in the mathematics of structural modeling that prohibits its application to experimental data; in fact, as Taylor and Fiske (1982) and Kenny (1979) have argued, it has particularly great potential for this domain. In a large proportion of experimental social psychology, the goal is to determine causal processes and mediating variables. For all of the reasons noted earlier, structural modeling is an appropriate and strong tool for this purpose, whereas traditional analysis of variance is not. Moreover, experimenter manipulation of the independent variable and random assignment of subjects to conditions eliminates many (but not all) "third variables" and alternative explanations in which cause and effect are reversed. Consequently, there are fewer sensible competing models to be considered, and a more definitive structural model is likely to emerge. A good example is provided by Fiske, Kenny, and Taylor (1982). For present purposes, the reader would do well to remember that the ability to infer causality from experiments does not arise from the method of statistical analysis, but rather from the procedures under which the investigation is conducted. All of the advantages of structural equation methods over other statistics apply to experiments as well, perhaps more so.

To sum up, while structural models cannot ascertain causality, they can help differentiate potentially valid propositions from those that are untenable. If the aim is to learn about causality, the researcher should seek consistency with plausible theoretical models specified in advance. If the aim is to snoop within a data set, the researcher should seek a trimmed, logical depiction of its internal structure.

THE FUTURE OF STRUCTURAL MODELS

For any new data-analytic system to have broad appeal to the psychological community, it must be flexible. Fortunately, the techniques described in this chapter were developed as a form of regression analysis, most usually of the ordinary least-squares kind. As a result, most of the advances that make regression analysis a pliant technique can be exploited within structural models as well. That is, group membership and nominal scales can be represented through dummy variable, effects, contrast, or any other coding scheme; power polynomials and other nonlinear functions can be incorporated through appropriate transformations of scale; interaction terms can be created; within-cases designs can be included; and specifically partialed terms can be conceived and analyzed. (See Cohen & Cohen, 1975, for a presentation of these methods). In short, any hypothesis that can be expressed as variables can be investigated in a structural model.

Particularly great promise is afforded by the advent of procedures that combine structural modeling with factor analysis. Most prominent in these endeavors is the development of LISREL (Jöreskog & Sörbom, 1979), RAM (McArdle, 1980; Horn & McArdle, 1980), or LVPLS (Wold, 1981). The logic used is a straightforward extension of what we have already seen. However, the variables analyzed in the structural model are not the actual variables assessed in the data collection, but rather a set of latent variables

thought to underlie those that were measured. A latent variable is analogous to the psychometrician's true score. By measuring more than one
indicator of each construct, it is presumed that a pure score, with greatly
reduced error, can be obtained. In very crude terms, these multiple
measures of each construct are first factor-analyzed separately. The factors
that result are then investigated as the components of the structural
model. Thus, structural analyses such as those described earlier are performed on latent (purified) variables not actually measured themselves but
derived from multiple indicators of the single construct they are thought
to represent. As an example, Figure 7, taken from Maruyama and
McGarvey (1980), is offered. The structural analysis uses five latent
variables, shown by the circles in Figure 7. These variables in turn are
obtained from factoring the variables in rectangles, which are the only data
actually collected from subjects. The numbers in the model simply represent the parameters that need to be specified or are estimated in the
analysis. Two great, although simple, advantages are added by incorporating factor-analytic procedures into structural models. The first is that
by using multiple measures of a unitary construct, researchers can avoid
the instrument-specific "error" inherent in any single index of a broader
phenomenon. The second is due to the great increase in reliability a factor
score possesses, yielding more meaningful variance for the structural model
to decompose. As noted earlier, measurement error can have serious
misleading effects, which the latent variable approach greatly minimizes.
While structural analyses of latent variables require a great deal more care
in meeting statistical assumptions and specifying parameters (see Kenny,
1979, chaps. 7-9 for an excellent introduction), they offer to add substantial power to the types of answers we can provide to long-standing
questions. But they must be utilized in the proper spirit of structural
methods—that is, either as a descriptive (specifying an optimal model) or
inferential (testing competing models) technique. Three excellent examples of the use of LISREL in contrasting competing structural models are
Weeks, Michela, Peplau, and Bragg (1980); Huba, Wingard, and Bentler
(1981); and Fiske et al. (1982).

A FINAL WORD

The goal of this chapter was to provide a superficial acquaintance with
structural modeling for the noninitiate, with the aim that it might facil-

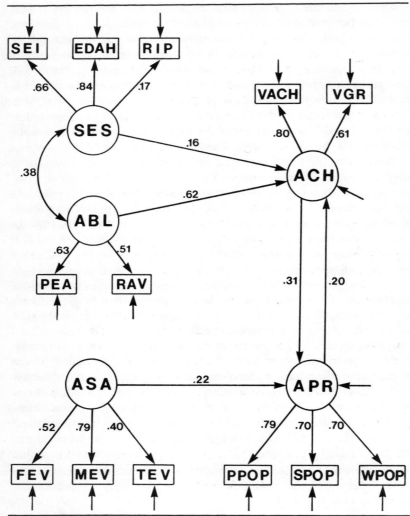

Figure 7: Maruyama and McGarvey (1980) latent variable model of achievement and acceptance. SES = socioeconomic status; ABL = academic ability; ACH = achievement; ASA = acceptance by adults; APR = acceptance by peers; SEI = socioeconomic index of occupation; EDAH = educational attainment of head of household; RIP = rooms per person in the house; VACH = verbal test scores; VGR = verbal grades; PEA = Peabody Picture Word Vocabulary Test; RAV = Raven Progressive Matrices; FEV = father's evaluation; MEV = mother's evaluation; TEV = teacher's evaluation; PPOP = playground popularity; SPOP = seating popularity; WPOP = school-work popularity. Copyright 1980 by the American Psychological Association. Reprinted/adapted by permission of the publisher and author.

itate critical reading of research using these strategies and that researchers might be encouraged to experiment in their own content areas. Given the goal of simplicity and the limitation of space, it has not been possible to present all of the necessary procedures and qualifications for concrete operation. However, it is hoped that some readers have been seduced to look further. A few references might be helpful in this regard. A full underpinning in regression analysis is given by Cohen and Cohen (1975). Kerlinger and Pedhazur's (1973 , pp. 305-333) account of path analysis is a good, although limited, statement most notable for its clear-cut algebra. Thinking in terms of path diagrams might be assisted by the early chapters of Heise (1975), although this can be accomplished as well by a fuller reading of the examples presented in this chapter. Duncan (1975) probably confers the most thorough and understandable education on the mathematics of straightforward structural models and should be sufficient for investigators wishing to apply the technique to their own research. An excellent discussion of the latent variable approach, particularly focusing on their advantages, relative to manifest variables, in causal modeling is given by Bentler (1980). Finally, the broadest treatment is that of Kenny (1979), who uses a general structural model paradigm to explain a myriad of correlational techniques such as latent structure analysis, factor analysis, cross-lagged panel correlation, and an excellent chapter on non-equivalent control group designs.

Certainly, structural modeling is no panacea for the perils of correlational research. As we have seen, it is all too easy to slip into inferences of causality from depictions that more properly remain descriptive. Nevertheless, the advent of structural models should induce researchers to conceptualize systems of interrelationships as more than independent and dependent variables. The attention researchers are beginning to pay to simple mediating processes is one sign of the theoretical import of this goal. But once social-personality psychologists become facile in such three-variable systems, we should expand our thinking to encompass larger networks of more variables and more intricate direct and indirect effects. In fact, much of the theory in our literature has long shown such complexity of thought, despite the fact that the empirical research strategies used to test derivations has usually been more singular. Explicit use of structural models should enhance our ability to evaluate these notions substantially.

APPENDIX A

Suppose we wanted to represent the simple Pearson product-moment correlation between z_3 and z_1. Any introductory statistics textbook should show that r can be expressed as follows:

$$r_{13} = \frac{1}{n-1} \sum_{i=1}^{n} z_1 z_3 \qquad [A1]$$

Equation 2, introduced in the main body of this chapter, indicated that:

$$z_3 = p_{31} z_1 + p_{32} z_2 \qquad [A2]$$

So if we then multiply both sides of equation 2 by $\frac{1}{n-1} z_1$ and takes its summation over all subjects, we would obtain

$$\frac{1}{n-1} \Sigma z_1 z_3 = r_{13} = \frac{1}{n-1} \Sigma z_1 p_{31} z_1 + \frac{1}{n-1} \Sigma z_1 p_{32} z_2 \qquad [A3]$$

Since the regression coefficients (p's) are the same for all subjects, equation 3 can be rearranged to

$$r_{13} = p_{31} \left(\frac{1}{n-1} \Sigma z_1{}^2\right) + p_{32} \left(\frac{1}{n-1} \Sigma z_1 z_2\right) \qquad [A4]$$

The rightmost term in parentheses is r_{12}; the same statistics textbooks as before should tell you that the lefthand term in parentheses equals 1. Therefore we have

$$r_{13} = p_{31} + p_{32} r_{12} \qquad [A5]$$

The exact same manipulations of equation 2 can produce r_{23} (try it yourself!) yielding

$$r_{23} = p_{31} r_{12} + p_{32} \qquad [A6]$$

Now, the three rs are known, since they can be calculated from the data. That means we have 2 equations (5 and 6), with two unknown quantities $(p_{31} + p_{32})$. Simple algebra lets us solve them, if we multiply both sides of equation 6 by $-r_{12}$ and then add:

$$r_{13} = p_{31} + p_{32} r_{12}$$

$$-r_{12} r_{23} = -p_{31} r_{12}^2 - p_{32} r_{12}$$

$$\overline{r_{13} - r_{12} r_{23} = p_{31} - p_{31} r_{12}^2} \qquad [A7]$$

The righthand side of the equation can be simplified to $p_{31}(1-r_{12}^2)$. Dividing both sides of equation 7 by $(1 - r_{12}^2)$ yields

$$\frac{r_{13} - r_{12}r_{23}}{1 - r_{12}^2} = p_{31} \tag{A8}$$

which is the value of the path coefficient, p_{31}. Interestingly (and fortunately), this is exactly the value of the standardized regression coefficient, β. (For example, see Cohen and Cohen, 1975, p. 77.)

NOTES

1. Although this wording is cumbersome and awkward, it is necessary. See the section entitled "Testing Competing Models."

2. Other studies, of course, fall even further short by not including measures of proposed mediators. One cannot empirically test constructs for which one has no data.

3. Use of this particular study for pedagogical purposes is not meant to criticize it any more than other, less explicit studies or those which do not even measure hypothesized mediators. I do not mean to single out one study for the generic problem, which is made clearer by an example.

4. The coefficient p_{31} should be read as "p, predicting variable 3 from variable 1." For all regression and path coefficients, the first subscript refers to the criterion, the second to the predictor.

5. In truth, this correspondence holds only because of a set of assumptions that make this the most reasonable and workable case. Under some conditions, it is not so. See Duncan (1975, chaps. 6 and 7) for a discussion of the logic of this assumption and procedures for situations in which other solutions are more appropriate.

REFERENCES

Alwin, D. F., & Hauser, R. M. The decomposition of effects in path analysis. *American Sociological Review,* 1975, *40,* 37-47.

Bachman, J. G., & O'Malley, P. M. Self-esteem in young men: A longitudinal analysis of the impact of educational and occupational attainment. *Journal of Personality and Social Psychology,* 1977, *35,* 365-380.

Bentler, P. M. Multivariate analysis with latent variables: Causal modeling. *Annual Review of Psychology,* 1980, *31,* 419-456.

Bentler, P. M., & Speckart, G. Models of attitude-behavior relations. *Psychological Review,* 1979, *86,* 452-464.

Blalock, H. M., Jr. Four-variable causal models and partial correlations. In H. M. Blalock, Jr. (Ed.), *Causal models in the social sciences*. Chicago: Aldine, 1971.

Cohen, J., & Cohen, P. *Applied multiple regression/correlation analysis for the behavioral sciences*. Hillsdale, NJ: Lawrence Erlbaum, 1975.

Cook, T. D., & Campbell, D. T. *Quasi-experimentation: Design and analysis issues for field settings*. Chicago: Rand McNally, 1979.

Dion, K. K., Berscheid, E., & Walster, E. What is beautiful is good. *Journal of Personality and Social Psychology*, 1972, *24*, 207-213.

Duncan, O. D. *Introduction to structural equation models*. New York: Academic Press, 1975.

Fishbein, M., & Ajzen, I. *Belief, attitude, intention and behavior: An introduction to theory and research*. Reading, MA: Addison-Wesley, 1975.

Fiske, S. T., Kenny, D. A., & Taylor, S. E. Structural models for the mediation of salience effects on attribution. *Journal of Experimental Social Psychology*, 1982, *18*, 105-127.

Galton, F. Regression towards mediocrity in hereditary stature. *Journal of the Anthropological Society of Great Britain and Ireland*, 1886, *15*.

Galton, F. *Natural inheritance*. London: Macmillan, 1894.

Goldberg, A. S. Discerning a causal pattern among data on voting behavior. In H. M. Blalock, Jr. (Ed.), *Causal models in the social sciences*. Chicago: Aldine, 1971.

Hart, H.L.A., & Honore, A. M. *Causation in the law*. London: Oxford University Press, 1959.

Heise, D. R. *Causal analysis*. New York: John Wiley, 1975.

Helmreich, R. L., Spence, J. T., Beane, W. E., Lucker, G. W., & Matthews, K. A. Making it in academic psychology: Demographic and personality correlates of attainment. *Journal of Personality and Social Psychology*, 1980, *39*, 896-908.

Horn, J. L., & McArdle, J. J. Perspectives on mathematical/statistical model building (MASMOB) in research on aging. In L. W. Poon (Ed.), *Aging in the 1980's: Psychological issues*. Washington, DC: American Psychological Association, 1980.

Huba, G. J., Wingard, J. A., & Bentler, P. M. A comparison of two latent variable causal models for adolescent drug use. *Journal of Personality and Social Psychology*, 1981, *40*, 180-193.

Jöreskog, K. G., & Sörbom, D. *LISREL: Analysis of linear structural relationships by the method of maximum likelihood*. Chicago: National Educational Resources, 1978.

Kenny, D. A. *Correlation and causality*. New York: John Wiley, 1979.

Kerlinger, F. N., & Pedhazur, E. J. *Multiple regression in behavioral research*. New York: Holt, Rinehart & Winston, 1973.

Land, K. C. Principles of path analysis. In E. F. Borgatta (Ed.), *Sociological methodology: 1969*. San Francisco: Jossey-Bass, 1969.

MacCorquodale, K., & Meehl, P. E. On a distinction between hypothetical constructs and intervening variables. *Psychological Review*, 1948, *55*, 95-107.

Maruyama, G., & McGarvey, B. Evaluating causal models: An application of maximum-likelihood analysis of structural equations. *Psychological Bulletin*, 1980, *87*, 502-512.

McArdle, J. J. Causal modeling applied to psychonomic systems simulation. *Behavior Research Methods and Instrumentation*, 1980, *12*, 193-209.

Newcomb, T. M. The prediction of interpersonal attraction. *American Psychologist,* 1956, *11*, 575-586.

Popper, K. R. *The logic of scientific discovery.* New York: Basic Books, 1959.

Reis, H. T. (Ed.). *Naturalistic approaches to social interaction.* San Francisco: Jossey-Bass, in press.

Simon, H. A. *Models of man.* New York: John Wiley, 1957.

Simon, H. A. Spurious correlation: A causal interpretation. In H. M. Blalock, Jr. (Ed.), *Causal models in the social sciences.* Chicago: Aldine, 1971.

Suppes, P. *A probabilistic theory of causality.* Amsterdam: North Holland, 1970.

Taylor, S. E., & Fiske, S. T. Getting inside the head: Methodologies for process analyses in attribution and social cognition. In J. Harvey, W. Ickes, & R. Kidd (Eds.), *New directions in attribution research* (Vol. 3). Hillsdale, NJ: Lawrence Erlbaum, 1982.

Weary, G. Examination of affect and egotism as mediators of bias in causal attributions. *Journal of Personality and Social Psychology,* 1980, *38*, 348-357.

Weeks, D. G., Michela, J. L., Peplau, L. A., & Bragg, M. E. Relation between loneliness and depression: A structural equation analysis. *Journal of Personality and Social Psychology,* 1980, *39*, 1238-1244.

Wold, H. Model construction and evaluation when theoretical knowledge is scarce. On the theory and application of partial least squares. In J. Kmenta & J. Ramsey (Eds.), *Model evaluation in econometrics.* New York: Academic Press, 1981.

Wright, S. Correlation and causation. *Journal of Agricultural Research,* 1921, *20,* 557-585.

Young, J. W. The function of theory in a dilemma of path analysis. *Journal of Applied Psychology,* 1977, *62,* 108-110.

Zuckerman, M., & Reis, H. T. A comparison of three models for predicting altruistic behavior. *Journal of Personality and Social Psychology,* 1978, *36,* 498-510.